# A TASTE FOR
# THE CLASSICS

*Patrick Kavanaugh*

Sparrow Press
Nashville, Tennessee

Published 1993 in Nashville, Tennessee, by Sparrow Press.
Distributed in Canada by Christian Marketing Canada, Ltd.

Printed in the United States of America

97  96  95  94  93    5  4  3  2  1

**Library of Congress Cataloging-in-Publication Data**

Kavanaugh, Patrick.
      A taste for the classics / Patrick Kavanaugh.
         p.  cm.
      ISBN 0-917143-29-9 : $16.95
      1. Music appreciation.
  MT90.K38  1993
  781.6'8—dc20                    93-2593
                                      CIP
                                      MN

Design by Barnes & Company

*This book is dedicated to Christopher, John, Peter and David—*
*four of the most talented people I have ever known.*

# CONTENTS

# ACKNOWLEDGMENTS

*This book could not have been written without the support
and inspiration of many other people—indeed, more than I could mention—
but I must thank at least a few of the "first-chair" persons:*

- My many musical friends, for their expert opinions and advice,
  especially Barbara Kavanaugh, Jim Kraft, Dean Christman,
  Steve and Linda Wall Schnurman and Linn Maxwell Keller.

- The greatest secretarial staff anyone could ever imagine—
  Marthellen Hoffman, Jan Patrick, Ann Marean and Wanda
  Skinner—for painstakingly preparing the manuscript.

- Paul Thigpen, David Hazard and Kathleen Stephens,
  for their skillful and creative editing.

- Bill Hearn, Billy Ray Hearn, Ron Griffin, Susan Heard, Debbie
  Emery, Lucy Diaz and all the other great people at the Sparrow
  Corporation, for the beautiful spirit that you share and the
  excellence that distinguishes your work.

- Finally, I want to thank all the hundreds of inspiring professors,
  composers and performers who have touched my life with their
  passion for great music.

# INTRODUCTION

Once you get a taste of the world's greatest music, you're bound to want more. But how do you find your way around that rich yet confusing world of classical works? What if you can't quite tell a Brahms from a Beethoven, but you'd like to get better acquainted with both?

Maybe you've heard a few symphonies on National Public Radio, and you liked what you heard. You want to be able to appreciate what you know is "good" music. You'd like to recognize the difference between a Mozart concerto and a Bach cantata—maybe even go to a local symphony concert and enjoy the experience.

If you're anxious to explore the realm of fine music and you need a few signposts on the way, this book was written for you. In it you'll find the essentials for understanding and appreciating:

- the basic types of classical works, such as orchestra and choral music, opera, chamber music and song.
- the instruments that play and the voices that sing these works, and how they work together to create a magnificent sound.
- the greatest classical composers and their unique contributions to the world of music.
- some of the most popular and inspired works that have stood the test of time.
- enough of the basics of music theory to help you better appreciate what you hear.
- some fascinating facts and anecdotes from music history, with a basic framework for understanding the progression of musical periods.
- the most common musical terms you're likely to encounter.

In short, I want to provide you with a solid yet lively introduction to classical music. Why? Because I know what it's like to stand on the edge of that vast world without having a clue about how to investigate it.

You see, though I'm a professional musician, I was a late bloomer. Most of the hundreds of people I know in my field became acquainted with classical music as young children and have been immersed in it ever since. But I wasn't born in Boston or Philadelphia or raised in a concert hall. I was born in Tennessee, the son of a postman and a nurse who weren't concert-goers at all. In fact, I was well into high school before I'd ever even heard of Beethoven's famous *Fifth Symphony.*

How did I encounter the classics? By accident. I fell for a girl whose mother was a piano teacher. She'd been raised with Bach and Brahms, so I had considerable motivation to get to know them as well. Since no one was around to prejudice me with warnings that such "highbrow" compositions were difficult or dull, I fell incurably in love with classical music.

Ironically enough, the romance with the piano teacher's daughter soon passed from my life. But the romance with great music had taken root, and a passion for classical music blossomed in my life. I saved up for albums of my favorite composers and artists. I read with great interest about the antics of eccentrics like Beethoven and Wagner. Huge orchestra concerts thrilled me—I even started hanging around backstage to get conductors' autographs.

In time, life became so seasoned with the classics that great music became a passion. Today, I conduct orchestras and compose symphonic music myself. This is my specialty; perhaps your specialty lies in another field. But that doesn't matter. In our day of occupational specialization, no one can know it all. Even people with the best of education have gaps in their knowledge. If you have a gap in your understanding of classical music and want to fill it, just turn the page.

My goal is not to provide you with intellectual stimulation, bore you with music trivia or introduce you to the art of music snobbery. No, I simply hope you'll come join me in the musical world I've come to love so deeply. Whether you're just starting out or you've already begun exploring, you've got quite an adventure waiting for you.

# 1
# GETTING THE BIG PICTURE

*The language of music is common to all
generations and nations. It is understood by everybody,
since it is understood with the heart.*

—Gioacchino Rossini

The young Austrian composer Franz Schubert had stopped in at a favorite cafe in Vienna one evening, joining some friends for a cup of coffee. Thumbing through a German edition of Shakespeare's *Cymbeline,* he suddenly started reading aloud a poem in the play that begins, "Hark, hark, the lark." As he did, a lovely melody came to his mind.

Schubert insisted that he must write it down, but there was no paper. So a friend turned over a menu, scratched out the lines of a musical staff and gave it to him. The composer set to work, scribbling rapidly in the dim candlelight of the cafe, and finished the project completely...in only a few moments!

Later that evening Schubert and his friends gathered around a piano for the first performance of the new composition—one of the most beautiful songs of the nineteenth century.

Those of us who have never experienced such a compelling moment of inspiration may well marvel. What kind of extraordinary gifting would it take for Schubert to translate so quickly the beauty of a few words of poetry into the leaping energy of such a song?

An equally amazing anecdote comes from the life of George Frideric Handel, best known for his masterpiece *Messiah.* One day, as the German composer walked to chapel, he was surprised by a cloudburst and sought shelter in a blacksmith's shop. While waiting for the rain to subside, he caught the melody the blacksmith was humming at his work, accompanied by the bass rhythm of his hammer strokes on the anvil.

On returning home, Handel's genius turned what he had heard into a musical masterpiece. The exquisite little piece became known as the "Harmonious Blacksmith," and was included in a larger work, *Suites de pieces pour le clavecin*, dedicated to Princess Anne of England.

Just as remarkable as these two creations are the many musical works prompted not by a flash of creative insight or the alertness of a fine musical ear, but rather by the most mundane of motivations—financial pressure. Consider, for example, how Wolfgang Amadeus Mozart's need for cash once led him to accept a commission to write a concerto for flute and harp.

The piece was to be composed for a particular man and his daughter to play—a man whom Mozart disliked. Worse yet, the composer abhorred the pair's musical abilities and had a general aversion (at that time) to the flute. Yet his genius combined with his need for money to overcome the lack of inspiration. The result— Mozart's brilliant labors produced the beautiful *Concerto for Harp and Flute,* one of the most popular works of its kind.

Whether a fine musical piece is born in a moment of inspiration, woven from an everyday scene or hammered out in hours of skilled labor, the result is the same. The composer conveys something of beauty that evokes from us a heartfelt response—joy or sorrow, awe or anxiety, peace or passion.

No doubt that response doesn't depend on how much we know about music. Beauty soars past the head and straight to the heart, giving us a pleasure independent of any thoughts about musical styles or standards. Nevertheless, our appreciation of music can be deepened and our pleasure in it sharpened with even a little knowledge about the elements of composition and the people and circumstances behind the pieces we enjoy.

Consider, for example, the works we've already mentioned. Sitting in a concert hall, we could certainly delight in Schubert's song or Mozart's concerto without knowing how they came to be. Yet there is something that seasons the enjoyment for me in picturing that moment—the friends at a cafe table, the panic of Schubert as inspiration struck with no paper in sight, the point of his pen riding the front edge of genius, the beauty of the song. Such knowledge transforms the listening experience for me.

Attending a concert of classical music, after all, is somewhat like sitting down to a gourmet feast. Without any culinary knowledge at all, we could still enjoy the exotic delicacies prepared by a master of cuisine; the taste of a fine French bouillabaisse would still delight us even if we couldn't understand the menu. But how much greater the pleasure would be if we could meet the chef, know the cultural origins of each dish, appreciate the skill required for the meal's preparation, and distinguish the various nuances of flavor.

In a similar way, we can enrich our musical experience—and our lives as a whole—by learning more about the art of classical works. What is distinctive about each period of this music? What unique contribution was made by each of its great composers? Which instruments are typically employed, and what role does each play in achieving the total effect? What circumstances lie behind great compositions that shaped them in interesting ways?

This book will provide some answers to these and other questions. Think of it as a "menu" of sorts for feasting on a number of the best classical creations. In these pages you'll find a fascinating mix of history, analysis and technical information that will cultivate your musical palate and whet your appetite for more.

## NO EXPERTISE NEEDED

As a young student in music school, I had a great desire to study the Bible. One day I took the opportunity to meet a well-known theologian and ask him how I should approach my personal study of Scripture. But his scholarly advice was rather discouraging.

"You really shouldn't even begin reading the Scriptures," he said somberly, "until you've at least acquired a thorough knowledge of Hebrew and Greek."

A thorough knowledge of Hebrew and Greek is no doubt essential for becoming a biblical scholar. But surely we shouldn't consider such training a prerequisite for a layperson's personal Bible reading.

The same is true of those who want to learn more about classical music. All too often, newcomers to the classical scene are given the impression that they can't truly enjoy it unless they become experts. They may feel as if they have to earn a doctorate in music with years of professional experience before they are able to understand what classical music is all about.

Nothing could be further from the truth. Music can be appreciated at a number of different levels, and to enjoy it, we need only listen to it. Then, if we increase our knowledge little by little, we'll find our pleasure increasing as well.

For the position of classical music lover, *no previous experience is necessary.* All we need is a desire to explore the art and enjoy it for its beauty and power.

## A SIMPLE APPROACH

We can approach the world of great music from a number of different directions, all of which have their merits. But I believe that some approaches are less helpful than others. One strategy we'll avoid in this book is the *theoretical approach.*

Well-meaning music teachers sometimes insist that to appreciate the subject, you must first learn an extensive body of music theory. You must know how to read music; you must understand the principles of melody, harmony, rhythm, form, analysis, orchestration and certainly all the instruments of the orchestra with their various ranges, tone colors, repertoire and much more. In this approach, theory and technique seem to be an end in themselves.

Personally, I love music theory. I've taught it for years, and you'll no doubt pick up some necessary technical knowledge about music in this book. But that kind of information isn't essential to your appreciation of the music. It's simply an aid in understanding—not an end in itself.

Another popular approach is the *chronological-historical method*. This strategy starts at the dawn of musical history many centuries ago and works up to the present day. That sounds logical enough.

But there's a problem here. Almost all the music played in classical concerts today in every concert hall in the world—what we call the *standard repertoire*—was written since the year 1700. So most likely the music you're interested in hearing and learning about has little to do with all the long centuries you would study in a chronological-historical approach.

The result? People try bravely to make their way through all those years of history, but tend to lose interest before they finally get to the first universally recognized giant of musical composition—Johann Sebastian Bach (1685-1750). Too many classical music appreciation students drop out when they have to endure long lectures on the mysteries of Gregorian chant, the techniques of medieval sequences and the intricacies of Renaissance counterpoint.

Don't misunderstand. I revel in the distinctive beauties of such "early music," as it is often called by musicians. And if you've ever heard a Renaissance Mass, chances are you love it as much as I do. But I realize that appreciation for music from such a distant time and culture is usually an acquired taste. So we'll spend most of our time in the last three centuries—not to limit your experiences, but to begin with the most basic repertoire.

That's the focus of this book—what the pros call the "standard rep." We'll become familiar with composers and works of classical music that are indispensable to a basic knowledge of the art, just as an acquaintance with certain literary authors is essential for becoming a well-read person. You'll be meeting the Shakespeares and Tolstoys and Hemingways of music. (For an in-depth look at twelve of these great composers, see my first book, *The Spiritual Lives of Great Composers*, Sparrow Press, 1992.)

Above all, our emphasis throughout will be the music itself. That's the heart of our approach, rather than technical or historical information. Of course, in the

4

process you'll encounter plenty of useful and interesting material: historical anecdotes, insights into musical forms, glimpses into how music is written, information about how instruments work, a smattering of facts about orchestration and acoustics—even a few tips about concert etiquette (such as the answer to "When do I applaud?").

But all that is optional. Make use of whatever information enhances your pleasure of the music, and ignore whatever distracts you from it. Enjoyment of the music is the overarching goal.

## AN OVERVIEW OF MUSICAL PERIODS

Though we're limiting our repertoire to music of the last three centuries, we still have a lot of territory to cover. So we need some broad categories to help us understand the big picture.

First, we should note that we're dealing only with *Western* music here—that is, the music that has developed over the centuries in Europe (including Russia) and the cultural offshoots of Europe in the Americas. Of course, other cultures of the world, such as those native to America, Africa, Asia and the Pacific, have their own beautiful music traditions. But those other musical cultures are beyond the scope of this study.

Music historians have divided the last three hundred years in the West into musical epochs, with labels reflecting the common aspects of the compositions written in each period. The names used are inexact, differ from book to book, and often provoke arguments—for example, the debate continues on whether Beethoven is best categorized as *classical* or *romantic*. Nevertheless, despite the variations in meaning, these terms will aid us in discussing and comparing various composers' music.

Here are the four principle epochs of music we'll be getting to know, with their approximate dates (there are of course no firm boundaries between periods):

**Baroque (1650-1750).** The sixteenth-century Reformation of the Western Church splintered Europe not only spiritually, but socially and politically as well. Consequently, the first half of the seventeenth century encompassed a long series of wars and upheavals, known as the Thirty Years War, throughout much of the continent.

When the war ended in 1648, Europe's military and spiritual energy was largely exhausted. Yet out of the devastation came a burst of new life in the artistic culture of the West that came to be known as the Baroque period.

In its musical aspect (the other fine arts also had their expressions of the Baroque), the new epoch was characterized by a grand style. The music featured multiple simultaneous melodies (known as *polyphony*), and within these melodies were numerous ornaments—that is, extra notes with which composers adorned their work. Often, complicated rhythms were added as well, resulting in a thick texture of sound, especially when written for chorus and orchestra—perhaps, the greatest musical genre of this period.

The dynamics of Baroque music are either loud or soft, with little crescendo or decrescendo—that is, without gradually increasing or decreasing volume. Yet these loud and soft sections are often juxtaposed to create an echo effect.

This age was the last hurrah for several instruments, among them the recorder (a wooden flute blown from the end rather than the side); the viola de gamba (a bowed string instrument with bass range); the clavichord (a stringed keyboard instrument); and the harpsichord (a piano-like instrument whose strings were plucked rather than struck with hammers). Some of these are making a comeback in the twentieth century.

The vocal lines in Baroque music often sound as if they were written for instruments, and this music was performed more often in the church than in the concert hall. The period had countless minor composers, but its two champions are certainly Johann Sebastian Bach (1685-1750) and George Frideric Handel (1685-1759).

**Classical (1750-1830).** The common title for the next musical epoch may be confusing because we use the word *classical* as a casual reference to *all* the styles we're studying. Nevertheless, the term was long ago assigned to this period and is probably too well-established to replace it with another. Some musicologists have suggested resolving the difficulty by calling this the "classic" period, but the new label has never caught on—perhaps because there are "classics" among the musical works of every age.

Other musicologists have tried to clear up our confusing terminology by replacing the broad term *classical music* with *serious music.* I abhor this idea, since I don't go to concerts with a long face and I don't think Mozart did either. After all—if this is "serious" music, why did so many of its composers enjoy writing what is called a *scherzo*—the Italian word for *joke?*

In any case, in the Classical period music becomes much more stately, balanced, elegant and even predictable. One uniform phrase follows another, and this compositional simplicity produces a lighter music, tunes that were made to whistle. Unlike the Baroque, even instrumental lines of the Classical period sound vocal or singable. Yet the overall effect is still restrained and graceful.

If the Baroque is "cathedral" music, then the Classical is "powdered wig" music—compositions for the cultured parlor. The newfangled piano emerges as the instrument of all time, both as a soloist and as an accompanist for voices and other instruments. Such new forms as the symphony and the string quartet are a sign of much to come.

The two masters of this age are Franz Joseph Haydn (1732-1809) and Wolfgang Amadeus Mozart (1756-1791). We might also include as Classical compositions the earlier works of Ludwig van Beethoven (1770-1827), who single-handedly takes us into the next epoch.

**Romantic (1830-1900).** Bring on the passion! Intensity is critical for what one observer described as "that infinite longing which is the essence of Romanticism." For the Romantic style, powdered wigs are out and melodrama is in. Whether it's Beethoven shaking his fist at fate or Wagner shaking his fist at creditors, agitated composers of this period find new modes of self-expression.

Judging from the growing size of orchestras and operas, the new motto seems to be "big is beautiful." There's more of everything: fast, slow, loud, soft, agony, ecstasy—passions of every type. Melodies become long and expansive with complex harmonies and a full range of dynamics. Rhythmically, there's much use of rubato, or free-time, with its abrupt tempo changes.

By this time the art of constructing wind instruments has been perfected, so prominent woodwinds and brass solos compete with a much-enlarged string section. At the same time, music becomes much more national in flavor: Instead of simply sounding "European," marked differences appear between composers from, for example, Germany and France, Italy and Austria, Russia and Czechoslavakia.

A myriad of composers represent the finest work of this period, including in addition to Beethoven such familiar names as Franz Schubert (1797-1828), Felix Mendelssohn (1809-1847), Robert Schumann (1810-1856), Johannes Brahms (1833-1897), Frederic Chopin (1810-1849) Richard Wagner (1813-1883, and Peter Ilyitch Tchaikovsky (1840-1893).

**The Twentieth Century.** You may be wondering, "Don't we have a term to classify the music of our own century?" We do, but the problem is that we have too many of them! Various styles have been called everything from Impressionistic to Expressionistic to Neoclassical to Modern. Rather than split hairs over fine points of classification, we'll simply call this latest epoch the *twentieth century*. In keeping with the standard repertoire, most of the compositions we examine in this last category will be from the first half of the twentieth century.

The key word in this epoch is *dissonance;* in fact, some observers of this musical century even speak of "the emancipation of dissonance." Harmonies no longer resolve into nice major chords, and the unusual becomes usual. Polytonality (the simultaneous use of many keys) and atonality (no key whatsoever) battle to rid the world of tonality (the system of major and minor keys used for centuries).

During the first half of the twentieth century comes a strong reaction against the excesses of emotional Romanticism, resulting in a music that strives to be intellectually interesting. The two most influential composers of this era are Igor Stravinsky (1882-1971), with his wild polyrhythms (the use of different meters at the same time); and Arnold Schoenberg (1874-1951), with his complicated serial music (using twelve tones in a repeated order or series).

The last half of the century is preoccupied with experimentalism, a wide variety of techniques that range from electronic music to the use of "prepared piano," in which that instrument may have a collection of paper clips, tapes and clothespins attached to its strings. The motto here is "anything goes." Works for such ensembles as "piccolo, bass clarinet, tuba, xylophone and microwave oven" become the norm.

Of our many contemporary composers, the best-known seem to be those who create music that impresses both the emotions and the intellect. Among my favorite living composers are George Crumb, Krzysztof Penderecki, Elliott Carter, Mario Davidovsky and Charles Wuorinen.

These four periods—Baroque, Classical, Romantic and Twentieth Century— provide us the large framework for our study. You may be aware of other epochs and movements, such as the Rococo or the Impressionist composers. But for our broad purposes, these others will be considered subcategories, and their music will be covered within the four primary periods of Western music.

### CONCERTI OR CONCERTOS—THAT IS THE QUESTION

We want to try a sampling, not just of all the musical epochs, but of all the musical genres as well. So we'll examine everything from the symphony to the string quartet, from the concerto to the opera. Part of the joy of classical music is learning to appreciate the wide variety of its forms. In light of that goal, we need an overview of musical genres.

The two most basic categories of music are *instrumental* and *vocal.*

**Instrumental.** In instrumental music, the orchestra is king, followed closely by the concerto, which is a piece for a solo instrument plus orchestra. Next comes chamber music—so named because small ensembles originally performed in the chamber rooms of music patrons—including such groupings as piano trios and string quintets.

The names of these smaller groups are easy to remember if you are familiar with the Latin roots of some of our number words. Two instruments form a duet; three, a trio; four, a quartet; five, a quintet; six, a sextet; seven, a septet; eight, an octet; and nine, a nonet.

The smallest category of instrumental music, then, is the solo. Although there are some unaccompanied solos for every instrument, the bulk of this genre is for keyboards, especially piano. In this book's section on solos I've included the standard solo literature for other instruments as well, even if their "solos" are accompanied by their friends at the keyboard.

We'll begin our study with the larger forms. For the beginner in classical music, the big sound of orchestral works usually command interest longer than the intimacies of chamber music and the solo literature. The smaller works are just as excellent musically, but it's easier to begin with the thrill of the wide, dynamic range of orchestral tones and colors before approaching an entire concert of one or two instruments.

**Vocal.** Classical vocal music includes some of the greatest songs that humankind has ever created. Even beginning students in this area should feel somewhat at home for two reasons. First, though not everyone plays an instrument, everyone sings (even if only in the shower). Second, most popular music today is vocal, so we're more accustomed to the sound of singing than of instruments alone.

Even so, many people are puzzled by their first taste of classical singing, especially opera. There are two principle reasons for this confusion, both of which we can overcome. First is the language barrier. Because so much classical vocal music was written by Europeans, the words not surprisingly often are written in Italian, French, German or Latin. For those who want to attend vocal performances but don't speak all those languages—and few of us are fluent in them all—some easy solutions to the problem are available, such as good translations, previous acquaintance with the libretto (the text of an opera), and helpful subtitles. We'll say more about this later, when we discuss some simple ways of getting through the language barrier.

The second source of confusion for newcomers to classical vocal music arises from a previous immersion in popular music. Most pop vocalists have in common the use of a light, microphone-aided voice with at least electronic reverberation added. If that's what you've heard most of your life, a classically trained singer may sound foreign to you.

Nevertheless, as you become more familiar with classical vocal music, the difference is one you'll grow to appreciate. Even a beginning student can respect the discipline, talent, and sheer power of the opera singer's voice, which has to carry over the resonant accompaniment of a huge orchestra to be heard all the way to the back of a large concert hall. Many pop singers, if their microphones malfunction, can't be heard further than the first row.

The three principle divisions of vocal music are *choral* (usually with an orchestra), *opera* (also with orchestra), and *song* (usually with piano). In this last group are thousands of compositions, often called by the German term for songs—*Lieder* (LEE-der). As in popular music, their lyrics deal with countless topics—love, war, faith, sorrow, the weather, every possible aspect of life.

The great majority of classical repertoire lies within the categories we've now outlined. As we examine works of each genre, choosing from the Baroque, Classical, Romantic and Twentieth Century periods, you'll enjoy a broad sampling of the greatest music Western civilization has produced.

## How to Tell a Symphony From a Suite

In any genre, the chief distinguishing traits have to do with the size of the performing medium. As we noted before, the larger forms, such as orchestra music, choral music and operas, tend to impress us with their majesty and power. We stand back from them in awe.

On the other hand, the smaller forms, such as chamber music, songs and solo literature, impress us as intimate and personal. Through them we come closer to the performers and perhaps to the composer as well.

Further distinctions of genre are revealed as we get to know each form's history and repertoire. For instance, chamber music conveys a certain atmosphere of elegance and affluence, having been first performed in the chambers of the royalty and the nobility. A concerto, on the other hand, dazzles us with such virtuosity that we cheer as if we were at the Olympics.

For musicians, the differences in genre are even more interesting. Wind players usually want to play in orchestras, string players often prefer chamber music, top instrumental soloists go for concerti or solo pieces, and top vocal soloists seek out opera or solo songs—while more average singers delight in choral music.

## Coming to Terms

One of the first things you'll note about musical terms is that most of them are Italian. That is because in the earlier musical periods of the West (the Middle Ages and Renaissance), the Catholic Church and Italian culture were major influences on composition.

Even when Germany became the dominant European musical power in the eighteenth century, no one wanted to abandon the lyrical sound of Italian terms. I'm relieved that we seldom see such tempo indications as *Plotzlich Zuruckhaltend* ("slow down suddenly"), such percussion commands as *Mit Schwammschlagel* ("use a cymbal mallet"), or such categories as *Volkstumliches Lied* ("German art songs").

You'll find a musical glossary in the back of this book for your convenience. Meanwhile, we'll define the basic terms as we use them.

## "SIR...MADAM...YOUR PROGRAM..."

Most of us discover classical music, not according to some rigid plan, but in a more casual way—a symphony concert here, a song recital there. Because that mix seems to me both more natural and more interesting than some strict scheme of ordering—with all the instrumental works grouped together before all the vocal works—we'll look at the various genres in a similar way. The topics of the following chapters will alternate between instrumental and vocal music to provide more variety as we go. Here are the genres we'll sample:

Orchestra Music
Choral Music
The Concerto
Opera
Chamber Music
Song
Solo Repertoire

Since most of us these days struggle with packed schedules, I've organized the study into bite-size portions—each one a concert "program" that you could spend an evening exploring. You'll find a fascinating variety here: Some of the programs are longer than others; some are more exhilarating, while others are more contemplative.

So turn off those television sit-com reruns and get ready for a new musical adventure. Whether alone or with fellow-explorers, you'll soon be reading about and listening with new ears to some of the world's finest music.

I should note how painfully difficult it was for me to select the pieces discussed in each chapter. There are literally dozens of great symphonies that deserve your attention, hundreds of pieces of chamber music, thousands of beautiful songs. And there are so many wonderful people I want you to meet— not just Bach and Beethoven, but Mendelssohn, Schumann, Verdi, Stravinsky and dozens more!

No doubt you'll recognize some of the titles I've chosen, while others may be new to you. If you've already developed some favorites and I've left out some of them, remember that I've left out plenty of mine too. I talked to a number of other professional musicians about these choices, and none of us completely agree on which works are the most important. But you'll certainly encounter much of music's "top 40" material listed here. Every work we'll discuss is without dispute a masterpiece you need to know about. Together they form a healthy representation of the major features in music's last three centuries.

At the same time, keep in mind that this book is only a beginning. Though I was dismayed at having to pass over many excellent works and composers, I'm happy to know that the following programs provide an opportunity to whet your musical appetite. After you finish them, the sky's the limit.

A note about musical titles: Those who spend many years in the company of classical musicians tend to use the most common names for every piece of music. This leads to some odd inconsistencies in language. For instance, in America we generally refer to Mozart's famous opera as *The Marriage of Figaro,* rather than using its original Italian name, *Le Nozze di Figaro.* Yet at the same time we call such works as Carl Maria von Weber's opera *Der Freischutz* by their original names (in this case, German) and never by the title's English translation, *The Marksman.*

Since I don't want the language barrier to hinder your appreciation of great music, I'll use the English titles whenever possible. Nevertheless, you'll occasionally see a title in French, German or Italian, especially in vocal music. Don't let it dismay or confuse you; in time you'll appreciate it as simply part of the history and charm of classical music.

## A MATTER OF TASTE

One last point before we crank up the stereo equipment and begin to listen. What about the matter of different tastes? Is there anything wrong with liking one piece but disliking another?

No, indeed! Discovering your own tastes in classical music—finding out what *you* appreciate the most—is our paramount aim, and the joy of it all. We'll all start at the same place, listening to a broad sampling of diverse music. But once we take a liking to one kind or another, the deepest kind of enjoyment begins.

Perhaps you'll gravitate either toward vocal music or toward instrumental. Then further preferences will appear. Some will go for chamber music in a big way; others will develop into opera buffs. Some may revel in Romanticism while others live for the Baroque. That's why I've listed so many extra works in the back of the book; if any particular genre or period becomes your specialty, you'll want lots of material for pursuing it further.

You'll probably also grow fond of particular composers. You may become a Debussy fan or an Ives fanatic, reading their biographies, stocking up on their CDs, even watching the newspaper and the TV guides for performances of their works.

Meanwhile, keep in mind a wonderful secret of classical music lovers: The more kinds of music you can learn to love, the greater your ultimate pleasure will be. So open your ears as wide as possible. A vast and beautiful world of sound awaits your discovery.

# 2

# ORCHESTRA MUSIC

*A symphony must be like the world;*
*it must embrace everything!*

–Gustav Mahler

The universally acknowledged king of classical instrumental music is the symphony orchestra. Nothing else can match the excitement created by its rich, massive sound. So well-assured is the symphony's central role in the standard classical repertoire that when we hear someone speak of "Beethoven's Ninth" or "Mozart's Fortieth," we immediately know that the reference is not to sonatas or quartets, but to symphonies.

Orchestral popularity may be surprising when we consider that this genre is one of the most expensive, impractical and difficult to produce. Consider how much easier it would be to get four string players together to perform quartets than it would be to secure a large concert hall, complete with all the various pieces of symphonic equipment such as dozens of music stands, a podium, percussion instruments, printed music and more. Add to that the task of rounding up the multitude of performers needed—not to mention the challenge of paying them all!

Nevertheless, every major city in the world has at least one orchestra, and many have several orchestras, each performing for thousands of devotees. How did the symphony orchestra achieve such prominence?

To answer that question we have to go back many centuries to trace the orchestra's development over a long time. But first, we need a few definitions, because the words *symphony* and *orchestra* are tossed around so freely that they sometimes seem to mean the same thing.

*Orchestra* actually refers to a large group of musicians who perform music together. *Symphony* is loosely used in several ways but correctly refers to a specific type of music written for an orchestra to play.

Like many other music forms, the symphony has undergone some changes throughout the centuries. But classical symphonies, such as those by Mozart or Beethoven, are orchestral works composed of several movements, usually four, with the movements labeled by their tempo—that is, the rate of speed at which they're performed (typically, "fast, slow, very fast, and fast"). There are dozens of variations, but this is the standard form.

Alongside these technically correct definitions lie several forms of musical slang. For instance, an orchestra of classical musicians is usually called a "symphony orchestra" whether or not they happen to be playing a symphony in a particular concert. This usage developed to distinguish such a group from other kinds of orchestras, such as those that play big-band music. With these definitions in mind, we can now look at the history of the orchestra.

## A HISTORY OF THE ORCHESTRA

For nearly fifteen centuries, the music of the early Christian church was almost exclusively vocal. Even when the earliest instrumental parts were written in the fifteenth century, the composers seldom noted which instrument to use. Any available instruments had to suffice, and they usually were relegated to accompanying the human voice.

In the late Renaissance, however, instrumentalists came into their own, and small ensembles began to appear. Throughout the 1600s these enterprising groups increased in sophistication and size, becoming the prototypes of our modern orchestras.

In the Baroque era orchestras found themselves not only accompanying a church cantata or an opera, but also performing music written especially for them. Soon they were playing public concerts as well.

The original orchestras had been composed almost exclusively of about a dozen strings, usually with the leader seated at a harpsichord. But by the time of Bach, a few winds were getting involved, notably oboes and horns. By modern standards still relatively small—with about twenty to thirty-five members, these orchestras gained in popularity, in part because music lovers were discovering that instrumental works had a universal advantage over vocal ones—they had no language barriers.

In the eighteenth century, rich noblemen often employed private orchestras. Notable among these was Prince Paul Esterhazy of Hungary, an art-loving aristocrat who took the composer Franz Joseph Haydn into his employ for years. Haydn, known as the "father of the symphony," produced a hundred and four of these works, including dozens for the prince.

In addition to a larger group of strings, the Classical orchestra of Mozart used pairs of flutes, oboes, clarinets, bassoons, trumpets, horns and tympani (kettledrums). The musical leader began to leave the keyboard and conduct the ensemble full-time. Soon trombones, tubas, harps and a host of percussion equipment were used. By the end of the nineteenth century, orchestras of one hundred players and more filled up the stage.

Fortunately, they didn't all play all of the time! But this expansion of the form into a large and diverse collection of instruments, along with the eventual complexities of nineteenth-century orchestra music, led to the need for a musical master to lead the effort. Thus emerged the role of the virtuoso conductor.

The orchestra simply couldn't keep growing in size—not if all the instrumentalists were to play on one stage. So in the twentieth century, the assortment of instruments diversified into new and sometimes bizarre combinations. For example, composers might write for orchestras containing four piccolos, but no flutes or oboes; or perhaps for one alto flute, three contrabassoons, five trombones and no violas.

Meanwhile, the twentieth century also has seen an astonishing growth of full-time employed orchestras—complete with their own staff of administrators, secretaries, stage hands, librarians and marketing experts. Through several centuries of growing popularity, then, the orchestra developed from a small and simple ensemble of occasional players to an extensive and complex professional company.

Finally, we should note that the orchestra's prominent place in music history has come not only because of its popularity with audiences. The form also holds an attraction for composers. Most of the famous composers of the last three hundred years have made the orchestra their primary vehicle, and many have been judged chiefly by the skill of their orchestral writing. With its huge array of tone colors, contrasts and dynamic variation, the orchestra has inspired composers to produce some of the greatest music ever conceived.

But enough history. It's time to get acquainted with the music itself. Let's walk together through a few centuries of orchestral repertoire, keeping in mind that we have to walk briskly. There are thousands of great works written for the orchestra, so we'll be sure to touch on the "must hear" pieces.

Check your public library or local music store for recordings of the works we'll examine. Then try to find a time and place to listen when you can get comfortable and avoid distractions. Relax and enjoy yourself!

## ORCHESTRAL PROGRAM #1
## BACH: ORCHESTRA SUITE NO. 3 IN D MAJOR
## HANDEL: WATER MUSIC SUITE

Long before the Classical symphony as we know it was conceived, Baroque composers were writing "suites" for orchestra. These groups of somewhat related movements often were based on the dance music of an earlier age and still used such titles as "minuet" or "sarabande" (both names of dances).

## JOHANN SEBASTIAN BACH (1685-1750)

The four Orchestra Suites of J.S. Bach (pronounced BOCK) are matchless examples of this art form. (We usually include the initials "J.S." to distinguish him from his sons who were also composers, especially C.P.E. Bach and J.C. Bach.)

The first movement of each suite is an extended overture (musical introduction) that begins slowly, breaks into a faster tempo and finally returns to the opening music. As you listen, notice how the shorter dance movements that follow are always in two parts, with each of the different sections repeated to form a delicate balance of form.

The most popular of Bach's four suites are the *Suite No. 2 in B Minor,* for flute and strings, and the *Suite No. 3 in D Major,* which in certain movements add trumpets and tympani to the strings and oboes. In the hands of a virtuoso soloist, the former work becomes a magnificent concerto for flute, with the last movement exhausting the technical possibilities of the instrument.

The *Suite in D Major* contains an especially beautiful air that you may recognize (an air is an optional movement of the suite with a melodic rather than dance-like character). This movement became famous in a different genre. Decades after Bach composed it, violinist August Wilhelm transcribed it for the violin, changing the key so that the melody could be played entirely on the lowest string of the violin. Consequently, thousands now know the exquisite "Air on the G String" who may have never heard its original orchestral setting.

When you listen to this piece, you'll enjoy how the stately bass line begins the movement as the violins' principal melody emerges with exquisite beauty.

## GEORGE FRIDERIC HANDEL (1685-1759)

Another Baroque composer of orchestra suites was George Frideric Handel, the master who created the beloved oratorio *Messiah* (an oratorio is a vocal composition of religious or contemplative character; more about this in chapter 3). Compositions such as the *Water Music Suite,* written for King George I of England, remind us how much eighteenth-century musicians depended on royal patronage.

Handel, a native of Germany, came into the employ of King George, at that time the Elector of Hanover. Traveling in England on what was to have been a brief leave of absence from that post, the composer found great appreciation for his genius in London; Queen Anne even honored him with a life pension. Handel enjoyed himself in England so much, in fact, that he failed to return to Germany as he had promised.

Imagine the composer's dismay when, at the death of the queen, the disgruntled George was summoned to the throne of England to be the new monarch. But Handel solved this rather ticklish dilemma in characteristic fashion. When a royal aquatic pageant with decorated barges was planned, he obtained from the Lord Chamberlain a commission to furnish the music.

The series of pieces he wrote, now known as the *Water Music Suite,* were played by an entire orchestra that floated down the Thames on a barge behind the king—with Handel himself conducting. If there was any seasickness in the orchestra, history has politely failed to record it. In any case, the king was delighted, sent for Handel, forgave him and granted him an additional pension. Fortunately for us, the *Water Music* soon moved from the barge to the concert hall and has delighted audiences ever since.

Perhaps the most famous movement of this work is the powerful "Hornpipe." Note the spectacular contrast between the trumpets and horns, which is characteristic of the grand Baroque orchestration. Then you'll hear a different type of beauty in the lovely "Air," with its long and elaborate melody.

Despite the noble orchestration, we're always aware that these movements are indeed *dances,* whose forms in some cases are centuries old. Thus the Baroque period is itself a transition from the old world of Medieval and Renaissance music into the new world of the modern orchestra.

ORCHESTRAL PROGRAM #2
HAYDN: SYMPHONY NO. 94 IN G MAJOR
MOZART: SYMPHONY NO. 40 IN G MINOR

## FRANZ JOSEF HAYDN (1732-1809)

Moving ahead a few decades into the Classical Period, we find the orchestra reaching a new level of evolution at the hands of the "father of the symphony"—Franz Joseph Haydn (HIDE-uhn, not HAYD-uhn, as some mispronounce his name). As we noted earlier, he was hired by a wealthy music-lover, Prince Esterhazy of Hungary; and for years Haydn had a full orchestra at his disposal. This resulted in dozens of symphonies with four movements: a fast one, a slow one, a minuet and a fast finale. Keep this structure in mind as you listen; it served as the model for composers throughout the nineteenth century.

Haydn wrote such a vast amount of symphonies that the best way to learn them is to begin with the ones that have programmatic titles. These include such whimsical entries as "The Chicken" *(Symphony No. 83),* in which a clucking noise is heard in the first movement; "The Military" *(Symphony No. 100),* named by its trumpet and drum fanfares; "The Clock" *(Symphony No. 101),* whose slow movement features a tick-tock accompaniment; and, perhaps best-known, "The Surprise Symphony" *(Symphony No. 94).*

In this last work, Haydn demonstrates his wry humor. The second movement

## INSTRUMENTS OF THE ORCHESTRA: STRINGS

The string section forms the largest group of players in the orchestra. At first sight you will see what seems to be three kinds of stringed instruments, which you may recognize as the violin, the cello and the bass (or double bass or contrabass). If you look more closely, however, you'll notice that one group of players seem to have very large violins. Don't ever ask these players why their violins are so big. They're not violins at all; they're violas.

These four instruments make up the foundation of the orchestra. The violins have such prominence that they're always divided into two groups, the first violins and the second violins (hence the phrase "playing second fiddle" to someone—but don't ever say *that* to a player, either). You'll notice that, unlike the winds (who each have their own distinct musical part), each string group is playing the same music (we hope), "doubled" by everyone in that group. While this custom eliminates almost all possibilities for a solo if you're a string player, the blend creates a beautiful, deep sonority that has enriched the orchestra sound for several centuries.

Each of these instruments has four strings, made of wire or animal gut. That's right—sheep gut. As Shakespeare aptly noted: "Is it not strange that sheeps' guts should hale [pull] souls out of men's bodies?"

These strings vibrate when a bow made of wood and horsehair is drawn by the right hand across the strings, usually one string at a time. The quivering string then vibrates a small piece of wood called the bridge, which vibrates the top of the instrument, which vibrates a smaller piece of wood inside called the soundpost, which vibrates the instrument's back, shoots the sound back out the front via the "F-holes" (shaped like the letter "F"), vibrating the air itself and finally vibrating your eardrum.

This entire process, happening in the twinkling of an eye, is responsible for all those beautiful string parts of the symphonies you've been hearing for years.

The fingers of the left hand push the strings down at specific places to shorten the length of the string that's vibrating. The shorter the length of string that's allowed to vibrate, the higher the pitch.

The strings can also create other effects, the most common being *pizzicato*—achieved by plucking the strings instead of using the bow. Furthermore, the bow itself can be bounced on the string, hammered, played near the bridge or over the fingerboard, or even played using the wood instead of the hair. Sometimes the bow is used to play two adjacent strings simultaneously, or full chords using three or four strings.

The melodic pre-eminence of the string section is also due to their very large range, that is, the number of notes (from very low pitches to very high) that each string instrument can play. Put them all together, from the lowest note of the bass to the highest of the violins, and you can cover almost the complete range of the piano. That's a lot of notes coming from all those vibrating strings!

begins with quiet music from the strings, followed by even quieter music. But watch out—suddenly a loud (fortissimo) chord from the whole orchestra rocks the concert, and wakes any would-be sleeper in the audience.

The composer commented on the piece simply: "This will make the ladies scream." At the very least, your heart will skip a beat. Throughout the work, notice the regular phrases and the elegant style characteristic of music in the Classical Period.

## WOLFGANG AMADEUS MOZART (1756-1791)

Haydn had a dear friend also destined for musical greatness, the young prodigy Wolfgang Amadeus Mozart (MOTE-sahrt; the "z" here is like the "z" in pizza). Their mutual respect was untouched by jealousy. Haydn's admiration for his colleague was evidenced by a statement to Mozart's father: "I assure you before God, as an honorable man, your son is the greatest composer I know personally or by reputation."

Mozart wrote symphonies even as a child; he composed forty-one of them before his untimely death at the age of thirty-five. The last seven or so have all entered the standard repertoire, and particularly noteworthy are the final three. Though Mozart was typically desperate for money and usually composed large works only after a commission, he wrote these three great symphonies (in less than two months) without explanation or even a chance of performance.

Of the hundreds of memorable melodies Mozart left us, few are more famous than the opening of his *Symphony No. 40 in G Minor*. An easy way to remember this tune is with the words music students have used for years: "It's a bird, it's a plane, it's a Mozart!" Pay special attention to the harmonic complexities found in the last movement; they are so ahead of Mozart's time that they could have been lifted from the twentieth century. If you want further evidence of the composer's genius, listen as well to the grand finale of *Symphony No. 41 in C Major* (The "Jupiter" Symphony). It points the way for the later Romantics.

If you compare Haydn's and Mozart's orchestrations, you'll find that Mozart likes to use a few more wind players than his friend, whose symphonies were mostly for strings with a few oboes, bassoons or horns added. Mozart was a fanatic about clarinets; he once wrote his father enthusiastically, "Ah, if only we had some clarinets, too! You cannot imagine the effect of a symphony with flutes, oboes and clarinets!"

By the end of his short life Mozart had established the standard woodwind section of two flutes, two oboes, two clarinets and two bassoons, joined by two trumpets, two horns and two tympani. You'll hear them all in *Symphony No. 40*. Since these last Mozart symphonies fall late in the Classical Period, their phrases have become less regular, anticipating the freedom of the coming Romantic composers.

## ORCHESTRAL PROGRAM #3
### BEETHOVEN: SYMPHONY NO. 3 IN E♭ MAJOR ("EROICA")
### BEETHOVEN: SYMPHONY NO. 5 IN C MINOR

## LUDWIG VAN BEETHOVEN (1770-1827)

Seldom in the history of art has one man had such a dramatic influence on those who followed him. As a young man Ludwig van Beethoven (BAY-toh-vuhn) had performed for Mozart, who remarked prophetically: "Keep your eyes on him. Someday he will give the world something to talk about." Although Haydn wrote one hundred and four symphonies and Mozart wrote forty-one, the nine symphonies of Beethoven were of such genius that for years composers were almost too intimidated by them to attempt the form themselves.

All nine symphonies are staples for major orchestras today, and several are monumental works. From the opening sounds of his *Symphony No. 1,* Beethoven was original. He began with a discord needing resolution—something that had never before opened a symphony composition.

In 1804 Beethoven completed his *Third Symphony.* In the preceding years Napoleon, a rising star on the French horizon, had fast distinguished himself on European battlefields, and the composer decided to dedicate the piece to the general. But when Napoleon entered Paris in triumph and was proclaimed Emperor, Beethoven's admiration turned to scorn. The composer crumpled the title page, retitled the massive work "Eroica" ("Heroism"), and dedicated it to "the memory of a great man." This memorial concept is culminated in the somber second movement, which the composer entitled "Funeral March."

The first movement is almost a symphony in itself, with scores of themes and innovative harmony. Note how at one point Beethoven cleverly brings in the horn two measures earlier than expected, and in the process superimposes two different chords on top of each other. A contemporary listener, unaccustomed to such fare, complained that either the horn player did not know how to count, or that Beethoven did not know how to write music!

One particular area of Beethoven's genius and innovation is rhythm. Although this first movement is written in 3/4 time (counted "one, two, three; one, two, three"), notice how the composer constantly uses strong chords of only *two* beats. The tensions created by these asymmetrical accents is both vintage Beethoven and vintage Romanticism.

Beethoven's *Fifth Symphony* is perhaps the most celebrated of all time. From the drama of its opening notes, which you will no doubt recognize, to the entrance of the trombones in the finale—their first appearance in a symphony—Beethoven's stamp is unmistakable. When Goethe first heard it, he exclaimed, "How big it is—quite wild! Enough to bring the house about one's ears!"

Compare this with the Classical pieces you heard by Haydn and Mozart, and it will be clear how such "wildness" distinguishes Romantic music from the works of that earlier epoch. Beethoven's Fifth proclaims the passion and intensity of the Romantic style.

An interesting historical note: The symphony's recognition jumped during World War II. Since the rhythm of the opening four notes (da, da, da, daaaaaa) is the same as the Morse code for the letter "V" (short, short, short, long), Beethoven's Fifth became a signal of victory whenever the Allied forces triumphed on the battlefield.

## ORCHESTRAL PROGRAM #4:
## BEETHOVEN: SYMPHONY NO. 6 IN F MAJOR ("PASTORAL")
## BEETHOVEN: SYMPHONY NO. 9 IN D MINOR ("CHORAL")

Beethoven's *Symphony No. 6* has been greatly popularized in our time by its animation in the film *Fantasia*. Even without Walt Disney's nymphs, this "Pastoral Symphony" is the perfect record of Beethoven's love for the countryside. He used descriptive programmatic titles above each movement, such as "The cheerful impressions excited on arriving in the country" and "By the brook."

Listen to the clever ways that the music imitates nature. In the second movement, "By the brook," the rippling sixteenth notes in the lower strings suggest ripples of quietly moving water. At the end of that movement, the flute, oboe and clarinet perform a delightful dialogue between the cuckoo, the quail and the nightingale. In the fourth "storm" movement, the rapid rumblings of the basses and cellos, along with the ferocity of the tympani, take us into the heart of a tempest. The composer paints a rural panorama in sound to match those of the nature-loving poets of his day.

The climax of Beethoven's symphonic works comes in the colossal "Choral" *Symphony No. 9.* Many of us have heard this masterpiece so often that we easily overlook the outrageous innovations it contains. Note especially the addition of a chorus and vocal soloists for the final movement.

Every movement here is sublime. The first is the epitome of drama; the second, of power; and the third, of beauty. The last movement is more like a grand opera than a symphony as it ties all the previous movements together. Listen to how it brings the simple tune popularly known as the "Ode to Joy" to a climatic state that overwhelms us even before the chorus and soloists arrive.

In this work, Beethoven shows no more mercy to the singers than to the instrumentalists as he challenges them with passages that are tortuously difficult to perform. Once, when a violinist friend complained about the difficulties in one of

Beethoven's compositions, the composer roared, "Do you think I consider your wretched violin when the spirit moves me?"

No doubt the *Ninth Symphony* demands the greatest of musicians for its performance. But when they rise to the challenge, the effect is closer to heaven than to earth.

The music of Beethoven contained such genius that he almost single-handedly led music from the eighteenth century into the nineteenth, and from the Classical era to the Romantic. His influence was felt by composers for many decades. In 1852, Franz Liszt confessed that "to us musicians the work of Beethoven parallels the pillars of smoke and fire which led the Israelites through the desert."

He must still be influencing musicians in our day: When asked once about classical music, Beatle Ringo Starr replied, "I love Beethoven, especially the poems."

## ORCHESTRAL PROGRAM #5:
### SCHUBERT: SYMPHONY NO. 9 ("THE GREAT")
### BERLIOZ: SYMPHONIE FANTASTIQUE

### FRANZ SCHUBERT (1797-1828)

Beethoven had a young admirer, almost a "groupie," named Franz Schubert. When the older composer was shown some music by the younger, he exclaimed, "Surely there is a divine spark in Schubert." But the younger composer remained awed by his mentor; he once moaned, "Who can do anything after Beethoven?"

Nevertheless, in his brief thirty-one years Schubert matched his master by creating nine symphonies of his own. This seems to have started an odd trend for others composers who followed: Dvorak, Bruckner, Mahler and Vaughan Williams all wrote nine symphonies as well. Schubert's final two are the symphonies we hear the most, and each has an interesting name, though not given by Schubert himself.

The "Unfinished Symphony" (*Symphony No. 8*) is doubtless the most celebrated musical fragment in history. The mystery behind its unfinished state has never been solved. It's not, after all, the familiar case of a composer failing to complete a work on his deathbed. On the contrary, in 1822, Schubert wrote the first two movements; then, for no known reason he mailed them to a friend and forgot all about the project. The manuscript was discovered years after the composer's death.

Despite some absurd attempts by modern composers to "finish" the symphony with additional movements, the exquisite two that Schubert completed have stood on their own as one of the world's most frequently performed symphonies. You'll notice that neither movement is fast, but both are intense. After the haunting opening melody by the oboe and clarinet (a favorite combination of Schubert), we soon come to the famous second theme given by the cellos.

Schubert's last orchestral work is called "The Great." And it is. But that's not how it got its name. Schubert has two symphonies in the key of C Major, numbers 6 and 9. To distinguish them, some unknown music cataloger labeled them "The Little" and "The Great."

From the quiet horn melody that opens the work to its climactic trombone fanfares, this symphony is the perfect epitaph for Schubert's short but creative life. You'll find it full of movement, perfectly balanced and featuring melodies that are so singable you'd have thought they came from an opera rather than a symphony.

## HECTOR BERLIOZ (1803-1869)

Now we turn away from this formidable line of German musicians to the Frenchman Hector Berlioz (BAIR-lee-ohz), a highly emotional and self-proclaimed "bad boy" of music. His personality is reflected in an incident that took place when he attended a concert of a Beethoven symphony. Berlioz was weeping so profusely that a gentleman near him tried to comfort him.

"You seem to be greatly affected, sir," said the stranger. "Had you not better retire for a while?"

Berlioz answered intensely, "Are you under the impression that I am here to *enjoy* myself?"

Known more for his imaginative orchestration than for his melodies or harmonies, Berlioz established himself in musical history by showing the nineteenth-century Romantics what a grand orchestra could do. One example of the genre's magnificent potential is his most performed work, *Symphonie Fantastique* (fan-tas-TEEK, with the older meaning of unusual, bizarre or mysterious).

As you listen, note especially Berlioz's use of the "idee fixe"—that is, the recurring theme that finds its way into every movement of the symphony. In this work, the theme is that of the "Beloved." It is first clearly stated at the beginning of the fast part of the opening movement.

Berlioz utilizes innovative orchestral technique, especially in the last movement. There he opens mysteriously with divided strings playing tremolo (a trembling effect). Later he asks the violins and violas to play "col legno"—that is, rapidly bouncing the wood of the bows onto the strings.

*Symphonie Fantastique* musically portrays a lover's dream that somehow turns sour. In the first few movements, the artist encounters his lover in such pleasant places as out in the countryside and at a ball. But he goes insane, kills her, is marched to the gallows (a great movement, especially if you're a bassoonist) and is eternally condemned. It's a bizarre story, but as we noted, that's what he meant by *Fantastique.*

# ORCHESTRAL PROGRAM #6
## MENDELSSOHN: MIDSUMMER NIGHT'S DREAM OVERTURE
## SCHUMANN: SYMPHONY NO. 3 IN E♭ MAJOR ("RHENISH")

### FELIX MENDELSSOHN (1809-1847)

After this brief visit to France, we head back to Germany, which continued to produce Europe's major symphonic composers throughout the nineteenth century. At the center of this renowned circle of musicians was Felix Mendelssohn, who knew most of them well and championed their music. He also is credited with the rediscovery of J. S. Bach, whose works had been neglected for years.

Mendelssohn was perhaps the greatest child prodigy since Mozart, both as a pianist and a composer. His beautiful *Midsummer Night's Dream Overture* was written when he was only seventeen.

We've listened to suites and symphonies; now we're going to enjoy our first *overture*. As the name suggests, it's a kind of introduction or announcement. Originally (and primarily) the overture is the first movement of an opera, an instrumental collage of all the musical themes that will be found in the opera. As we'll see in chapter 5, the orchestra plays the overture as a "prelude" before the curtain goes up.

Mendelssohn and other Romantic composers, however, began to write instrumental "concert overtures" that stand on their own in a symphonic program. Some are inspired by a play, usually one of Shakespeare's masterpieces. Others center on a place, such as Mendelssohn's *Fingal's Cave Overture*, written about his visit to the Hebrides Islands. Sometimes an event spurs the creation of an overture; the most famous example surely is the *1812 Overture* of Tchaikovsky (more about that later). The composer seeks to suggest the play, place or event musically in a way that foreshadows the work of the French Impressionists at the end of the nineteenth century (more about that later too).

Naturally, Mendelssohn's concert overture—inspired by Shakespeare's magical play—has many passages that suggest fairies, charms and whimsical humor. If you listen with imagination to the light rustle of the violins, you can almost see Oberon and his fairies from *A Midsummer Night's Dream*.

Incidently, as you get better acquainted with classical music, you'll notice that composers have always been fans of Shakespeare. Beethoven's *Tempest Piano Sonata*, Verdi's *Othello*, Tchaikovsky's *Romeo and Juliet Overture*, Schubert's *Who Is Sylvia?*—all were inspired by Shakespeare. As a source of material for composers, the English playwright's works are surpassed only by the Bible.

If you want to hear more of Mendelssohn, you should know that he wrote five excellent symphonies. The last four are staples for all orchestras. They're subtitled

"The Hymn of Praise"; "The Scottish" and "The Italian" (these two refer to the composer's visits to these countries); and "The Reformation."

The "Hymn of Praise" (*Symphony No. 2*) uses a chorus in the last movement (Beethoven's shadow lengthens!) that's twice as long as all the other other movements combined. "The Italian" (*Symphony No. 4*) is best known for its opening rapid chords in the woodwinds, as well as the excitement generated by the fourth movement, whose breakneck tempo is derived from an Italian dance known as a "Saltarello."

*Symphony No. 5*, "The Reformation," is a statement of faith from this Lutheran composer. Mendelssohn wrote it for the tricentennial of that religious revolution's birth. Its last movement contains clever musical references to "A Mighty Fortress Is our God," a song written by the German Protestant reformer Martin Luther.

## ROBERT SCHUMANN (1810-1856)

Mendelssohn once was praised as "the Mozart of the nineteenth century" by fellow composer Robert Schumann (SHOE-mon). Although these two men had much in common—notably their talent for recognizing other talent—they displayed very different temperaments.

Mendelssohn, whose first name, Felix, means "happy man," typically was optimistic and confident. Schumann, on the other hand, was an emotional Romantic. Having barely won the hand of his beloved from a cantankerous father-in-law, he was unable to turn a beautiful marriage into a beautiful life. At one point he attempted suicide by throwing himself in the Rhine River. Soon after, he became insane and died in an asylum.

Of Schumann's four symphonies, the most well-known are the "Spring" (*Symphony No. 1*) and the "Rhenish" (*Symphony No. 3*). The first was inspired by a couplet of the poet Adolph Bottget: "Oh, follow, follow on the run, for the valley blooms with the spring." It's a vivacious work; the beauty of the second movement is especially reminiscent of the freshness of the season.

The "Rhenish" was intended to depict a panorama of life in the Rhine valley. It features musical references to old German songs, a "Cathedral Scene" in the fourth movement, and a concluding Rhenish festival. This symphony was inspired by the composer's first visit to the lofty Cologne cathedral, whose magnificence is reflected throughout the first movement—especially in the rousing brass ending.

The fourth movement shows Schumann to be a Bach fanatic like his friend Mendelssohn. Its solemn counterpoint is a nineteenth-century tribute to the work of the Baroque master.

Schumann may have ended his life without joy, yet this sample of his orchestral works illustrates just how joyous his music could be. His finest compositions were masterpieces of power, majesty and victory.

## ORCHESTRAL PROGRAM #7
### BRAHMS: SYMPHONY NO. 2 IN D MAJOR
### BRAHMS: VARIATIONS ON A THEME BY HAYDN

## JOHANNES BRAHMS (1833-1897)

After Schumann's death, his friend Johannes Brahms wrote, "Schumann's memory is holy. The noble, pure artist forever remains my ideal. I will hardly be privileged ever to love a better person."

Brahms indeed loved both Schumann and his wife Clara. After Robert's death, some historians conjecture, Brahms might have married Clara had he not been an incorrigible bachelor, strictly wedded to his art. He was terribly scrupulous in composition; though writing many smaller works, he waited years before attempting a symphony. Then he spent more years still laboring over it before he was satisfied. But for those of us privileged to hear the results, it was worth the wait.

Brahms's four symphonies are second only to Beethoven's in frequency of performance. This century Brahms has become so popular that you rarely hear the old joke, "Sure, I know classical music; I know what Brahms are."

Each of this composer's symphonies is a perfectly crafted masterpiece. The first is so dramatic and powerful that it's been nicknamed "Beethoven's Tenth." When someone once pointed out to Brahms the obvious similarity between the theme of the last work's movement with that of Beethoven's Ninth, the composer shot back, "Any fool could see that!"

While Brahms busily wrote his second symphony in 1877, across the ocean Thomas Edison invented the phonograph. Little did the composer know that one day that newfangled American invention would make it possible for millions of music lovers to hear the piece he was laboring to create.

Many consider Brahms's *Second Symphony* his greatest work, from the sunshine of the opening horns to the final brass chords. Sometimes called his "Pastoral Symphony," its opening three notes contain the germ of many melodies to follow. See how many variations in this three-note motive you can find throughout the work, especially in the first and last movements.

Other Brahms fans argue that the top symphonic award should go to the sublime No. 3, or the mysterious and beautiful No. 4. The argument could go on forever, yet all would agree that all four of Brahms's symphonies are in a class by themselves.

Even so, the composer himself was unassuming about his creations. He once sent the manuscript of his fourth symphony (of which no other copy then existed) to the conductor Hans van Buelow in an ordinary postal package—not even by registered mail.

In a fury, Buelow protested, "What would we have done had the package gone astray?"

The composer simply stated: "In that case I would have to write the symphony anew."

Brahms also wrote some great overtures, serenades and the classic we examine here, *Variations of a Theme by Haydn*. After the chorale-like theme is fully stated, Brahms begins the first of nine contrasting variations. Some obscure the theme almost completely, and the last is the most complex of all—a broad passacaglia (a dance form) that contains a set of variations within itself. Finally the theme is triumphantly restated, with a typically Romantic, Brahmsian flourish.

Listening to Brahms's works, we can easily understand the sentiment behind Schumann's statement: "I believe Johannes to be the true apostle, who will also write Revelations."

## ORCHESTRAL PROGRAM #8
## DVORAK: SYMPHONY NO. 9 IN E MINOR
## ("FROM THE NEW WORLD")
## SMETANA: THE MOLDAU
## JOHANN STRAUSS: BLUE DANUBE WALTZ

### ANTONIN DVORAK (1841-1904)

Without a family of his own to care for, Brahms generously provided for many others, especially a younger composer from Bohemia (part of the present-day Czech Republic) named Antonin Dvorak (AN-taw-neen DVOR-zhahk). Brahms "discovered" Dvorak as a composer, befriended him, talked his own publisher into buying the younger man's music and even gave money to his family. We can tip our hat to this bit of philanthropy, for without it Dvorak's genius might have forever been buried in Czech poverty and obscurity. Instead, this simple man became—to his own bewildered amusement—an international star, traveling all over Europe and even America.

When Dvorak came to the United States in 1892, he was not alone. Another wave of European immigration was in progress; only a few years before, the Statue of Liberty had been erected in New York's harbor to welcome the newcomers, many of them from the composer's homeland. As if to welcome them—and perhaps to give the loved ones they left behind a glimpse of the new homeland—Dvorak wrote while he lived in the United States the last of nine symphonies, subtitled "From the New World." This most popular of his works contains themes that openly suggest African-American spirituals and the music of Native Americans. Dvorak denied literally quoting specific American tunes in this symphony, although the second theme to the first movement sounds suspiciously similar to the old spiritual "Swing Low, Sweet Chariot." He once told a reporter for *The New York Herald* that "the future music of this country must be founded on what is called the Negro Melodies."

The "New World" Symphony is wonderful fun, from its quiet moody opening to its rousing boogie-woogie ending. Since Dvorak conducted its premiere with the New York Philharmonic, it has been acclaimed by many to be the greatest composition ever written and premiered in the Western hemisphere.

Whether in Chicago, London or New York, this humble composer never forgot his Bohemian roots. Among his many works that reflect this flavor are the two sets of his fabulous *Slavonic Dances*. These irresistible pieces are vintage Dvorak, orchestrated to give a panorama of the joyful peasant dances of the Czech countryside.

I prefer the first set of dances (Opus 46—"opus" is simply the Latin term for "work"), especially the ones in C Major, F Major and C Minor. But if you try them, you'll love them all—even snobby musicologists do, though some won't admit it. After all, sometimes nineteenth-century Romanticism can get rather heavy, so it's nice to lighten up a bit.

## BEDRICH SMETENA (1824-1884)

While we're visiting Czechoslovakia, we should take time to listen to Bedrich Smetena (SMEH-tah-nah). Occasionally history presents us with a so-called "one-work" composer; that is, someone who wrote few, though excellent, pieces. Smetena is just such a composer.

Smetena is remembered for one opera, one string quartet and one principle orchestra piece, "The Moldau"—a movement from a larger suite entitled *Ma Vlast* ("My Native Land"). I've never seen the Czech river that inspired this last work, but if it's half as beautiful as its orchestral counterpart, then someday I want to float down it leisurely in a lone canoe. *Tres Romantique!* This music ought to be used in commercials to attract tourists to Eastern Europe.

The water of many streams is suggested here by flutes, clarinets and other instruments that flow irresistably into the Moldau's main theme. The river travels through woodlands, villages and rapids (you can't miss them), then finally reaches the great city of Prague, when the principal theme is restated triumphantly in a major key. A beautiful boat ride!

## JOHANN STRAUSS, JR. (1825-1899)

Speaking of music about rivers, you've probably heard the "Blue Danube." It's a great piece, and one of dozens of waltzes by (who else?) the renowned "Waltz King," Johann Strauss, Jr. All of these are fun to hear, fun to play and presumably fun to dance to, though sadly enough most waltzing is now done only in old movies.

All waltzes are in a rather quick 3/4 time, often with a slight emphasis on the second of the three beats. Orchestras that specialize in Strauss waltzes add subtle retards and accelerandos (gradual slow-downs and speed-ups) that give the music an authentic flavor. If you can get a recording of Strauss's waltzes by the Vienna Philharmonic, pay any price for it!

An important note: This man should never be confused with the later composer Richard (re-KARD) Strauss, the creator of wild and woolly "tone poems" we'll discuss soon. Thousands of his records have been purchased inadvertently by innocent novices who only wanted some light waltzes by our friend Johann, Jr. You should see the shock when someone invites a sweetheart over for a romantic dinner, lowers the lights for effect and then turns on the stereo—only to be assaulted by Richard's decidedly bombastic sounds.

## ORCHESTRAL PROGRAM #9
### LISZT: LES PRELUDES
### WAGNER: THE FLYING DUTCHMAN OVERTURE
### WAGNER: PRELUDE TO TRISTAN UND ISOLDE

Leaving the Moldau of Bohemia and the Danube of Austria, we now go back toward Hungary and Germany to take an important new turn in music. What we come upon in the days of Brahms is the beginning of a musical war between two very different camps. We've looked at some of the works on the "Brahmsian" side. But now we need to examine a strong new influence opposing that tradition, created by the "wild men" of music—Franz Liszt and Richard Wagner.

We should also mention that other musical wars were taking shape as well. In the world of opera, there would soon be developing a battle between the Wagner fans in Germany and the fans of composer Giuseppe Verdi in Italy. Furthermore, the emerging musical traditions of many countries—especially France and Russia, but also England, Finland, Norway, Spain, Hungary and even America—were collectively undermining the dominance Germany had long held in music.

### FRANZ LISZT (1811-1886)

Remember the child prodigies Mozart and Mendelssohn? Little Franz Liszt topped them both; he was dubbed "the eighth wonder of the world," and grew up to become the greatest and most uncontrollable pianist of his century. Comparing him with some popular modern musicians, we might describe Liszt's temperament as a bit of Elton John, Liberace and maybe Elvis Presley all in one.

Liszt took Europe by storm. He made thousands of fans and enemies with his personality of striking contrasts. Listz was known, for example, as a deeply religious man, yet his passion for rich women was a scandal.

## The Instruments of the Orchestra: WOODWINDS

Woodwinds aren't all made of wood. The flutes and piccolos, which belong to this family, are metal. But they were once made of wood, and the classification remained even when the substance of these instruments changed.

The classical symphony contained pairs of the four basic woodwind instruments: flute, oboe, clarinet and bassoon. You may have noticed the similarity between this and the basic classifications of the human voice: soprano, alto, tenor and bass. In fact, this system was noticeable in our string groups as well and will be again seen with the brasses.

The woodwind instruments, however, each come with partners. Flute players also play the smaller (and higher) piccolo. The oboes have a cousin, the slightly larger English Horn (a charming instrument with a curious name, since it is neither English nor a horn).

The clarinets have not only a much larger and lower partner in the bass clarinet, but also a whole family that includes the alto clarinet and the piccolo clarinet. The bassoon's sixteen-foot big brother (folded over four times) is the indomitable contrabassoon, capable of the orchestra's lowest pitches. In addition, a newer family sometimes found in the orchestra contains the soprano, alto, tenor and baritone saxophones, perfect for blending the woodwinds and the brass.

The woodwinds each play their own separate parts, so they're known for their many solos in the orchestral literature. Because of their varied construction, they offer a greater variety in tone color than the strings. For instance, a violin in its lowest register can sound almost exactly like a viola, but a flute in *any* register will never be mistaken for an oboe. Yet the woodwinds also function well as a woodwind choir, whose sound is often used to contrast the string choir, a favorite technique of Beethoven.

Although these wind instruments don't use strings and a bow to produce sound, they still use the same principle to make sound: vibrations. Instead of vibrating a string, they vibrate an air column within their instrument. You'll notice that each instrument has holes drilled in it, which the player covers with his fingers. The column of air is shortened (and the pitch gets higher) when the holes on the instrument are opened. Lower notes are made by lengthening the air column, that is, closing the holes with the fingers (and a variety of gears, pads and other plumbing).

Clara Schumann, a world-class pianist herself, labeled Liszt "a smasher of pianos." An awed contemporary described the scene at a typical concert: "Terrified pianos flee into every corner...gutted instruments strew the stage, and the audience sits mute with fear and amazement."

Wouldn't you have loved to be there? By now you should be on the edge of your seat waiting to hear his compositions. Actually, they're not too crazy, and many are quite nice.

We'll deal with Listz's piano pieces later; first let's look at a new type of orchestral form he created. It's called the "symphonic poem" (or "tone poem"). He wrote thirteen of them; the one performed most frequently today is probably *Les Preludes.*

The work is a series of episodes based on a single theme, given at the beginning of the slow introduction and finally culminating in triumph. These episodes, or consecutive "preludes," are inspired by an epigraph from the poet Alphonse de Lamartine: "What is life but a series of preludes to that unknown song of which death strikes the first solemn note?"

Like the concert overture, the symphonic poem is basically a free-form orchestral movement usually suggestive of a place, mood or other subject. Historically, the symphonic poem is yet another attempt by the Romantic composers to throw away the restrictions of Classical forms. Such were the Romantics; they had fun breaking any tradition they could get their hands on.

## RICHARD WAGNER (1813-1883)

One of the great Romantic iconoclasts was Richard Wagner (Re-KARD VAHG-nuhr). Someone once claimed that more books have been written about this colorful figure than about anyone else except Jesus Christ and Napoleon. Since you already have so many potential sources for information about the bizarre life of the composer himself, we'll focus on the music rather than the man.

Wagner is best known for his operas, which he called "musical dramas." But so many symphonic programs are filled with his overtures and excerpts from his opera compositions that we don't want to overlook his contributions in this area. His contemporary, Tchaikovsky, is worth quoting here.

"Wagner was a great symphonist," Tchaikovsky said, "but no operatic composer. Had that extraordinary man written symphonies instead of devoting his life to operatic illustrations of Germanic myths, he would have enriched the world with masterpieces comparable to Beethoven's immortal endeavors."

Whether or not you find anything about Wagner the man to like, his orchestral writing is brilliant. Of his many overtures, the ones you must know are those from the *Flying Dutchman, Lohengrin, Die Meistersinger, Tannhauser* and the *Prelude to Tristan und Isolde.* We'll be listening to two of these.

Some of Wagner's overtures, such as *The Flying Dutchman,* are a rip-roaring roller-coaster ride, the perfect orchestral showpiece. This exciting work was actually the sign-in music for the *Captain Video* television show of the 1950s.

Other Wagnerian overtures, especially "Tristan," are gorgeously romantic. The mysterious opening cello theme is answered by the equally mysterious woodwinds. After several repetitions, the orchestra bursts in and begins a drama that builds melody on rapturous melody.

Upon hearing the climax of this work, you may want to passionately kiss the next person you see. So be careful—playing this piece may get you in trouble.

Another of Wagner's works often performed is *Siegfried Idyll*. This piece was written secretly for his wife, Cosima (daughter of Franz Liszt), and played as a surprise birthday gift as she descended her staircase. Now that's romantic! It's a lovely piece—no doubt Cosima liked her present, though it's not quite as well known as those fantastic overtures.

## ORCHESTRAL PROGRAM #10
## TCHAIKOVSKY: SYMPHONY NO. 6 IN B MINOR ("PATHETIQUE")
## TCHAIKOVSKY: 1812 OVERTURE

### PETER ILYICH TCHAIKOVSKY (1840-1893)

The first great symphonic composer from the country of Russia was Peter Ilyich (IHL-yihch) Tchaikovsky (Chy-KAWF-skee). I've always loved his music, but until I recently conducted in Moscow I had no idea how much he's adored by the Russian people. While discussing Tchaikovsky with a Muscovite, I noticed that every time his name was spoken, the woman bowed her head slightly in deference to his memory. Tchaikovsky wrote four orchestral suites and six symphonies, all of them excellent music. The last three symphonies are classics. Number six, the "Pathetique" (not "pathetic," but pahth-e-TEEK) is the epitome of the nineteenth-century symphony.

Listen to how the first movement begins with mystery but develops into a dramatic interplay between a romantic slow theme and faster material that has climaxes on top of its climaxes. Note a clever innovation in the second movement—a waltz in 5/4 time, that is, having the unusual number of five beats to each measure rather than the expected three.

The power of the triumphant third movement, with its fanfare ending, may tempt you to applaud this as the symphony's conclusion. But it's followed by a broad, poignant slow movement, whose tragic themes have provoked tears, especially by those who know that this is the composer's final statement. Tchaikovsky died unexpectedly soon after the work's premiere.

Can you name a piece of classical music that uses a cannon? It's Tchaikovsky's *1812 Overture*, of course. A fragment of this music is familiar to my generation from its use in the old commercial about "the cereal that's shot from guns."

The overture was written to commemorate the seventieth anniversary of Napoleon's retreat from Moscow. Perhaps Tchaikovsky thought the Russian people needed some patriotic music; it was a chaotic period of revolutionary rebellion in that land, and just the year before the work was premiered, the czar had been assassinated.

The *1812 Overture* opens quietly with the Russian hymn "Save, O God, Thy People," which you'll hear return triumphantly with massive church bells at the work's close. Meanwhile, as Napoleon's troops attack, you may recognize the first phrase of the French national anthem, "La Marseillaise." The notes are repeatedly quoted, most notably as a rousing trumpet call. In the music, Russia's cannons score the victory—a much more exciting ending than the reality of history, in which Napoleon was ultimately defeated by starvation and Russia's bitter winter cold.

Cannons, bells and quoted themes aren't the only features of interest in this stirring composition. You're sure to appreciate the profound counterpoint—that is, the technique of combining two or more independent melodies to make a harmonious texture. You'll also enjoy this composer's melodic development and his phenomenal orchestration.

In fact, Tchaikovsky's unmistakable orchestration is one of the keys to his success. Russian composers all seem to have cultivated this skill, but Tchaikovsky—who was also a noted conductor—knew exactly how to get what he wanted from his eighty or so musicians.

Of Tchaichovsky's other orchestral compositions, the most frequently performed works are the *Nutcracker Suite* (every Christmas), the *1812 Overture* (every Fourth of July), the *Romeo and Juliet Overture* (Valentine's Day fare) and his *Marche Slave* (because of its great appeal, played whenever an orchestra needs more subscriptions). Since these are so popular, a word of caution is needed: Don't succumb to the problem of "familiarity breeds contempt."

However grossly overplayed these works may be, remember that they're still great masterpieces. Their appearance in television commercials and kindergarten plays makes them no less serious as art. We don't want to play the snob who pretends to appreciate only obscurity.

In fact, I enjoy poking holes in such pompousness. If you ever meet someone who says foppishly that he likes Beethoven's Second rather than his *Third Symphony,* try responding that *your* favorite was always his *Tenth Symphony* (remember, Beethoven only wrote nine of them). See if he even notices.

While the scope of this book doesn't include the dance per se, we can't overlook Tchaikovsky's famous ballets, which stand on their own as concert music. The two most popular are the *Sleeping Beauty* and *Swan Lake. Tres magnifique!*

## ORCHESTRAL PROGRAM #11
## RIMSKY-KORSAKOV: RUSSIAN EASTER OVERTURE
## MUSSORGSKY-RAVEL: PICTURES AT AN EXHIBITION

### NIKOLAI RIMSKY-KORSAKOV (1844-1908)

Another great Russian orchestrator from this period was Nikolai Rimsky-Korsakov (RIHM-skih KWAR-suh-kawf). He's best known for his exotic symphonic suite entitled *Scheherazade,* based upon old stories from the *Thousand and One Arabian Nights.*

Another popular work by Rimsky-Korsakov is his *Capriccio Espagnol* (a capriccio is an orchestral work that includes popular melodies). But my favorite is his *Russian Easter Overture.*

In this composition, which I've chosen for our program, the composer quotes the Easter chants of the Russian Orthodox Church, surrounding them with orchestral fireworks of resilient spirit. The composer's colorful scoring gives important solos throughout the orchestra, especially in the violin and flute cadenzas (a cadenza is a free musical passage by one soloist ususally performing technically difficult material). This kind of scoring anticipated much twentieth-century orchestration.

Striking contrasts are typical of all Rimsky-Korsakov's works. You may hear, for example, luscious slow themes in the strings along with hair-raising fast passages with the brass that keep you on the edge of your seat.

### MODEST MUSSORGSKY (1839-1881)

While we're in Russia, we should listen to a piece from one more composer of that land, Modest Mussorgsky (Moo-SAWRG-skih). Although his first name was Modest, his strange personality was not. Nevertheless, he did write some interesting music.

Mussorgsky is another example of a "one-work" composer. He's remembered primarily for one opera, *Boris Godunov,* and one orchestral work, *Pictures at an Exhibition.* Actually, the latter wasn't originally an orchestral piece; Mussorgsky wrote it for piano and he never heard it played by an orchestra. The work was later orchestrated by the French composer Maurice Ravel, and today, it's this Mussorgsky/Ravel version that's more popular than the original piano work.

In any case, this great composition was inspired by an exhibition of paintings of the Russian artist Victor Hartmann. The peculiar titles of each movement correspond to specific paintings, such as "The Ballet of the Unhatched Chickens," and "A Hut on Fowl's Legs."

As you listen, imagine yourself walking through an art exhibit, glancing at various pictures. Mussorgsky opens his work with the "Promenade" theme, given by a brass choir, and this theme walks us from movement to movement. Each picture and corresponding movement has its own interest; listen for rare solos from the saxophone in "The Old Castle" and tuba in "Bydlo" (Polish for "cattle," referring to the pulling of a slow ox cart). When the "Promenade" theme returns in the last movement (called "The Great Gate of Kief"), get ready for a true orchestra showpiece.

## ORCHESTRAL PROGRAM #12
### FRANCK: SYMPHONY IN D MINOR
### SAINT-SAENS: CARNIVAL OF THE ANIMALS

### CESAR FRANCK (1822-1890)

Welcome to France in the late nineteenth century. The first symphonic writer you should meet is yet another one-work composer, named Cesar Franck (SAY-zar FRAHNK). A fine organist who wrote much for his own instrument, today he's primarily known for his one symphony, his one string quartet and his one sonata (played on violin, cello, flute or whatever—an easily transcribed piece).

Franck's *Symphony in D Minor* has a peculiar place in today's repertoire. Most youth orchestras play it, as it is not technically difficult; yet major professional orchestras can have difficulty with it since its full interpretation is rather elusive. This is a big, grand work full of vitality and color.

Note that *Symphony in D Minor* only has three movements rather than the four movements of the standard classical form. After a slow introduction, the first movement bursts with energy—notice how the opening theme is treated both slowly and quickly. An extended solo for English horn sets the mood for the middle movement, a slow section with an added scherzo. The vitality of the last movement combines themes from the first two movements, recalling Berlioz's "idee fixe" concept.

### CAMILLE SAINT-SAENS (1835-1921)

Another Frenchman of note has the very French name of Camille Saint-Saens (san-SAHN). His most frequently performed works for orchestra are his "Organ Symphony" (*Symphony No. 3*)—a huge work for organ and orchestra—and the *Carnival of the Animals.*

In this latter piece, subtitled "A Grand Zoological Fantasy," each of Saint-Saens's movements represents a different animal, such as the lion, the elephant and the kangaroo. Try to guess which creatures are represented simply by cues from the music itself. A favorite is "The Swan," a beautiful cello solo, which the ballerina Anna Pavlova later made famous with an exquisite solo dance. Although the "Carnival of the Animals" is often performed in children's concerts, the composition should be in adult collections as well.

# ORCHESTRAL PROGRAM #13
## DEBUSSY: NOCTURNES
## RAVEL: BOLERO

We now come to the great French Impressionists, a term which has come to refer musically to Debussy, Ravel and their lesser followers. Impressionism supposedly refers to similarities between this style of French music and the French Impressionistic painters, such as Renoir and Monet. Although Debussy himself rejected the term, it will always be associated with his music.

Instead of presenting the strong, commanding messages of Germanic music, this music suggests impressions to the listener. In any case, the Impressionistic period represents the epitome of the French art of making beautiful music.

## CLAUDE DEBUSSY (1862-1918)

The kingpin of this group is definitely Claude Debussy (dehb-yoo-SEE). This interesting composer became a kind of French Beethoven, breaking icons and brushing convention aside. A stuffy professor of the Paris Conservatoire once confronted him with the questions: "So you imagine that dissonant chords do not have to be resolved? What rule do you follow?"

Debussy simply replied, *"Mon plaisir."* (That means, "My pleasure," but it's often translated as, "My rule is what I like.") His new harmonies created an entirely new way of composing and had an enormous influence on composers of the twentieth century.

Although Debussy insisted that he was a lazy composer, he wrote a good deal of orchestra music, much of which has entered the standard repertoire. Most everyone's favorite is his captivating *Prelude to the Afternoon of the Faun.* From its opening flute solo to its hushed ending, it's spellbinding—very French, full of surprises, a delicate masterpiece.

Like the Russian composer Rimsky-Korsakov, whose *Capriccio Espagnol* we've already noted, Debussy had a love for Spain. He wrote a wonderful symphonic work named *Iberia,* with three movements that suggest the Spanish culture better than the music of most Spanish composers. (Other examples of Iberian-themed works include *Rapsodie Espanole* by Ravel and *Carmen,* the opera about Spain by the Frenchman Georges Bizet.)

Debussy's *Iberia* actually is one of three parts of his *Images for Orchestra.* The other two works take you to England and France. Much of Debussy's music is rather like a travel guide. His magnificent *La Mer* ("The Sea") is perfect for anyone who's always wanted an ocean voyage and couldn't afford it. All the beauty and spectacle of the sea—without the dramamine.

Another great Debussy composition is his *Nocturnes,* which we've chosen for

## INSTRUMENTS OF THE ORCHESTRA: BRASS

---

The brass choir is often the thunder of the orchestra. When God wanted the walls of Jericho to fall, He didn't score it for strings or woodwinds; He called up the trumpets. Nevertheless, we shouldn't think of brass as always loud. Each of the brass instruments has a full dynamic range, and some of the best orchestral solos in the repertoire are quiet passages from the brass section.

Again, we notice counterparts to human voices: the trumpet, French horn (usually shortened to "horn," although that word is often used in slang to describe *any* brass instrument), trombone and tuba. Like all wind instruments, they vibrate an air column within them to produce a sound. The woodwind players change the length of this column by uncovering holes with their fingers, but this wouldn't work too well with a brass trumpet, so the early brass instruments couldn't play all the melodies of their woodwind friends. From the composer's point of view, this was a problem that had to be fixed.

Except for the trombone, which could change its length by means of a long slide, the players of early brass instruments could only produce different pitches by changing the pressure from their lips. This was easy on the fingers, which had nothing to do, but rather tough on the "chops," as brass players sometime call the facial muscles they use to blow into their mouthpieces—the actual term is *embrochure*. For years, horns could only be lengthened by inserting different lengths of additional pipes, called "crooks." But this was rather cumbersome, and who wants to show up at rehearsal with a bunch of crooks?

Fortunately, a system of valves finally was developed, which put the brass section on an even keel with the other orchestral instruments. By pushing specific combinations of valves—which open other pipes and therefore extend the vibrating air column—the trumpet, horn and tuba could play the same melodies as the strings or the woodwinds. Furthermore, more variety of sound was introduced with various extra brass members, especially in bands, such as the cornet, the bugle, the fluglehorn, the baritone, the euphonium and the sousaphone, named after John Philip Sousa, who proposed its newly designed bell.

As we noted before, brass can play lovely quiet sections; but there's nothing quite like the powerful sound of fortissimo brass choir. The excitement can be hair-raising—you feel as if that much energy could power a large city all week—and few conductors can fully control it. No wonder that Richard Strauss once wryly advised conductors, "If you think that the brass is not blowing loud enough, mute it by a couple of degrees."

this program. As you listen, you'll find that this piece has perfectly named movements: "Clouds" (the puffy chords in the strings will convince you); "Festivals" (wait till you hear the parade section); and "Sirenes," whose impression of Homer's Greece is supported by a "wordless" female chorus that sings simply an "ah" throughout. It's gorgeous.

## MAURICE RAVEL (1875-1937)

The other great Impressionist, always linked with Debussy on programs and albums, is Maurice Ravel (Ruh-VEHL). We've already noted his popular orchestration of Mussorgsky's *Pictures at an Exhibition.*

Ravel was the French orchestrator par excellence. One of my favorite examples of his work is *Daphnis and Chloe,* specifically Suite No. 2. As the delicious sounds of the opening pour over you, an astounding 15,000 notes and more are played in the first sixty seconds!

This outstanding work features two contrasting sections. The first part is very slow (unless you're among the woodwinds playing those millions of fast little notes); note how the sound presents a broad panorama. The last section, however, is the wildest roller-coaster ride this side of Disney World.

The Ravel piece chosen for this program is the controversial work *Bolero,* which some call "the world's longest crescendo." At its premiere, an enraged woman in the audience shouted, "He's mad!" Ravel simply smiled and replied that she had understood the piece.

The composer described this work as "a piece for orchestra without music." What he meant is that he decided to write a piece whose primary material is not the usual "melody, harmony and rhythm," but rather orchestration itself. So he used a minimal amount of thematic material, started with very little sound and simply added layer upon layer of instrumental color.

Listen for each solo—flute, clarinet, bassoon, saxophone, trombone—on and on it goes, building hypnotically. Whether you like the result or not, you can't ignore *Bolero.*

## ORCHESTRAL PROGRAM #14
### BRUCKNER: SYMPHONY NO. 4 IN E♭ MAJOR ("ROMANTIC")
### MAHLER: SYMPHONY NO. 1 IN E♭ MAJOR ("TITAN")

We've now spent so much time in France that you might have thought the Germans had gotten out of the musical business. But they've kept busy too, both the Wagnerites and the Anti-Wagnerites. So let's pick up the action that survived the Brahms-Wagner wars by examining the composers who came on the scene next. They're sometimes referred to as Post-Romantics.

## ANTON BRUCKNER (1824-1896)

Anton Bruckner (BRUK-nuhr), a musical follower of Wagner, is primarily known not for operas, but for his nine symphonies (there's that magic number again) and his choral works. The last three symphonies, with their huge quantities of heroic grandeur, are well established in the standard repertoire today. My favorite, however, is an earlier one—his *Symphony No. 4,* which he nicknamed "Romantic." Listen carefully in this work to the unifying element of a certain rhythm he creates, especially noted in the second theme of the first movement and throughout the hunting calls of the third movement. Some have even called this the "Bruckner rhythm." Now wouldn't it be "romantic" indeed to have a rhythm named after you?

## GUSTAV MAHLER (1860-1911)

Gustav Mahler (MAHL-er) tried to break the mold of the nine-symphony career, but died before he finished what would have been number ten. (This "nine-symphony" fetish is beginning to sound ominous). Mahler was a world-class conductor—at one time the director of the New York Philharmonic—and though he created amazing sounds with his scores, he always looked for more. When he traveled to Niagara Falls, his first exclamation was, "Fortissimo at last!"

Mahler's symphonies are often categorized in three groups: the first four, with their intensity and struggle; the next four, which seem more philosophical; and the Ninth, in a class by itself—his farewell to the world. His music is as vast as the canvasses of great landscapes. In fact, he once was with fellow conductor Bruno Walter in a lovely section of rural Austria. When Walter stopped to admire the mountain scenery, Mahler told him, "Don't bother to look. I've composed this already."

All of Mahler's symphonies employ enormous orchestral forces, some even gargantuan. The best example of this tendency is his *Symphony No. 8,* known as the "Symphony of a Thousand" and labeled by one critic "a monster cantata." It requires eight vocal soloists, two large choruses, a boy's choir and a massive orchestra with a number of instruments uncommon to any ensemble. The first and second symphonies (known as the "Titan" and the "Resurrection") are the most frequently performed, followed closely by his fourth, which contains a lovely soprano solo in the last movement. The first symphony is the most accessible. Mahler named it after Jean Paul's novel *The Titan;* he separated the four movements into two sections entitled "From the Days of Youth" and "The Human Comedy."

Mahler's basic idea was the musical portrayal of a life, from the innocence of youth to the trials and triumphs of adulthood. The famous third movement is indeed full of trials and confusion: The bizarre principal theme is unforgettable, followed by a minor-key rendition of the nursery song "Frere Jacques," and even a street band song. But the massive finale brings in the note of victory, far overshadowing the earlier trials.

Although there are flashes of exhilaration and even touches of humor, these works often reflect the pain of Mahler's unappreciated greatness in much of his own lifetime. He often insisted, "My time will come!" His time did come at last, but he suffered ample discouragement in the meantime.

## ORCHESTRAL PROGRAM #15
## RICHARD STRAUSS: A HERO'S LIFE
## GRIEG: PEER GYNT SUITE
## SIBELIUS: FINLANDIA

### RICHARD STRAUSS (1864-1949)

Earlier you were warned not to confuse the waltz king, Johann Strauss, Jr., with Richard (Ree-KARD) Strauss. Now you'll learn the vast difference between them.

Actually, Strauss and Mahler, the composer we just discussed, have one thing in common: They spent lots of time with a baton. Strauss even wrote ten golden rules for the young conductor. Among them: "When you think you have reached the limits of prestissimo (the fastest possible tempo), go twice as fast." And this: "Never look at the trombones; it only encourages them."

Strauss's orchestral offerings were huge tone poems—a form that brings us well into the twentieth century. They're fun, bombastic, wild and usually off the wall. Debussy—who was hardly a conventionalist—once called a Strauss tone poem "an hour of original music in an insane asylum."

Even Strauss himself once remarked to Mahler, "I employ cacophony to outrage people." But after a few decades of puzzlement, we've become accustomed to Strauss. In fact, many orchestra musicians (especially brass players) swear by him. His tone poems may seem strange on first hearing, but with repeated listenings, they grow on you.

My favorites are *Don Quixote, Til Eulenspiegel's Merry Pranks, Death and Transfiguration* and *Ein Heldenleben* ("A Hero's Life," in which the composer refers to himself—no one ever accused Richard Strauss of having low self-esteem). This last piece is a kind of musical autobiography, which uses themes from his earlier works. If you start with this composition first, you can find the themes that interest you the most, then go back and listen to whichever tone poems originally contained them. This work functions as Strauss's private musical card catalog.

Earlier we mentioned that around this time in music history, we find the rise of composers drawing from the musical traditions of many different cultures. Now let's go on a little tour that starts in the late nineteenth century and leaves us in the late twentieth. We'll begin in Scandinavia and proceed counterclockwise on Europe's map, passing through England, Spain, Italy, Hungary and Russia. Sooner or later we'll make it back to the German Fatherland—and we'll even travel to America as well.

## EDVARD GRIEG (1843-1907)

We begin our tour of Nationalistic music in Norway, which may seem a long way from Vienna and the usual haunts of Western music. But Norway's composer laureate, Edvard Grieg (GREEG) was proud to be a Norwegian, remarking, "I am sure my music has a taste of codfish in it." His principle work for the orchestra was his scenic *Peer Gynt Suite,* inspired by the Henrik play of the same title.

There are ten movements in this suite, but few performances or recordings include them all. By far the most popular movements are "Morning" (you'll recognize the pastoral flute suggesting a bird song at dawn); "Ase's Death" (reflecting the drama of the demise of Peer's mother); "Anitra's Dance" (a strangely sensuous dance—every piccolo player's favorite); and of course, "In the Hall of the Mountain King." This hall is filled with a multitude of subterranean trolls, sometimes quietly working (the lumbering bassoons), sometimes in a fighting frenzy (full orchestra). The music will take you right down to their world.

## JEAN SIBELIUS (1865-1957)

In nearby Finland, national pride produced another genius, Jean Sibelius (Sih-BAY-lee-uhs). His seven symphonies are all performed frequently, but his most popular work is the tone poem *Finlandia.* The work is a musical representation of the Finnish people and their long history of struggle against foreign oppression.

The power of the percussive sections and the massive ending sharply contrast with the poignant melody, which symbolizes Sibelius's Finnish homeland. In 1900, when *Finlandia* was premiered in Helsinki, Russia ruled Finland. The work inspired such patriotism that the Russians outlawed its performance for years. By the time the Russians left Finland in 1918, it had become the anthem of the Finnish independence movement.

You may recognize the lovely Finlandia theme. It is known universally and has even found its way into hymnbooks, accompanied by the lyrics of Katharina von Schlegel that begin "Be still my soul..."—a paraphrase of the Forty-Sixth Psalm.

## ORCHESTRAL PROGRAM #16
### ELGAR: ENIGMA VARIATIONS
### VAUGHAN WILLIAMS: FANTASIA ON A THEME OF THOMAS TALLIS
### BRITTEN: A YOUNG PERSON'S GUIDE TO THE ORCHESTRA

By now you may be asking, "What about English composers?" Unfortunately, through all the years of Mozart, Beethoven and even the Wagnerian wars, England apparently forgot to show up for music class—or at least for composition class. There are simply no great English composers between the death in 1695 of opera-

## INSTRUMENTS OF THE ORCHESTRA:
## PERCUSSION AND OTHER INSTRUMENTS

If the orchestra only contained strings and winds, much of its color would be left out. Many of the dramatic effects created in a symphonic concert come from the percussion, as well as the "added" instruments such as harp, piano and organ.

The percussion department covers a wide range of instruments; anything that's not a string or a wind fits here. But there are two basic divisions of percussion: those producing definite pitches and those producing indefinite pitches—the ones that simply go *pow!*

Although most of the drums are in the second category, one drum fits in the first, and it's the most popular of all symphonic percussion instruments. This is the tympani, also called kettledrums, though I've never seen a kettle that big. Its adjustable "head" of stretched calfskin (or various modern synthetics) gives it exact pitches that can be tuned by means of a foot pedal. This powerful instrument has been used by every composer for the orchestra, from Bach to Bernstein.

Other percussion instruments producing definite pitches include the "mallet" instruments (xylophone, vibraphone and marimba) and the "bell" department, encompassing the glockenspiel, chimes, tubular bells and the celesta, a small keyboard instrument made famous by Tchaikovsky's *Nutcracker Suite.*

The unpitched percussion section has it all. Drums of all sizes: snare drums, side drums, tenor drums, bass drums. You'll also find a variety of cymbals and gongs (or tam-tams). Then we have the assortment of small miscellaneous instruments such as castanets, tambourines, triangles, temple blocks, wood blocks and so on. Percussionists have to be able to play a wide variety of toys.

They also have to count *very* well. Certainly their realm is the realm of rhythm, not melody; you don't play many lovely melodies on the snare drum. But counting is really a challenge if you have 153 measures of rest (that is, doing nothing), and then crash your cymbals together as loud as possible at precisely the right time. Percussionists have to have nerves of steel to endure this kind of pressure. It helps, of course, if the conductor remembers to give you a cue for such a critical entrance. Percussionists pray for such small graces.

writer Henry Purcell and the late nineteenth century. (Unless you believe the transplanted German Handel should be considered an English composer, as the English themselves do.)

Why the dearth of outstanding English composers? Your theory is as good as mine; perhaps they were too busy playing cricket.

## EDWARD ELGAR (1857-1934)

In any case, by the turn of the last century, English composers began to be heard again. The first of these was Edward Elgar, eventually to be *Sir* Edward Elgar. Nearly everyone who graduates from high school hears his "Pomp and Circumstance," but his work more apt to be played on a symphony concert has the enigmatic title of the *Enigma Variations.*

These fourteen variations are musical portraits of twelve of the composer's close friends, his wife and the composer himself. This must have been an interesting circle, for the variations range from the explosive (such as #7, for Arthur Troyte Griffith) to the serene (#8, for Winifred Norbury).

Musically, the variations are of the opening violin solo. You can easily recognize this theme as it's transformed from the delicate softness of Variation 9 to the martial sounds of Variation 14. But there is one theme you probably won't hear—what has been called "the Enigma theme."

It's there, somewhere, according to the composer, who said: "Through and over the whole set another and larger theme 'goes' but is not played." Musicians have tried for years to crack the code without success. The secret "Enigma Theme" hidden in the music could be anything from Beethoven's "Fifth" to "Yankee Doodle." What's *your* guess?

Elgar also has two nice symphonies, greatly contrasting in mood. The first is depressed; the second, elated.

## RALPH VAUGHAN WILLIAMS (1872-1958)

Next is Ralph Vaughan Williams (at last a name that's easy to pronounce). He may not be one of the three "B's," but he was a fine English composer all the same. Can you guess how many symphonies he wrote? Yes, nine—if only Beethoven had known what he started.

Some people like Vaughn Williams's first symphony best, called the *Sea Symphony,* with a chorus and an ocean of sound. I prefer his fifth, but you won't go wrong with any of them. The most popular of his works in this genre, chosen for our program, is actually scored for two string orchestras and entitled *Fantasia on a Theme of Thomas Tallis* (Tallis was an English composer of the sixteenth century).

This English work is worth the wait of several centuries. Listen for the contrast of the solo viola and the solo violin sections, then later the solo string quartet. What an effect it has with such huge chords of so many strings! Listening to it, you feel as if you were inside the violin itself, or maybe even as if you *were* the violin.

## BENJAMIN BRITTEN (1913-1976)

Since we're in England, let's move forward a few years and explore the greatest twentieth-century composer of Britain, Britten. This prolific musician seems to make up for his country's lack of compositions, especially in the field of opera. His best-known symphonic works are his massive *Sinfonia da Requiem,* commissioned by the Japanese government to celebrate the Imperial

Dynasty but later rejected as "too Christian," and the popular *Young Person's Guide to the Orchestra.*

Although the *Guide* was commissioned for an educational film and is, after all, intended as children's music, grownups love it in regular symphony concerts. It uses variations on a theme by the early English composer Henry Purcell to bring out the nuances of the different instruments. Expertly arranged, this work has turned on kids of all ages to the joy of orchestral music.

You may have noticed that our program has no composers from Spain. Well, for all you who studied Spanish in high school and are ready to use it at last, I've got bad news. There haven't been many Bachs and Beethovens come out of the Iberian Peninsula.

Instead of producing many great composers, Spain's musical culture has given birth to great performers: the master classical guitarist Andres Segovia, the great tenor Jose Cararas, the great conductor Frubeck de Burgos, and many more. The best Iberian composers are all from around the turn of the last century—Issac Albeniz (he has an interesting *Suite Espanola* for orchestra); Enrique Granados (you'll love the *Intermezzo* excerpted from his opera *Goyescas;* and Manuel De Falla (you'll stomp your feet in the three famous dances from his ballet music, *The Three-Cornered Hat).* Listen to them all when you have the opportunity.

## ORCHESTRAL PROGRAM #17
### RESPIGHI: THE PINES OF ROME
### BARTOK: CONCERTO FOR ORCHESTRA

### OTTORINO RESPIGHI (1879-1936)

Now on to Italy. Though it's known chiefly as the land of opera, Italians like orchestras too. A key figure in this development is Ottorino Respighi (Reh-SPEE-gee). He was interested in old music as well as new, and three very popular suites for orchestra are his *Ancient Airs and Dances.*

In this set of compositions, Respighi took a number of obscure Renaissance dances, jazzed them up a bit and gave each a fabulous twentieth-century orchestration. The resulting synthesis is a must-hear, especially the second suite.

He also wrote some large orchestral pieces to show off his homeland, the best known of which is the *Pines of Rome,* chosen for this program. A great guided tour of the Eternal City, this piece is complete with a visit to the catacombs (you can't miss the "subterranean" music), a tape recording of bird songs, and a big parade at the end. The parade, like the one we mentioned earlier in Debussy's "Festivals," starts small but slowly crescendos until the sound almost runs you over. The antiphonal brass is breathtaking.

## BELA BARTOK (1881-1945)

Hungary, anyone? Then feast your musical palate on the works of the Hungarian composer Bela Bartok (BAR-tok), a major musical influence of the twentieth century. Perhaps his greatest orchestral achievement is the powerful *Concerto for Orchestra.*

This isn't the chapter on the concerto, but Bartok's work isn't a piece for soloist and orchestra—it's a work in which everyone in the orchestra is the soloist. A virtuoso showpiece, it's only playable by a virtuoso orchestra.

The symmetrical Bartok planned his five-movement concerto carefully: fast (after a slow introduction), moderate, slow, moderate, fast. The outside movements are full of excitement and feature some of the most spectacular writing for brass ever conceived—especially the massive buildup of imitated themes in the middle of the first movement.

Yet this serious composer is not without humor. Consider the delightful duets of the second movement, entitled "Game of Pairs," or the bizarre interlude within the fourth movement—you'll know it clearly by the exaggerated trombone slides. The many-faceted *Concerto for Orchestra* offers the perfect example of the many-faceted Bela Bartok.

## ORCHESTRAL PROGRAM #18
### STRAVINSKY: THE RITE OF SPRING
### PROKOFIEV: PETER AND THE WOLF
### SHOSTAKOVICH: SYMPHONY NO. 5 IN D MINOR

## IGOR STRAVINSKY (1882-1971)

We now return to Russia, which has produced a great variety of musical styles in the last hundred years. For musicians, the major Russian revolution of the twentieth century wasn't carried out by the Bolsheviks, but rather by Stravinsky. He burst upon the scene in his thirties with creations called the *Firebird, Petrushka* and the *Rite of Spring.* All of these were commissioned by Serge Diaghilev, the famed director of the Russia Ballet. Nevertheless, as with Tchaikovsky's ballet music, these three masterpieces have had a life of their own on the concert stage.

The *Rite of Spring,* chosen for this program, is a musical landmark; it's been called "The Ninth Symphony of the Twentieth Century" (Beethoven's shadow continues to grow). If you've seen Walt Disney's animated feature *Fantasia,* you may remember this piece as the music for the dinosaur scene.

Note the rhythmic complexity and harmonic vocabulary of the *Rite.* These elements were so far ahead of their time that the work provoked a riot in the Parisian audience attending its premiere. From the mysterious bassoon solo (in its highest register) to the frenzy of the concluding "Dance to the Death," the striking features of this composition continue to raise eyebrows.

Stravinsky produced other orchestral works in his long life, yet the *Rite of Spring* always will be considered his greatest accomplishment.

## SERGEI PROKOFIEV (1891-1953)

Russia is a big country, with ample room for diverse compositional styles. A completely different music, yet equally Russian, came from the composer Sergei Prokofiev (Praw-KAW-fyehf). Though the name may not be familiar, you've probably heard his *Peter and the Wolf* (thanks again to Walt Disney).

This is a clever piece, portraying an old Russian folktale using themes for the different people and animals much as Saint-Saens had done. The accompanying narrator relates the tale to us, but it would be fun to guess the action simply by identifying the characters. The flute represents a bird; the oboe, a duck; the clarinet, a cat; the bassoon, the old grandfather; the horns, the wolf; the tympani, the hunters' guns; and the strings, Peter himself.

Prokofiev excels, however, in his larger orchestral ventures. He wrote seven symphonies (my favorite is his fifth), and the popular *Classical Symphony* is indeed a classic. It's an early work, perhaps not as profound as his later symphonies, but musicians and audiences agree that it's great fun both to play and to hear.

## DMITRI SHOSTAKOVICH (1906-1975)

For yet another style of Russian music, we turn to Dmitri Shostakovich (Shahs-tuh-KOH-vich). His music bears little resemblance to that of Stravinsky or Prokofiev, but it still sounds unmistakably Russian. Dmitri wrote so much music that he broke the record going all the way back to Mozart for the number of symphonies by a single composer. He created fifteen, thus escaping the nine-symphony "spell."

Like many of his Russian comrades, Shostakovich was often in and out of favor with his government. His wild musical style soon got him into big trouble with Stalin; the Soviet newspaper *Pravda* condemned his "modernist formalism." Since he didn't relish the idea of composing in labor camps, he tactfully called his fifth symphony "a Soviet artist's practical, creative reply to just criticism." This unjust humiliation at least pacified Stalin, saving Shostakovitch's neck and enabling him to continue producing masterpieces.

This politically-influenced *Fifth Symphony* actually became his greatest hit. Though the composer controlled himself enough to give the work an outwardly traditional form—four movements of fast, scherzo, slow, fast finale—it contains movements of surprising power. The writing for brass in the outside movements is justifiably famous, but the inside movements are equally creative, especially the heart-felt slow movement with its intense string sections. The playful scherzo shows that this mistreated artist still kept his sense of humor, even with Stalin breathing down his neck.

Don't overlook Dmitri's later works. Sometime you'll want to hear his last symphony—it's a gem, with interesting quotes coming from sources as diverse as Wagner and Rossini.

## ORCHESTRAL PROGRAM #19
### SCHOENBERG: VARIATIONS FOR ORCHESTRA
### IVES: THREE PLACES IN NEW ENGLAND
### COPLAND: APPALACHIAN SPRING SUITE

## ARNOLD SCHOENBERG (1874-1951)

You've probably already noticed that most nineteenth-century music is wilder than that of the Baroque and Classical eras, and that most twentieth-century music is even wilder than that. Not surprisingly, many music lovers began to ask, "Where are we headed?"

One unusual answer to that question was provided by German composer Arnold Schoenberg (SHOHN-berg) and his followers, who created a whole new way of composing called *serial music*. Most composers always had created music that revolved around a specific "key." But Schoenberg believed that no one tone was more important than another, so he did away with what we usually call a "tonal center" (see "Keys and Tonality" on page 156).

Schoenberg's music is thus often "atonal"—that is, it has no particular key. Instead of "melodies," he uses "tone rows," and they owe their existence as much to mathematic formulas as to emotion or inspiration.

You may ask, "Why would I want to listen to this weirdness?" Believe it or not, some of the resulting music can be very interesting and—dare I say it?—quite beautiful. Instead of listening for simple melodies, abandon yourself to the exotic aural colors that meet your ears.

It may not be good dinner music, but does everything have to sound like Schubert? Whether or not you can appreciate it, the genius of Schoenberg has had a tremendous influence on modern composers and can't be ignored. Though none of his atonal works has yet to become popular on symphonic programs, you need to be aware of his music.

For this program, I want you to try his *Variations for Orchestra*. They can be rather strange, but they employ some magnificent orchestral color. The opening theme is given by the cellos, and the nine variations and finale that follow offer an interesting ride into the world of atonality. My favorites are the fourth (a rather bizarre waltz), the fifth (gloriously massive orchestration), and the seventh (listen for the innovative combinations of very high-pitched instruments: celesta, glockenspiel, piccolo and violin). Enjoy the wild ride to the end!

Who knows? You just might become Schoenberg's biggest fan, and if not...well, I told you that you don't have to like everything.

## CHARLES IVES (1874-1954)

Are you ready to cross the ocean and see what the New World has to offer? As it was with Columbus, there's much to be explored. America may have taken a century or so to clear the land and start growing composers, but the twentieth century has at last yielded a rich harvest. Since your ears are still ringing with the outrageous dissonance of Schoenberg's atonal works, you're ready to meet the rowdiest musician of all time, and one of the most lovable—Charles Ives.

Ives was the first great American composer, yet he was virtually unknown until years after he stopped writing music. Most of his life he spent as an insurance executive, and a very successful one. But from his youth he broke every musical rule he could find and created some of history's most innovative compositions. Stravinsky would one day be in awe of "this fascinating composer...who was exploring the 1960s during the heyday of Strauss and Debussy."

If there is any one word that characterizes Ives's orchestral music, it's *dissonance*. So be prepared; there's plenty of it. Ives himself exhorted us to "take it like a man!"

He loved to superimpose songs like "Yankee Doodle" on top of old hymns like "What a Friend We Have in Jesus," with notorious results. Even Ives once asked himself, "Why do I like these things? Are my ears on wrong?"

No—we love them too, Charlie. Few composers are more challenging yet rewarding to try to appreciate. Of his five symphonies, which get progressively more untamed, you might want to start with the last, which he entitled *New England Holidays*. You can take it!

For this program, we've chosen his excellent orchestral suite *Three Places in New England*. As you listen, don't be afraid of the dissonance; revel in it. This composition may not ever be used by the local chamber of commerce for tourist commercials, but they can stir great emotions in a serious listener.

The first movement, "Boston Common," evokes the spirit of the Massachusetts Fifty-Fourth Regiment (the first African-American troops used in the Civil War), quoting such tunes as "Old Black Joe," "Marching Through Georgia," and the "Battle Cry of Freedom." In the second movement, "Putnam's Camp, Redding, Connecticut," the Revolutionary War is celebrated. Wait until you hear the passage depicting two military bands passing each other—playing at two different speeds!

# THE DISTINCTIVE VOICES OF THE INSTRUMENTS

You may hear people speak about the different "voices" of the instruments—the traits that give each one a unique musical character. Actually, it's difficult to generalize about these qualities because instruments can be so versatile. For example, although the brass has always been thought to produce a "military" sound, a skillful composer can produce martial effects even with a string quartet or piano. Nevertheless, we can make some general observations.

Flutes often convey a pastoral setting, perhaps reminding us of the shepherd's panpipes of old. The oboe can express an amorous, even erotic feeling, especially in a slow passage. The clarinet's various registers (that is, the different parts of its range) are versatile: The lowest register gives us a dark, somber mood, and the highest, a bright, piercing quality. Bassoons can also be very dark, as well as humorous in certain staccato passages (that is, when notes are played quickly, lightly, and separated from one another).

Trumpets, of course, sound the battle call, while horns either announce the hunt (in fast movements) or give us romantic melodies of passion (in slow movements). The versatile trombone provides strength with its volume and humor with its slide. When not in a supportive role, the tuba—like its comrade the bassoon—is often used comically. As noted before, all the brass can denote a military spirit.

The diversity of percussion instruments produces an abundance of effects. From the power of the tympani to the skeleton-like eeriness of the xylophone, the percussion add colorful touches to the orchestra. Meanwhile, keyboards convey either their location or their epoch: An organ means church, a harpsichord or clavichord means Baroque. And the piano can do everything!

Like the piano, the strings are so versatile they defy easy categorization. The violin certainly denotes leadership in the orchestra, but can be used to express every feeling from terror to tenderness. The viola has a darker quality and is at its most distinctive in its lowest register. The cello, however, loves to sing on its highest string, often using a technique called *thumb-position* to soar higher than the nearby violas. The basses usually support the cellos, but—like the tympani—they have the commanding power of accent.

The last movement, "The Housatonic [River] at Stockbridge," is surprisingly mild and pastoral. Even Ives could enjoy a quiet river scene—though he still gave us an explosive ending.

## AARON COPLAND (1900-1991)

Wow! What happened to Bach and Mozart? You thought everything was going to be in C major, right? You'll be relieved, then, to find that the history of music composition—as with so many other realms of human endeavor—swings like a pendulum from one extreme to the other. After the cacophony and dissonance of

Ives and Schoenberg, you'll welcome the music of our next American, Aaron Copland (COPE-lund).

He gives us a sense of balance: "Music that is born complex is not inherently better or worse than music that is born simple." Good point, Aaron. His music is grand, but not pretentious; never dissonant for its own sake.

For our program we've chosen one of Copland's ballet suites, *Appalachian Spring*, which will delight you when it quotes such Americana as the Shaker tune "Tis a Gift to Be Simple." Opening quietly in the morning of a country village, the tempo soon picks up as the pioneers begin their day. Before long the community is in a great dance, complete with a bride and groom for a centerpiece. Copland builds the Shaker melody to mammoth proportions, but then ends his suite with the hush of an Appalachian evening.

Don't forget Copland's symphonies (especially No. 3), his *Billy the Kid Suite,* and the stirring *Lincoln Portrait,* for narrator and orchestra.

Bravo! You've just completed a brisk walk from Baroque Germany to twentieth-century America, covering over forty major symphonic composers and gaining some working knowledge of dozens of significant works. Encore!

Of course, the real fun has only begun. Listening to a great piece of orchestral music is more than a one-time experience. It's rather like a promising relationship: The more time you can get together with the music, the better it seems to get. So after you've listened to these eighteen recommended programs, grab some concert tickets, buy some good CD's, or just turn on your favorite classical music radio station and enjoy yourself. You've earned it.

# ORCHESTRA REPERTOIRE

## THE TOP 15

Beethoven
  Symphony # 5
  Symphony # 9 ("Choral")
Brahms
  Symphony # 2
Debussy
  Prelude to the Afternoon of the Faun
Dvorak
  Symphony # 9 ("From the New World")
Haydn
  Symphony # 104 ("London")
Mendelssohn
  Symphony # 4 ("Italian") Mozart
  Symphony # 40
Prokoviev
  Classical Symphony
Rimsky-Korsakov
  Scheherazade
Schubert
  Symphony # 8 ("Unfinished")
  Symphony # 9 ("The Great")
Stravinsky
  The Rite of Spring
Tchaikowsky
  Symphony # 6 ("Pathetique")
  1812 Overture

## THE TOP 50

Bach
  Orchestra Suite #3
Bartok
  Concerto for Orchestra
Beethoven
  Symphony # 3 ("Eroica")
  Symphony # 5
  Symphony # 6 ("Pastoral")
  Symphony # 9 ("Choral")
Berlioz
  Symphonie Fantastique
Brahms
  Symphony # 1
  Symphony # 2
  Symphony # 3
  Symphony # 4
Debussy
  Prelude to the Afternoon of the Faun
  Nocturnes
  La Mer
Dvorak
  Slavonic Dances
  Symphony # 9 ("From the New World")

Franck
  Symphony in D Minor
Handel
  Water Music
Haydn
  Symphony # 104 ("London")
Mahler
  Symphony # 1 ("The Titan")
  Symphony # 2 ("Resurrection")
Mendelssohn
  Symphony # 4 ("Italian")
  Midsummer Night's Dream Overture
Mozart
  Symphony # 40
  Symphony # 41 ("Jupiter")
Mussorgsky/Ravel
  Pictures at an Exhibition
Prokoviev
  Classical Symphony
  Peter and the Wolf
Ravel
  Daphnis and Chloe, Suite #2
  Bolero
Respighi
  The Pines of Rome
Rimsky-Korsakov
  Scheherazade
  Russian Easter Overture
Schubert
  Symphony # 8 ("Unfinished")
  Symphony # 9 ("The Great")
Schumann
  Symphony # 1 ("Spring")
Shostakovich
  Symphony # 5
Strauss, R.
  Till Eulenspiegel's Merry Pranks
  Ein Heldenleben
Stravinsky
  The Firebird
  Petrushka
  The Rite of Spring
Tchaikovsky
  Symphony # 5
  Symphony # 6 ("Pathetique")
  Nutcracker Suite
  Romeo & Juliet Overture
  1812 Overture
Wagner
  Tannhauser Overture
  The Mastersinger Overture
  Tristan und Isolde Prelude

*Peter Ilitch Tchaikovsky, King of Russian Romanticism.*

*Mendelssohn, one of history's happiest (and richest) composers;
also a man deeply at peace with his personal faith.*

# 3

# CHORAL MUSIC

---

*Since singing is so good a thing*
*I wish all men would learn to sing.*

—William Byrd

Onward to the choir room!

No doubt most folks reading this book have at some time in their lives sung in a choir, glee club, chorus or other vocal ensemble. But we couldn't make the same assumption about who might have played in an orchestra. After all, everyone has vocal chords, but not everyone has a violin or a tuba.

Choral singing is a joy in part because it's primarily an *amateur* experience. Of course, professional choruses exist, as do amateur and community orchestras. Yet the thousands of choirs and even choral societies around the world are full of wonderfully normal people who work at the office or factory each day but live a secret singing life at night. With a transformation at least as dramatic as that of Clark Kent to Superman, these closet performers sing their hearts out as sopranos, altos, tenors and basses.

Amazingly, the combined sounds of a company of relatively untrained singers can be remarkably good. In choral singing—unlike the other two kinds of vocal music, opera and song—beautiful sounds can result from the blending of many voices that would never make it to Carnegie Hall individually. What's true of armies is true of choirs as well: There's safety in numbers.

So if having a just-average voice has discouraged you from public singing, I recommend you give choral singing a try anyway. You'll find it a wondrous experience.

Before we delve into centuries of glorious choral repertoire, let's examine some of the differences between instrumental and vocal music.

The major difference is obvious: This music has *words!* That additional element introduces new challenges for everyone involved. The composer must write music to express a pre-existing bit of poetry or prose. The performers must learn the text and sing with the kind of expression that amplifies each word. And the listeners? Since the words and music are inseparable, listening is greatly enhanced if the text is known and understood. So whenever we talk about any vocal music, we first look at the words.

Within choral music, the two all-encompassing categories are *sacred* and *secular*. In the Western choral tradition, sacred music means primarily Christian music. With regard to texts, its major divisions are Catholic and Protestant. The words of this sacred music draw frequently on the Bible, and especially the book of Psalms.

Secular Western music, on the other hand, can be divided into pieces whose texts are taken from poetry and pieces who draw their words from every other source imaginable. This music makes frequent use of Shakespeare, Goethe, or other master poets.

In Europe the sacred texts were the first to dominate, since for centuries the only compositions preserved for posterity were sponsored by the Church. That brings us to the next major difference between vocal and instrumental music: an historical difference.

The story of vocal music begins long before the days of the symphony. Who knows whether the caveman first sang or first beat on a drum, but we do know that choirs came centuries before orchestras. In fact, we have record of a "School for Singers" in Rome during Pope Silvester's reign over sixteen hundred years ago.

Church orchestras might have appeared by then as well if many early Christian leaders hadn't been wary of using instruments in worship. But they were reluctant because such instruments were associated with pagan practices. Leaders also feared that fancy playing in church (and fancy singing, too, for that matter) would distract the worshiper from God.

I've often wondered how they explained such biblical passages as Psalm 150, which calls for a variety of musical instruments in worship. But that's another matter, and we'll be dealing with enough *musical* controversy without bringing up theological difficulties too.

Now I know I promised not to bother you with dusty old medieval chants that are seldom performed anymore, and that I would stick to the standard repertoire of the last three centuries or so. That was fine for orchestral music, but with choral music, let's compromise. Since so many great vocal works were composed before the Baroque era, I'll at least mention the four Renaissance composers you need to know and their most famous works. Then we'll soon be back to Bach, Handel and the rest of the friends you made in the last chapter.

Let's keep it simple: two composers from the sixteenth century and two from the seventeenth. Even the nationalities will be easy to remember—from each century we'll choose one composer from Italy and one from England. The sixteenth century gave us the Italian Giovanni da Palestrina and the Englishman William Byrd. The following century produced Claudio Monteverdi from Italy and the last great English composer until the twentieth century, Henry Purcell.

### CHORAL PROGRAM #1
PALESTRINA: MISSA PAPAE MARCELLI
BYRD: PSALMS, SONNETS AND SONGS
MONTEVERDI: VESPERS
PURCELL: REJOICE IN THE LORD

## GIOVANNI PIERLUIGI DA PALESTRINA (C. 1525-1594)

It's only right that a survey of choral music begin with Palestrina, whom Verdi would someday call the "real king of sacred music." (It may seem strange that we refer to him not by his own name but by the name of his hometown, Palestrina, Italy. But if you ask for the music of "Pierluigi" you'll only get funny looks.) Not that there wasn't beautiful music written earlier—medieval composers like Josquin Despres (c. 1440-1521) will never be forgotten. But Palestrina seems to sum up the music of the Renaissance in the same way that Bach was the culmination of the Baroque.

Working under the favored patronage of the Vatican, Palestrina produced a vast number of compositions. We've chosen for our program his most important masterpiece, the *Missa Papae Marcelli* ("Mass of Pope Marcellus"). Although this pope was only destined to reign for three weeks, the composition named for him is still performed today.

This mass was written for a six-part choir. Notice how its imitative counterpoint intertwines massive chords that emphasize the key doctrinal points of the text—such as the principle statements of the "Credo" (meaning "I believe," from which we get our word *creed).* Hearing this composition performed under any circumstances is a treat, but if you ever hear it sung in a great cathedral, you'll never forget the experience.

## WILLIAM BYRD (1543-1623)

From the Church of Rome we go to the Church of England. This religious transition is easily made in William Byrd, who wrote for both churches and was perhaps the greatest English composer in history. Instead of working for a pope, Byrd served Queen Elizabeth, yet he wrote three lovely masses. We really don't know why; they certainly could never have been performed in the Protestant England of his lifetime.

Among his other vocal works, perhaps the best moments are found in his two sets of *Psalms, Sonnets and Songs.* They represent Elizabethan English music at its best.

My favorite of these is "Lullaby, My Sweet Little Baby." It displays Byrd at his most lyrical, yet it's still peppered with occasional dissonances that add dramatic effect.

These pieces have a preface, an "Epistle to the Reader," in which Byrd expresses the prevailing sentiment of the choral composers of his day: "If thou finde any thing here worthy of lykeing and commendation, give prayse unto God, from whome (as a pure and plentiful fountaine) all good gifts of Scyence do flow: whose name be glorified forever."

## CLAUDIO MONTEVERDI (1567-1643)

The seventeenth century was one of transition from the music of the High Renaissance to that of the Baroque. In Italy the key figure was an innovator named Claudio Monteverdi. His progressive ideas would one day prompt an innovator from the twentieth century, Igor Stravinsky, to comment on Monteverdi's music: "Amazingly modern and, if one can say such a thing, near me in spirit."

Although we remember Monteverdi most for his contributions to the development of opera, he also wrote madrigals, masses, psalms and a beautiful collection of pieces we now call the Monteverdi *Vespers*. As you listen to this music for evening worship, you'll note that the work employs strings and brass in addition to chorus. The writing is both lyrical and expressive. It points toward the highly emotional word painting of the later Baroque composers. Another great piece to hear in a cathedral.

## HENRY PURCELL (1659-1695)

Back to England for their version of the seventeenth century, which is best summarized in the music of Purcell. He had a flair for the dramatic, writing much for the theater. But he also left us choral music: songs, motets, and anthems (see the glossary for definitions of these forms).

Purcell's brilliant use of the trumpet and drums must have been a powerful influence on the fanfares that Handel would later write while living in England. We've chosen for our program what is perhaps Purcell's best-known anthem, the exuberant *Rejoice in the Lord*. It's found on many choral programs today.

Pay attention to the similarities (as well as the differences) between the vocal and instrumental writing here. Although the choral parts are obviously the more important, it is noteworthy how much this little orchestra's status has been elevated. Already the string parts are doing more than simply playing the vocal line. This new importance of the instrumental accompaniment is one of the transitions that take us from the vocal-dominated music of the Rennaissance toward the orchestras of the coming Baroque Period.

Other composers also helped in the transition from the Renaissance to the Baroque, notably Heinrich Schutz and Dietrich Buxtehude in Germany and Jean

Baptiste Lully in France. But no one could anticipate the creative explosion that would soon take place in choral music through Bach and Handel. To do these men justice we need to spend more time on their works.

## CHORAL PROGRAM #2
### BACH: CANTATA NO. 140, "WACHET AUF!"
### ("SLEEPERS, AWAKE!")
### BACH: MASS IN B MINOR

### JOHANN SEBASTIAN BACH (1685-1750)

Bach wrote music for virtually every genre of his day; you'll see his name frequently in this book, in nearly every chapter. Since he worked for a number of churches, his choral output was stupendous: nearly three hundred cantatas—about two thirds of which have survived—huge masses, motets, oratorios, and passions (a passion is a musical setting of biblical texts describing the events in Jesus's life leading up to the crucifixion).

Staggering! Considering that he fathered twenty children as well, I wonder how he found the time for all these compositions.

We'll discuss only a few of Bach's major works, but maybe we'll whet your appetite for more. Bach's compositions provide an almost inexhaustible supply of beauty.

As an example of a Bach cantata, we'll choose #140, entitled *Wachet Auf!* ("Sleepers, Awake!"). In Bach's impeccable style, the opening choral movement announces the joyful coming of the Bridegroom to meet his beloved. The text refers to Christ's parable of the Wise and Foolish Virgins (Matt. 25:1-13), which admonishes His followers to be ready for His coming.

In the subsequent movements, the composer eloquently develops this theme with his Lutheran theology of "longing" for death, a meeting with the Lord. The final chorale (a chorale is a hymn intended to be sung by the congregation rather than just the choir) is like the hundreds of others Bach wrote: It brings the chorus together in a strong finale of joy.

I mention here several "must-hear" works not on our program, but worth checking out when you have the opportunity. First of all, Bach's *Magnificat* is surely the greatest musical setting in history for Mary's prayer from the first chapter of Luke's Gospel. Every part is a gem, from its exhilarating opening (which also closes the work) through a wide variety of colorful movements.

In addition, Bach's three great oratorios—the "Christmas," the "Easter" and the "Ascension" Oratorios, portraying the life of Christ—are quite popular. They're a bit long for some listeners, yet they're so well crafted that they merit their length.

Of Bach's motets, the acknowledged favorite is *Jesu, Meine Freude*, actually a series of chorale variations. Fun to sing, and fun to hear.

Next we come to two masterpieces that have been landmarks of Baroque choral art. The *Mass in B Minor,* chosen for our program, demonstrates the vastness of the composer's spirit: He was a Lutheran writing a Catholic mass that was far too huge a work to be used for liturgical purposes.

The opening "Kyrie Eleison" ("Lord, Have Mercy") explodes with religious drama, which is sustained through the final resolution of the "Dona Nobis Pacem" ("Grant Us Peace"). One of its most famous moments is found in the two movements of the *Credo:* "Cruxifitus" and "Et Resurrexit." After the passion of the crucifixion, the Lord's body is quietly lowered into the tomb, as the pitches descend lower and lower. But then the resurrection: The chorus and orchestra shout with joy, a breathtaking effect that composers imitated for decades afterward.

We must not forget the sublime *St. Matthew Passion.* Although Bach also composed a *St. John Passion,* the Matthew version is heard more today. This piece is the epitome of symbolic sacred music, the perfect portrait of the suffering Saviour. Even the titles of the movements—such as "Break in Grief," "For Love My Saviour Now Is Dying," "Come, Healing Cross"—express the fervor of Bach's faith.

A classic point here is the so-called "halo effect" provided by the quiet upper strings, which always play when Jesus sings. But they're abruptly removed at the words "My God, my God, why have you forsaken me?" to emphasize Christ's humanity. It's no wonder that Mendelssohn, who recovered for posterity this neglected masterpiece in 1829, declared it "the greatest Christian music in the world."

## CHORAL PROGRAM #3
### HANDEL: MESSIAH
### VIVALDI: GLORIA

### GEORGE FRIDERIC HANDEL (1685-1759)

The choral accomplishments of Bach would seem to be a tough act to follow. Yet his contemporary and countryman Handel didn't follow him; rather he worked in a very different sphere and locale. While Bach was working away at obscure churches (after his death, his music was all but forgotten for decades), Handel traveled and became world-renowned in his lifetime.

He first moved to Italy, where he became a successful composer of Italian opera, and later to England, where he almost starved as a composer of Italian opera. Fortunately, he learned in time how to please his British audiences by becoming the foremost composer of a dramatic form known as the *oratorio*—a musical setting of a long text for soloists, chorus and orchestra.

It is for oratorio that we best remember Handel. Without the elaborate sets, costumes and staging of opera, oratorio appeals instead to our imagination, somewhat like the reading aloud of a play. Since Handel is a master at using music to enhance a given text, your favorite oratorio will probably be the one whose story you happen to prefer.

Some especially love the powerful choruses of *Judas Maccabaeus,* others the tenderness and pathos of *Theodora,* still others the chromatic innovations of *Israel in Egypt.* All of them are worth hearing, especially in live performance, for the powerful drama they deliver. To quote Mozart: "Handel understands effect better than any of us—when he chooses, he strikes like a thunderbolt."

To hear Handel's powerful treatment of biblical passages, you'd never know that many of his fellow Europeans of "culture" were embracing the anti-religious skepticism of the Enlightenment. The year *Israel in Egypt* appeared (1739), Voltaire published one of his numerous attacks on the Christian faith, *La Pucelle.*

Evidently, Handel didn't pay much attention to the Frenchman's scoffing. Two years later, the composer gave the world what was to become the best-loved of all his spiritual works, *Messiah.* What can you say about such a colossal achievement—written in a whirlwind of only twenty-four days, yet the most popular choral work in history? It's a case of utter inspiration, a musical miracle.

The sheer fact that it's still clamored for after decades of annual revival seems miraculous. Year after year we welcome it back like an old friend. Even with grotesquely overblown re-orchestrations (it was once performed using almost 1000 players!) and tragic attempts by many under-rehearsed choirs, Handel's *Messiah* still reigns as the king of choral repertoire.

The entire text of this oratorio is from the Bible and is composed of three parts. The first deals with the coming of Christ to earth; the second with His sacrifice and victory; and the final with the hope and faith of Christianity. What more can be said, since you've probably heard it all anyway?

If by some chance you *haven't* yet heard *Messiah,* set this book down and run out right now to buy a recording of at least the "Hallelujah Chorus." You'll soon find out why the world still loves, has always loved and will always love this masterpiece.

## ANTONIO VIVALDI (1675-1741)

Before we leave the Baroque era, I must recommend an excellent choral work by Antonio Vivaldi (vee-VAHL-dee): his popular *Gloria.* Although this Italian violinist is best known for his instrumental music—especially *The Seasons,* which you'll encounter in the next chapter—he did a splendid job of putting voices and instruments on the same stage. Vivaldi was not only a composer; he became a priest, and his vocal writing reveals a deep sensitivity to the meaning behind his text.

A good example of what I mean is the movement "Qui Tollis," where his chromatic chords speak so poignantly of Christ's taking away the sins of the world. There is more depth in this work than is often realized, a depth that remains to be pondered long after the excitement of the shout, "Gloria!"

As you might expect, the Baroque era, with all its ornamental and contrapuntal exuberance, sometimes led to excesses. This was particularly true in choral works, where long strings of notes began to sound more like instrumental passages than vocal writing. Changes of style were inevitable and began in the mid 1700s.

The immediate result was a time of transition when the music of various countries searched for direction. One of the transitionary products is often referred to as the "Rococo" period, whose style was light and graceful yet still highly ornamented.

Meanwhile, geniuses were on the horizon, and their compositions eventually came together in the Classical period of music. Genius #1 was Franz Joseph Haydn. We've already talked about his symphonies; now let's examine his choral works.

## CHORAL PROGRAM #4
### HAYDN: LORD NELSON MASS
### HAYDN: THE CREATION

## FRANZ JOSEPH HAYDN (1732-1809)

At a time in history when church music was often melodramatic to the point of becoming lugubrious, Haydn's choral compositions are a breath of fresh air. The composer was sometimes criticized for writing sacred music that wasn't sufficiently solemn for some tastes; yet he defended himself with these words: "At the thought of God my heart leapt for joy, and I could not help my music's doing the same."

Haydn wrote a number of fine masses in this spirit. His ebullience shows through even in the mass he wrote in a minor key, the so-called *Lord Nelson Mass*. Most people recognize the trumpet calls at the end of the "Benedictus" movement, which celebrate Nelson's victory at the Battle of the Nile. (Lord Nelson and Lady Hamilton, a great Haydn fan, actually visited the composer in 1800). But the entire work is an excellent example of the composer's craft.

The opening "Kyrie" is thoughtful, almost somber (that is, for Haydn), but the "Gloria" displays the cheerfulness for which he's best known. Note how expertly Haydn balances the solo vocal passages with the passages of the chorus, especially in the dramatic "Qui Tollis" section. An interesting historical item is the three-note motive found at the beginning of the mass. This same motive became famous as the theme of Beethoven's scherzo of his *Ninth Symphony*.

Two of Haydn's choral works have gained a prominence even above his masses: *The Creation* and *The Seasons*. The former, which we've chosen for this program, is full of unforgettable images. Listen to the cacophony of the opening music as it depicts chaos. It sounds like something right out of the twentieth century. Enjoy the magic moment of "Let There Be Light," and the comic touches during the creation of certain animals such as the whales. This huge work took the composer two years to complete—a long time for such a prolific composer as Haydn.

*The Seasons* (not on this program) was written as the century turned and provides the perfect introduction to the later Romantics. The storm scene sounds a good deal like Beethoven at his wildest, while the light texture of many parts remind you of the lovely songs of Schubert or even Schumann.

## CHORAL PROGRAM #5
### MOZART: CORONATION MASS
### MOZART: REQUIEM

## WOLFGANG AMADEUS MOZART (1756-1791)

Haydn's good friend Mozart is our genius #2 of the Classical period. He too wrote many masses that are still performed today. My favorite, chosen for our program, is the famous *Coronation Mass,* written not for the coronation of a king but for an archbishop.

Here we find some of Mozart's most interesting effects. Listen to his treatment of the words "Et Incarnatus Est," where the descending violin line suggests the mystery of divinity descending into humanity through Christ. The somber trombones at Christ's burial may remind us of Bach's similar effect in the B Minor Mass. These operatic devices are typically Mozart, who moved with ease from the secular to the sacred in his multitudinous compositions.

Mozart's music affected countless later composers. In the following century Charles Francois Gounod confessed, "Mozart is to Palestrina and Bach what the New Testament is to the Old in the spirit of the Bible, one and indivisible."

Apart from Mozart's masses, several other of his choral works are quite popular today. These include his two "Vespers" settings, as well as the charming *Ave Verum Corpus*—one of those rare pieces that still sounds lovely no matter the level of expertise of the choir. But his most renowned work was his last, the sublime *Requiem.*

The requiem form—a mass for the dead—has a long history. If you're a newcomer to classical music, particularly if you're not familiar with the ancient practices of the Church, the idea of a "Mass for the Dead" may strike you as a bit odd. Yet this musical form has inspired composers from a variety of theological slants to compose some of history's greatest works. A requiem by one of the masters is performed nearly every week in the major cities of Europe and America.

The story of this particular requiem's creation is shrouded in mystery and intrigue. Supposedly, a stranger offered Mozart an anonymous commission for a requiem. The man planned to try to pass it on fraudulently as his own.

Mozart was still young, but dying. He worked frantically, saying to his wife, "It is for myself I am writing the requiem." Even on his death bed, he sang in an informal rehearsal of this work. His last action was to imitate the kettledrums of the piece. Then he died leaving it unfinished. What grist for the mills of Hollywood!

Nevertheless, it's the genius of the *Requiem* music, not the melodrama, that deserves our attention. It's a crowning masterpiece of a life that began as a prodigy. Listen to the power of the "Dies Irae" movement and the marvelous trombone solo that immediately follows; the dramatic contrasts of the "Confutatis"; the beautiful counterpoint in the "Recordare"; and the heartfelt cries of the "Lacrymosa." All these elements are evidence of Mozart's culmination as a musician.

We should note that before he died Mozart gave his student Franz Sussmayr instructions for completing the work. Sussmayr did so at the request of Mozart's wife. That was a controversial move, which has provoked much speculation and research. But after hearing the piece, we might well agree with Beethoven, who coyly commented: "If it wasn't all written by Mozart, then it must have been written by another Mozart!"

## CHORAL PROGRAM #6
### BEETHOVEN: MASS IN C
### BEETHOVEN: MISSA SOLEMNIS

### LUDWIG VAN BEETHOVEN (1770-1827)

Beethoven wrote much more for chorus than the fourth movement of his Ninth Symphony, which we noted in the last chapter. Despite his inclination toward instrumental technique—he never possessed the gift of lyric vocal writing as Mozart and Schubert did—Beethoven composed several worthy choral works, and finished with a masterpiece that some regard as the pinnacle of all: *Missa Solemnis ("Solemn Mass")*.

Yet before the creation of this monument, Beethoven had been "warming up" to choral writing. Two of his earlier works in particular deserve our attention.

The first is entitled *Christ on the Mount of Olives*, Beethoven's only oratorio, if indeed we can call it that. For if you close your eyes and only listen you might easily mistake it for an opera, based on the scene of Jesus in the Garden of Gethsemane. The choral writing has that dramatic opera quality, the orchestra parts are rather melodramatic, and the trio for the Seraph with Jesus and Peter is a bit more appropriate for the Barber of Seville than the suffering Savior. Though the work seems uneven at times, we have to remember that Beethoven was still young when he wrote it. You have to start somewhere.

# THE CONDUCTOR

The great conductor Sir Thomas Beecham once told his ten-year-old sister: "It's easy. All you have to do is waggle a stick."

Was he right? Why are the conductors up there anyway? They're not playing any of the instruments themselves; couldn't the orchestra play without them?

Maybe. Sometimes. But in most symphonic music, the conductor is indispensable. In complex works, the music would fall apart if the conductor decided to stop.

Obviously, conductors do *something.* They beat out the tempo with their right arm and use the left to give cues and to make the music louder or softer. And of course they perform great theatrical gestures whenever the music gets dramatic.

But what really is a master conductor's job? Among other things, conductors must:

- Thoroughly memorize the score, every note of every part.
- Spend endless hours alone, year after year, learning dozens of new scores.
- Be able to hear like Superman; within a blaring fortissimo they must notice if one of the string players has accidentally left on a mute.
- Give hundreds of cues to specific players or sections, with visual and hand gesturing to convey everything from a loud cymbal crash to a pianissimo flute entrance.
- Have a complete grasp of the working of every instrument in the orchestra: fingering, difficult registers and more.
- Know enough music theory simply to look at a large piece of music and know what it will sound like when played.
- Interpret the score before it is rehearsed: especially as it concerns themes, tempos, dynamics, accents, ritards, accelerations and articulation.
- Be constantly in control of orchestral balance, the delicate blending of the different instrumental groups, and of solo passages against their accompaniment.
- Have inexhaustible energy (conducting is *very* tiring), and enough mental stamina never to lose concentration on the music and the job.
- Know how to prepare rehearsals to their best advantage: when to stop and correct, what parts need the most work, how many precious minutes each piece will take, and so on.
- Be able to conduct the same symphony for the three hundredth time with original freshness.
- Know the entirety of music history, tradition, style and performance practice; how to interpret French Impressionism as opposed to Germanic Neo-Classicism, and so on.
- Have impeccable conducting technique: a clear right hand, beating a wide variety of standard patterns, with a huge array of different accents, dynamics and styles. Their left arm must be fully independent and capable of conveying visually a brainload of musical and interpretive details to over a hundred players.
- Be in complete control of their entire body at all times, knowing that a simple act like bending down could be interpreted wrongly by the orchestra, and that closing their eyes briefly can mean missing a dozen important cues.

Do conductors just "waggle a stick"? Not on your life. Maybe they deserve their paychecks after all. At least now you'll all clap a little louder when the one with the baton takes a bow.

A few years later in 1807, the *Mass in C* emerged at the request of Haydn's patron, Prince Esterhazy. This lovely work has now found the popularity it rightly deserves, but it had a difficult time at the start. Its premiere was unenthusiastically received, and the famous publishers Breitkopf and Hartel wouldn't touch it.

Beethoven's plea to them is touching. He begged them to publish it "chiefly because it is dearer to my heart and in spite of the coldness of our age to such works."

Typically, Beethoven breaks his own mold in this mass. Although it has bombastic moments, the overall feeling of this composition is best represented by the peaceful quietness of the opening and its closing.

You may remember the old question: "If you were stuck on a desert island with only five records, which ones would you pick?" Next for our program I've chosen what we in the music world call a "desert island disk." The *Missa Solemnis* is the climactic result of Beethoven's striving within choral music, somewhat of a sister-work to the *Ninth Symphony.*

This magnificent composition has such depth of emotion that it can seldom be appreciated at first listening. Yet after decades of repeated performances and recordings, you can always seem to find more, like digging in a deep vein of pure gold.

A few of its many nuggets must be mentioned. The ending of the grand first movement, "Gloria," is one of the classiest ever written, especially when played in a great cathedral. The last shouted "Gloria!" seems actually to be scored for reverberation.

The "Credo" is surely the greatest musical statement of the Christian faith ever written. You can feel the nails being driven in during the agony of the "Cruxifitus," and the explosion of the "Et Resurrexit" seems that it might still raise the dead. Between Beethoven's and Bach's settings of this text (Bach's *B Minor Mass*), it's a wonder that there are any atheists left.

The "Sanctus" conveys perfect holiness from its first four notes, and the solo violin of the following "Benedictus" is exquisite. Finally the "Agnus Dei, Dona Nobis Pacem" sums up all of the Christian faith into one triumphant musical prayer.

## CHORAL PROGRAM #7
### SCHUBERT: MASS IN E♭
### BERLIOZ: REQUIEM

## FRANZ SCHUBERT (1797-1828)

You might think that after Beethoven's intimidating masterpiece, no composer would try writing a mass for a while. Nevertheless, his young admirer Schubert was undaunted, and wrote *masses* of masses—well, at least quite a few. All of them are worth hearing, and some are superb.

However, Schubert's masses are sometimes hard to keep straight since they have no programmatic titles. Instead, we have the *Mass in F*, the *Mass in G*, the *Mass in Bb*, the *Mass in C*, the *Mass in Ab*, and the *Mass in Eb*. Maybe it's easier simply to remember your favorite movements. Mine are the "Kyrie" from the *Mass in G*, the "Sanctus" from the *Mass in Ab*, and the "Gloria" from the *Mass in Eb*. This is worse than a menu in a Chinese restaurant!

The piece we've chosen for this program is perhaps his greatest piece of sacred music, the *Mass in Eb*. It's a late work, written after all Schubert's nine symphonies, and it represents both a musical and a spiritual summation of his short life. This mass is full of effect, such as the powerful trombones in the "Domine Deus" of the "Gloria" movement and the mammoth sound of the "Crucifixus" in the "Credo" movement.

It's also full of harmonic variety. Although the mass is in the key of Eb, many other keys are used. The "Sanctus," for example, moves from Eb major to B minor to G minor to Eb major to Bb major. You can hear the way we're now moving into nineteenth-century Romanticism, where—at least harmonically—anything goes.

I'd also like to recommend a few Schubert pieces not on our program: his *Stabat Mater* (a musical setting of a poem that tells about Mary's vigil by the cross of Jesus); a nice setting of *Psalm 92;* and a late work for chorus and piano entitled *Song of Miriam*. This last composition contains an unforgettable musical illustration of how the Red Sea swallowed up Pharoah's bad guys, as well as some touching passages about the good guys. Simple but sincere, it's pure Schubert.

## HECTOR BERLIOZ (1803-1869)

You may have noticed that almost all of the pieces we've looked at so far have been sacred music. That's because most of the choral music of the Renaissance, Baroque and Classical periods used biblical or other sacred texts. Secular texts aren't entirely missing, of course; an interesting example is Bach's *Coffee Cantata*, written about one of his favorite subjects. But until the nineteenth century, much Western music was composed for the church, and virtually all of the major composers had deep religious beliefs themselves.

Now, however, we come to a strange new juncture: sacred music written by an avowed atheist. You may remember from the last chapter the Romantic free-thinker Hector Berlioz, a wild French master of orchestration. As if his orchestra for *Symphonie Fantastique* wasn't big enough, he decided to expand it a bit for a gargantuan *Requiem*. He scored it for four flutes, two oboes, two English horns, four clarinets, four bassoons, twelve trumpets, four cornets, twelve horns, sixteen trombones (at least he spared us seventy-six!), six tubas, two bass drums, four gongs, *six* tympani, five pairs of cymbals, fifty violins, twenty violas, twenty celli and eighteen basses—not to mention anywhere from three hundred to nine hundred singers!

You can see why instead of a "Mass for the Dead," musicians have nicknamed this *Requiem* the "Mass to Wake the Dead." Whether or not you purchase a recording of this one (and if you do, you'd better have good sound equipment for its full effect), don't miss any opportunity to hear a live performance of it. With that many kettledrums, this piece guarantees more rumbling than the movie *Earthquake*.

Another interesting Berlioz work (not on this program) is his *Te Deum* (the *Te Deum* is an ancient prayer of praise and thanksgiving often set to music). This composition is similar in size to the *Requiem* except that it employs two adult choirs plus a children's choir of six hundred. Perhaps his most effective choral attempt is *The Infancy of Christ*. The style is markedly French, light and pastoral, and the middle movement ("The Flight to Egypt") is gripping. Berlioz may have professed atheism, but his setting of these sacred scenes have stirred religious devotion in thousands of listeners.

## CHORAL PROGRAM #8
## MENDELSSOHN: ELIJAH

### FELIX MENDELSSOHN (1809-1847)

From an atheist who wrote Christian music, we now turn to a Jew who converted to Christianity, Felix Mendelssohn. In the last chapter we noted that he was a great lover of the music of Bach, and it seems that he shared Bach's gift for great choral writing. Yet Mendelssohn excelled in composing, not cantatas, masses or passions, but his two great oratorios.

His first effort in this genre was entitled *St. Paul*. Mendelssohn felt a kinship with this fellow Jewish convert to Christianity, and his treatment of the text is especially sensitive. Although it's been somewhat eclipsed by the overwhelming acclaim of his second oratorio, *Elijah*, *St. Paul* deserves more notice than it receives. It's full of magic moments, and the vocal writing is so fluid that it often approaches Schubert's gift of "speech-song" melody.

Though *St. Paul* isn't on our program, I urge you to hear it for yourself sometime. When you do, don't compare it to *Elijah;* just enjoy it for what it is. Its beauty is still undimmed.

*Elijah* is a very different oratorio from its predecessor. From the first chord it's much more dramatic, almost Hollywood-style, and it has achieved great popularity. Yet as we saw in the last chapter concerning such overplayed works as the *1812 Overture*, familiar masterpieces are still masterpieces. *Elijah* justly deserves its reputation as the finest oratorio of the nineteenth century.

The work is well-balanced, with an almost operatic blend of rousing choruses, lyrical arias and stormy recitatives (a recitative is a style of singing that closely resembles speech, with a free rhythm governed largely by the rhythm of the text). Some of you chorus veterans may have heard one-too-many under-rehearsed choirs butcher the movement "He, watching over Israel," and maybe two-too-many wailing sopranos from the choir squeeze through "Hear Ye, Israel." But that's not Mendelssohn's fault. *Elijah* is a true musical monument. Find a good recording of it and enjoy it anew.

You may have noticed that the order of composers in this chapter has so far been the same as in the last. But as we walk through music history in these different genres, differences will start to appear. Not every composer was equally gifted in every genre.

For instance, Frederic Chopin (shoh-PAN) was a marvelous composer, but he wrote no orchestral or choral music. We'll be introduced to him in the next chapter on the concerto and hear some of his best works in the solo literature section. Meanwhile, Schubert, whom you know quite well by now, will be left out of the next chapter, since he wrote no concerti.

In fact, such renowned composers as Schumann (his only real choral work, *Faust,* was such a failure that it has never entered the repertoire) and Wagner (his outrageous choral attempt, *The Love Feast of the Twelve Apostles,* has hardly been performed this century) are omitted in the present chapter. Don't worry; we'll meet with them again soon. In the meantime you'll also make some new friends, such as Giuseppe Verdi. He composed no symphonies but wrote outstanding pieces for the voice.

## CHORAL PROGRAM #9
### BRAHMS: REQUIEM
### FAURE: REQUIEM

### JOHANNES BRAHMS (1833-1897)

A precious few composers wrote well for nearly every genre. Such a musical genius is our old friend Brahms, who composed equally well for instruments or the voice. He wrote a good deal of choral music, even some unaccompanied choral music.

Many of these works, like the beautiful *Alto Rhapsody* and the *Lieberslieder Waltzes,* are frequently performed today. But when a choral singer thinks of Brahms, all thoughts immediately turn to a work that has become a pinnacle of this genre, the sublime *German Requiem.*

The typical requiem mass uses a centuries-old Latin text that deals rather grimly—or at least Brahms thought so—with the subjects of hell and judgment. This was rather foreign to a man who had been influenced by Protestant and Humanist culture. So at the death of his mother, Brahms chose his favorite passage from his German Bible that emphasizes the peaceful and joyful aspects of death. The result was a very personal masterpiece.

Brahms's *Requiem* begins and ends in quiet beauty, inspired by the biblical words "Blessed are they who mourn, for they will be comforted" and "Blessed are they who die in the Lord from now on." Of the many powerful moments found in this work, one of my favorites is the extended crescendo of the second movement, "All Flesh Is as Grass"—guaranteed to lift you right out of your seat. (This passage is comically dangerous for an overly-dramatic conductor.)

After Brahms combines soloists with the chorus, he brings to us the lyric beauty of "How Lovely Is Thy Dwelling Place," a favorite with church choirs. For sheer power of sound there is nothing quite like the sixth movement, from its portrayal of the final trumpet on Judgment Day to its glorious fugue, a hymn of praise to God. If you haven't yet had the opportunity to embrace the Brahms *Requiem*, you have a musical love affair coming your way.

## ANTONIN DVORAK (1841-1904)

While we're speaking of requiems, we should mention one not on our program by Brahms's Bohemian friend, Antonin Dvorak. While Dvorak's *Requiem* isn't performed as frequently as the one by Brahms, it's still a moving work.

The pious Dvorak took the Latin text very seriously, yet some of his finest passages have the lighthearted charm of folk tunes. His approach will remind you of Haydn's way of injecting joy into texts that others treated soberly and even morbidly. Dvorak also wrote an exquisite *Stabat Mater*, composed while living through the grief of several deaths in his beloved family.

## GABRIELE FAURE (1845-1924)

Now let's meet a new composer, the Frenchman Gabriele Faure (Foh-RAY). Like Brahms, he wrote a requiem occasioned by the death of a parent, in this case the composer's father. But there the similarities stop. Faure's work is light, austere and heavenly—beautifully French.

The composer once noted: "It has been said that my *Requiem* does not express the fear of death and someone has called it a lullaby of death. But it is thus that I see death: as a happy deliverance, an aspiration towards happiness above."

Many of Faure's melodies have their roots in ancient Gregorian chant, and his choral writing invokes the sound of distant angelic choirs. To complete the effect, the piece is scored for a rather small orchestra, with no violins (except for an exquisite solo in the "Sanctus") and a minimal role for the winds. You'll find that Faure's Requiem is simplicity at its best, especially its famous movement, "Pie Jesu." This is music of the clouds, music to relax by; put this on after a long, hard day and be at peace.

# CHORAL PROGRAM #10
## VERDI: REQUIEM
## BRUCKNER: MASS IN E MINOR

## GIUSEPPE VERDI (1813-1901)

Since we're meeting new composers, let's look at the other great *Requiem* of this period, composed by Giuseppe Verdi (VEHR-dee). His name translated into English simply means "Joe Green," but that doesn't sound very romantic, so we never translate names. If we did, J. S. Bach would become John S. Brook and Bedrich Smetana would be Fred Sourcream!

Like the Faure piece, the Verdi *Requiem* has some quiet, soothing moments, such as the serenity of the "Lux Aeterna" movement. But this work also packs a punch; watch out for the "Dies Irae." This portrayal of Judgment Day is massive beyond words.

Sometimes when I'm upset and want to hit something I imagine I'm the bass drum player in this movement's opening pages! From the torrents of sixteenth notes to the tension of the offstage brass choir, the seven hundred and one measures of the "Dies Irae" are electrifying.

Of course, such superdrama is what you might expect when you get the master of Italian opera to compose an ecclesiastical choral work. Someone once described the Verdi Requiem as "a bunch of opera singers let loose in a cathedral!" But this work is much deeper than that; it's a sincere expression of Verdi's faith. The gorgeous quartet writing of "Domine Jesu Christe," the prayerful duet in the "Agnus Dei," the final resolution of the "Libera Me"—these and many other moments give us glimpses of Verdi's inner self.

The composer's other choral works include a powerful *Te Deum* and an intensely moving *Stabat Mater*. But make sure you don't miss his *Requiem!*

## ANTON BRUCKNER (1824-1896)

After examining requiems from Czechoslovakia, France and Italy, let's head back to Germany to hear the choral music of Bruckner. Although he wrote some wonderful shorter works—such as his *Psalm 150* and his *Te Deum*—this composer's devout faith is best expressed in his masses. My favorite is the *Mass in E Minor*, which I've chosen for this program.

This work is small by Romantic standards. Yet its compact size keeps the very chromatic writing from becoming obscured. (Chromatic writing uses melodies and chords that have many notes foreign to the key of the passage in which they appear). One reason Bruckner loved chromatism was that he was a disciple of Wagner. Someone once commented that if Wagner had ever written a mass, it would have sounded like Bruckner's.

---

## VOCAL TYPES

There are basically two kinds of singers: male and female. And you might say there are basically two kinds of singing: high and low. So there are four primary categories of singers: the high female voice, or soprano; the low female voice, or alto, sometimes called contralto; the high male voice, or tenor; and the low male voice, or bass.

Both the males and the females have a "middle" category, sandwiched between the high and low voices. For the females, this medium voice is called a mezzo-soprano (MET-zo). The middle category for men is called baritone, which means "of heavy tone," usually for good reason.

Opera singers are described by a sub-category of those already mentioned. For instance, a soprano might be a "coloratura soprano" (very high and with great agility), a "lyric soprano" (with a light, charming voice), a "dramatic soprano" (with marked power and emotion), or a "spinto" (sort of a lyric soprano who also can project the power and emotion of a dramatic soprano). A tenor can be a "counter-tenor" (a very high, even falsetto voice), a "lyric tenor" (same as with the soprano), or even a "Heldentenor" (a strong, heroic tenor, right out of a Wagner opera).

Then it gets even more confusing. Sometimes specific types of opera roles are named after famous singers of the past. Some singers will tell you that they are a "Dugazon," a "Falcon," or a "Baritone-Martin." If they do, just smile and change the subject. To enjoy great music, all you really need to know are the basic voice types.

---

But this is only half true. Spiritually, Bruckner was a devout Roman Catholic, and his affinity with the mass text is evident in the care he takes as he sets it to music. Every accent in the words is placed to have the perfect stress in the music, which even helps with the orchestral accent.

Bruckner knew how to write well for the voice, and every year his masses become more popular.

## FRANZ LISZT (1811-1886)

Remember our wild pianist who later entered the priesthood? Liszt never did anything halfway, so when he composed a sacred oratorio the result was the four-hour *Christus*. As you might imagine, not many church choirs attempt this juggernaut, but it gives a true representation of the Romantic spirit in choral music. And it contains some fantastic music as well.

But I'd better not get your hopes too high for hearing this work: Its size makes it so expensive to perform that it's only produced once a decade or so. For that reason, it's not on our program.

## PETER ILYICH TCHAIKOVSKY (1840-1893)

How about Russian choral music? We have none on our program, and for good reason. While all that great orchestral music was being composed by Tchaikovsky, Rimsky-Korsakov and Mussorgsky, choral music in Russia was somewhat neglected. We should at least mention, however, that the lovely, unaccompanied *Legend* of Tchaikovsky is one of the few works of this kind still performed today.

Such national trends form fascinating patterns throughout history. Because of factors too numerous to analyze, different genres have been emphasized at different times and different places. We can't expect everything to show up everywhere.

## CHORAL PROGRAM #11
## ELGAR: THE DREAM OF GERONTIUS
## WALTON: BELSHAZZAR'S FEAST

### EDWARD ELGAR (1857-1934)

You may recall from the last chapter that for decades the British Isles produced very little in the way of orchestral composition. Yet the choral tradition has always been strong in England, with oratorio societies that seem to spring up on every street corner. The first example of British choral music to remain with us is by the composer of *Pomp and Circumstance,* Edward Elgar.

The work is called *The Dream of Gerontius;* it's set to a Christian poem by Cardinal John Newman. In this cantata, the soul of the main character, Gerontius, passes into the next life, where he sees visions of angelic choirs and scenes of hell. Fortunately for both Gerontius and the audience, he avoids the latter. It's the beginning of an English choral explosion—and a fun piece to hear.

Like Wagner before him, Elgar used the leitmotif concept. So whenever a certain element in the text appears, its specific theme is heard in the orchestra. This is helpful as the audience sorts through the characters—angels, demons and so on— and it gives unity to this large work. After hearing its performance in 1902, the composer/conductor Richard Strauss offered a toast: "To the success and welfare of the first English progressive musician, Meister Elgar."

### RALPH VAUGHAN WILLIAMS (1872-1958)

While we're in England, we should note in passing another Brit who knew perfectly how to compose for voices. Vaughan Williams's *Mass in G Minor* is purely English, yet it seems to belong to no age in particular. Certainly it contains many up-to-date harmonies, but it's cleverly mixed with the melodies and colors of medieval times.

Like many masses of the last two centuries, this work is inherently neither Catholic or Protestant. The style is universal, and its effect is pure and serene. This is

# THE MASS

The Roman Catholic church service known as the mass has been set to music by hundreds of composers throughout the centuries. This is true for composers of many religious backgrounds, Catholic, Protestant, Jewish, agnostic and even atheist. The basic sections of the mass as used in standard music settings are listed below. The names of each movement are derived from the Latin word or words that begin that movement:

Kyrie
Gloria
"Qui tollis"
    "Quoniam"
    "Cum sancto spirito" (sometimes with other subdivisions)
Credo
    "Et incarnatus"
    "Et resurrexit"
    "Amen" (sometimes with other subdivisions)
    Sanctus
Benedictus
Agnus Dei
"Dona nobis"

## REQUIEM MASS

The requiem mass omits the "Gloria" and "Credo" and adds the following movements:
    Requiem aeternam
    Lux aeterna
    Dies irae

**The English translations:**

Kyrie (from "Kyrie Eleison"): "Lord, have mercy."
Gloria (from "Gloria in excelsis Deo"): "Glory to God in the highest."
    "Qui tollis" (from "Qui tollis peccata mundi"): "Who takes away the sins of the world."
    "Quoniam" (from "Quoniam tu solus sanctus"): "For you alone are holy."
    "Cum sancto spirito": "Together with the Holy Spirit."
Credo: "I believe."
    "Et incarnatus": "And was made flesh."
    "Et resurrexit": "And He arose again."
    "Amen": "Amen."
Sanctus: "Holy"
Benedictus (from "Benedictus qui venit in nomine Domini"): "Blessed is He who comes in the name of the Lord."
Agnus Dei: "Lamb of God"
    "Dona nobis" (from "Dona nobis pacem"): "Grant us peace."
Requiem aeternam: "Eternal rest."
Lux aeterna: "Eternal light."
Dies irae: "Day of wrath."

a peaceful kind of cathedral music, liturgical without adornment, sincere and unpretentious. Check it out when you can.

## WILLIAM WALTON (1902-1983)

A new English composer we haven't yet studied is Sir William Walton. (Another "Sir"; the English love titles. But could you imagine a Sir Ludwig van Beethoven?) Walton's best-known work, *Belshazzar's Feast,* is well on its way to becoming a twentieth-century classic. The shout of the chorus at the death of Belshazzar is an unforgettable moment of drama, and it is surrounded with a wide variety of colorful music. This is possibly the greatest choral portrayal of the grandeur of the Old Testament.

CHORAL PROGRAM #12
BRITTEN: CEREMONY OF CAROLS
STRAVINSKY: SYMPHONY OF PSALMS

## BENJAMIN BRITTEN (1913-1976)

Let's finish up our look at British composers with the master. Not since Handel has anyone so expertly put English text to music as has Benjamin Britten. His choral work is best exemplified by the lovely *Ceremony of Carols,* written for women's chorus, two soprano soloists and harp. Not unlike Handel's *Messiah,* the *Ceremony of Carols* is becoming an annual Christmas tradition in parts of America and England.

The early twentieth century saw a great surge of interest in musicology and the medieval music that had been forgotten for centuries. In keeping with this new interest, Britten took his text from a number of medieval carols, giving them unadorned musical settings of great charm. By using only sopranos and harp, he created an atmosphere of innocence and antiquity, even within the framework of twentieth-century harmony—a remarkable blend.

The twentieth century, as you may suspect, has exploded with choral music from every conceivable point of view. There are too many works to name, and we'll need a few more decades to sort out the classics from the second-rate pieces. But we'll at least mention the ones most performed today.

This list includes the mystical *Hymn of Jesus* by Gustav Holst; Arthur Honneger's powerful *King David;* the lovely *Chichester Psalms* of Leonard Bernstein; Ernest Bloch's beautifully Jewish *Sacred Service;* two works from Eastern Europe, Zoltan Kodaly's *Psalmus Hungaricus* and Carl Orff's *Carmina Burana;* and two very French compositions: Theodore Dubois's *Seven Last Words of Christ* and the *Mass in G* of Francis Poulenc. You'll find listening to any of these a rewarding taste of the twentieth century.

For those of you who like a challenge, I suggest the gigantic *Gurre-Lieder* of Arnold Schoenberg, or even Krzysztof Penderecki's wild *Passion According to St. Luke.*

Now I know we're standing rather far away from those pretty Bach chorales and Mozart masses. But it's not our fault that we were born in the twentieth century.

Besides, once you get used to the intensity of modern choral music, you may find that many of these works express our complex modern situation better than the simple melodies of ages gone by. Of course, you'll have to decide for yourself whether that's the case, but at least give these moderns a sporting chance.

## IGOR STRAVINSKY (1882-1971)

I mentioned earlier that it will take some time before the true "classics" of twentieth century works take prominence. Yet already there are some works that seem destined to be admired for centuries. Probably the best example of modern choral writing is by our friend and icon-breaker, Igor Stravinsky—the classic *Symphony of Psalms.*

If you're bracing yourself for the fierce barbarism of Stravinsky's *Rite of Spring,* relax. The *Symphony of Psalms* is a different kind of modern, an example of what we call Stravinsky's "neo-classic" period. Written soon after his return to Christianity and dedicated "to the glory of God," it is a sincere statement of faith by an innovative genius.

This compositon is scored for a large orchestra minus the violins and violas. Stravinsky gave us an interesting commentary on it, his principal religious work: "The first movement," he said, "was written in a state of musical ebullience." The second movement, Psalm 40, "is a prayer that the new canticle may be put into our mouths." The Alleluia (third movement) is that canticle.

From the opening sixteenth notes, to the double fugue of the second movement, to the final hymn of praise, the *Symphony of Psalms* has found a unique place as a modern classic. I hope it will be soon followed by many more choral compositions from twentieth-century composers.

You've again made it through hundreds of years, from the Renaissance to our own day. I'm impressed, and you should be too. Now that you've twice found your way through music history, we're ready to try a different approach in the next chapter.

# CHORAL REPERTOIRE

## THE TOP 15
Bach
  Magnificat
  Mass in B Minor
  Passion According to St. Matthew
Beethoven
  Missa Solemnis
Brahms
  Deutsches Requiem
Britten
  A Ceremony of Carols
Faure
  Messe de Requiem
Handel
  Messiah
Haydn
  The Creation
Mendelssohn
  Elijah
Mozart
  Requiem
Stravinsky
  Symphony of Psalms
Verdi
  Requiem
Vivaldi
  Gloria
Walton
  Belshazzar's Feast

## THE TOP 50
Bach
  Magnificat
  Mass in B Minor
  Jesu meine Freude
  Christmas Oratorio
  Passion According to St. John
  Passion According to St. Matthew
  Ein' feste Burg ist unser Gott (Cantata #80)
  Wachet auf, ruft uns die Stimme
    (Cantata #140)
Beethoven
  Christ on the Mount of Olives
  Mass in C Major
  Missa Solemnis
Berlioz
  L'Enfance du Christ
  Requiem
Brahms
  Deutsches Requiem
  Alto Rhapsody
  Lieserslieder Waltzes
Britten
  A Ceremony of Carols

Bruckner
  Mass in E Minor
Dubois
  Seven Last Words of Christ
Dvorak
  Requiem
Elgar
  The Dream of Gerontius
Faure
  Messe de Requiem
Handel
  Esther
  Israel in Egypt
  Jephtha
  Judas Maccabaeus
  Messiah
  Theodora
Haydn
  Paukenmesse ("Missa in tempore belli")
  The Creation
  The Seasons
  Lord Nelson Mass
Mendelssohn
  Elijah
  St. Paul
Monteverdi
  Vespers
Mozart
  Coronation Mass (K. 317)
  Ave Verum Corpus
  Requiem
Palestrina
  Missa Papae Marcello
Penderecki
  Passion According to St. Luke
Purcell
  Rejoice in the Lord
Schoenberg
  Gurre-Lieder
Schubert
  Mass in E♭
  Mass in G
Stravinsky
  Symphony of Psalms
Vaughan Williams
  Mass in G Minor
Verdi
  Requiem
  Stabat Mater
Vivaldi
  Gloria
Walton
  Belshazzar's Feast

*Bach's favorite portrait of himself.*
*Who knows why? Since his frugality was legendary,*
*perhaps he had it made for the cheapest price.*

*Middle Ages Illumination. In the early days of chant, the manuscripts were beautifully decorated, both to glorify God and to inspire the performer—who was trying to read all those little notes.*

# 4

# THE CONCERTO

*I am delighted to add another unplayable work*
*[his "Violin Concerto"] to the repertoire. I want the concerto to be difficult and*
*I want the little finger to become longer. I can wait.*

—Arnold Schoenberg

This quote from Schoenberg illustrates the way composers often view the writing of a concerto. Or at least it illustrates the way performers *think* composers view a concerto—as one more impossibly difficult piece to try to play. Although Schoenberg doubtless said these words with a touch of humor, the point is clear: A concerto is always the most difficult music for a soloist to perform.

Dictionaries tell you that a concerto (con-CHAIR-toe) is a piece of music written for a virtuoso soloist, accompanied by an orchestra. Casual concert-goers will tell you that a concerto is the most exciting way to find out how fast a human being can actually play. Concert hall managers will tell you that a concerto (complete with a big-name soloist) is the best way to bring a huge crowd to their hall and pay their bills. And soloists will tell you that a concerto is a method that composers have devised to torture them.

Even so, those soloists love concerti (con-CHAIR-tee; that's the plural), live for them, and could hardly pay the rent without them. If you ask performers which of these four pieces they would practice the hardest for—their part in a string quartet, in an orchestral work, in a solo recital piece, or as a concerto soloist—they'll always give you the same answer: the concerto solo. Playing a concerto with an orchestra is the pinnacle for an instrumentalist, the big chance in the spotlight. However difficult concerti may be, performers love them and so do we.

*Every* instrument has at least one concerto, probably many, written for it. You may not have heard many concerti for tuba or English horn, but they've been written, especially in the twentieth century. Some are very interesting—as music, not just as acrobatic exercises.

Nevertheless, the concerto's trait as a virtuoso showpiece is critical to its essence, and it has been for many years. For the audience it's a bit like watching the Olympics—you want to hear great music, but you also want to see the soloists sweat.

Newcomers are often puzzled by the titles of the concerto repertoire. Most of these fiery, dramatic works have dull names such as "Violin Concerto #2 in E♭ Major." So get used to it.

Every once in a while, though, a concerto may acquire a more interesting title. Mozart's *Piano Concerto #21 in C Major* was once used as the soundtrack in a 1960s movie. Suddenly everyone was calling it the "Elvira Madigan" Concerto, after the movie's title.

Among performers, concerto titles are even more lackadaisical: Often only the last name of the composer is used. So just mention "the Tchaikovsky" to a violinist or "the Dvorak" to a cellist. They'll immediately become animated, recognizing their favorite concerto.

Since by now you've learned some basics about the last three hundred years of music, in this chapter we'll take a break from the straight chronological approach. Instead, let's categorize the concerto by its solo instruments. Since the majority of concerti in the standard repertoire are written for the piano and the violin, we'll spend the most time with these two. Afterward, we'll also mention the principle concerto repertoire for several other prominent instruments (with my apologies to the tuba and English horn players; this book can only be so long).

## THE PIANO CONCERTO

### CONCERTO PROGRAM #1
### MOZART: PIANO CONCERTO IN A MAJOR
### BEETHOVEN: PIANO CONCERTO NO. 5 ("EMPEROR")
### MENDELSSOHN: PIANO CONCERTO NO. 1 IN G MINOR

The earliest piano concerti still frequently performed today were written by Joseph Haydn. Since he wrote twenty works of this kind, all of which are similar, it's difficult to pick a favorite. But the most commonly heard is his *Piano Concerto in D Minor*, a favorite because of its graceful and lighthearted style, especially in the first movement.

Although "Papa Haydn" is known to have originated many musical forms, he inherited much of the concerto form from such forerunners as the Italian Antonio Vivaldi (you'll hear much more about him later). Especially noteworthy here is the well-established concerto format: three movements, the first and third fast, the second slow. This simple design was to serve composers for many decades.

# THE COMPONENTS OF MUSICAL SOUND: PITCH

Suppose a murder has been committed in your Boston apartment building. Just after a scream, you heard a few notes on a musical instrument, but you are unsure which instrument or what music was played. The detectives, eager for clues, interview you about the music you heard. If they've read this book, they'll ask you at least four important questions:

"Were the notes high or low?" (*pitch*)

"Were the notes long or short?" (*duration*)

"Were the notes loud or soft?" (*dynamics*)

"What type of a sound was it?" (*timbre*)

First, then, they begin with the basic question: "Were the notes high or low?" Perhaps the most important component of musical sounds is what we call pitch, that is, the relative highness or lowness of a specific sound. We recognize that a flute plays higher than a bassoon (usually), that a triangle sounds higher than a tympani (definitely), and that women sing higher than men (sometimes).

Furthermore, as we listen to or sing a song, we notice that the melody seems to go up and down. Indeed, it would be a very boring composition that only used one note. When you sing "Mary Had a Little Lamb," the first three notes descend and the next two ascend. The syllables "lit-tle lamb" are all sung on the same pitch. This is what pitch is all about. This going up or down is a basic building block of every musical composition.

Pitch is determined by how fast or slow something is vibrating. Every note in a song or symphony is heard because something is vibrating at a certain speed. For instance, if a violinist plucks the A string, it's vibrating back and forth at 440 times each second, while if the high E string is plucked, it vibrates 660 times per second.

What determines how fast or slow something will vibrate? There are several basic factors: the length or size of the vibrating material (such as a string), the amount of material (the mass) that is vibrated, and the tension or intensity of the force causing it to vibrate.

The simple rules are these:

1) Smaller equals higher pitch, and larger equals lower; a little trumpet plays higher notes than a big tuba.

2) Lighter material equals higher pitch, and heavier material equals lower; the thin strings inside your piano play higher notes than the fat ones.

3) Tighter equals higher pitch, and looser equals lower; when a violinist tightens a string, the pitch goes up; when the string is loosened, the pitch goes down.

So what were the pitches of the sounds you heard just after the scream in your Boston apartment building? You answer, "They were very low. Let me see...the first three were quite low in pitch, and the fourth was even lower." The Boston detective dutifully scribbles down your response and shouts to his assistant, "We have a clue. Quick! Bring me Kavanaugh's book and we'll check it out." *(To be continued.)*

## WOLFGANG AMADEUS MOZART (1756-1791)

As if to outdo his good friend Haydn, Mozart wrote twenty-seven piano concerti in his short life and performed most of them himself. All are charming, and most are still performed quite often today. In many ways, this genre seems the classic vehicle for Mozart's multiple talents.

I can easily picture the young virtuoso before an orchestra performing his exquisite melodies, perfectly orchestrated, while he himself directs the ensemble and plays the most difficult part. My two favorites are his dramatic *Concerto in D Minor* and the lyrical *Concerto in A Major*.

Which one should you try first? If you're looking for joy and sunshine, try the *A Major*, and if you're a stormy Beethoven fan, go for the *D Minor*. I've chosen the former for our program, but you should hear them both eventually, and others too.

Since many concerti are known primarily for their flashy, fast movements, let's begin by focusing on the slow movement of this work. Though all three movements have a singable quality, this one is the epitome of lyricism. The piano begins unaccompanied, followed by the strings and clarinets, with an echo in the bassoon.

The feeling is exquisite and pure. After such delicate beauty, you'll almost be shocked by the boisterous enthusiasm of the finale.

If you've ever heard even a few classical concerti, I'm sure you've already noticed an interesting convention: At some point the whole orchestra stops playing and the soloist suddenly launches into an extended solo, complete with masterful virtuosity. This is called a cadenza, and long before the "hot riffs" of jazz solos, performers used these occasions to show off their technique to a dazzled audience.

In the early days of the concerto, a cadenza was improvised on the spot. But Beethoven and his nineteenth-century devotees began to compose cadenzas, which by this time were considered an integral part of the concerto itself. Cadenzas are now often the centerpiece of a work, designed to keep the hushed listeners on the edge of their seats.

## LUDWIG VAN BEETHOVEN (1770-1827)

Beethoven's piano concerti are a bit like his symphonies: He composed fewer of each than did Haydn or Mozart, but each is a jewel and they culminate in a sublime masterpiece. All five are in a top pianist's standard repertoire, especially the last two.

Once, when Beethoven was to perform his fourth piano concerto, he asked a friend to turn pages for him. Imagine the man's trepidation when he found that the pages were blank except for "a few Egyptian hieroglyphs wholly unintelligible to me scribbled down to serve as clues to him." Sure enough, every few minutes, Beethoven would nod for his friend to quickly turn another blank page.

Yet it's in his *Piano Concerto #5* ("Emperor") that Beethoven created the model for a century of followers. Notice how the impetuous soloist, rather than wait for the traditional orchestra introduction, storms in from the first chord of music. Though no one knows how this concerto got its nickname, it must have been suggested by the grand manner of the piano's new-found leadership position. "The Emperor" is a must-hear and provides the perfect opening for the 1800s, known as "the century of the piano."

## FELIX MENDELSSOHN (1809-1847)

The next major piano concerto writer is Mendelssohn, who—like so many of the major composers—was a great pianist as well. He actually wrote two piano concerti. But you almost always hear the first one performed, and almost never the second.

Why is that? I'm not quite sure, but the phenomenon happens frequently in music. Sometimes history seems to choose one work of a composer to be representative and then discards the rest.

At any rate, history chose well with Mendelssohn's *Piano Concerto #1 in G Minor*. The work displays a typically Romantic device that will many times be imitated: The three movements are each connected or "attached" to each other, with the music moving continually from one movement to the next.

The first and third movements are wild and tempestuous, but the slow second movement has more than enough peace to counteract its surroundings. You'll probably recognize its lovely principle theme, which is quite famous. Then you'll say, as all of us have said about a thousand different famous melodies, "So *that's* where that theme comes from!"

## CONCERTO PROGRAM #2
### SCHUMANN: PIANO CONCERTO IN A MINOR
### CHOPIN: PIANO CONCERTO NO. 2 IN F MINOR

### ROBERT SCHUMANN (1810-1856)

Now we come to a true colossus among piano concerti, Schumann's *Concerto in A Minor*, or simply "The Schumann," as a pianist would call it. Its composer had dreamed of being a concert pianist, until he tried to strengthen his fourth finger with a harness contraption he had developed. Sadly, the attempt caused permanent damage and ruined any chance of a solo career. Nevertheless, this arch-Romantic married a great pianist, Clara Wieck Schumann, and continued to compose some outstanding piano music.

The *Piano Concerto in A Minor*, chosen for our program, explodes with fury in the opening chords. Notice how the pace fluctuates from lyrical tenderness to the frenzy of the finale. This work has won many competitions for young pianists and even made reputations for older ones. Many consider it Schumann's magnum opus (music jargon for "greatest work").

---

## THE COMPONENTS OF MUSICAL SOUND: DURATION

We're back with the Boston detectives who are looking for clues to help them solve the murder in your apartment building. Specifically, they want to know about the musical notes you heard right after the scream. Now that you've informed them of the notes' low pitch, one detective asks you the next critical question: "Were the notes long or short?"

He wants to know about the next major component of music, the *duration*. Some musical notes are played (or sung) for a longer amount of time than others. Otherwise, things would surely be dull on the concert stage. Just imagine if every note in a piece of music had the same length: Like the ticking of a clock, the sound would get boring fast.

This leads us to the general topic of time in music, which includes, in addition to duration, the elements of rhythm and tempo as well.

*Duration* indicates the relative length of each note in a music composition. Combinations of notes, each with their own duration, form *rhythm*. *Tempo*, on the other hand, refers to the overall rate of speed at which a specific composition is performed, such as adagio (slow) or allegro (fast). But they all have to do with the basic element of time.

Obviously, some instruments have limitations on their notes' duration. A wind instrumentalist (or for that matter, a singer) can only sustain sound for as long as his or her breath can last. A violinist can play a note only as long as the bow is moving across a string; think how different music literature would be if violin bows were only three inches long. The greatest length of a note on a drum or piano is determined by its gradual decay. And an electronic organ can sustain a note for as long as the electric bill is paid.

In the child's song "Row, Row, Row Your Boat," you can easily get a sense of each note's duration. The first two "Rows" are held for exactly the same amount of time, but notice how quickly you say the word *your*. These subtle differences of duration combine to make this melody's distinctive rhythm. The tempo you choose simply depends on how fast you feel like rowing.

The detective's voice rouses you from your musical reverie. "I said, were the notes you heard long or short?" You respond thoughtfully, "The first three notes were quick, but the fourth was very long." The detectives exchange grim looks. "We were afraid you'd say that." *(To be continued.)*

## FREDERIC CHOPIN (1810-1849)

"Hats off, gentlemen, a genius!" These words of Schumann referring to his new discovery, a young Polish pianist, were prophetic. Frederic Chopin was not only a phenomenal performer, but one of his century's unique composers in that he wrote almost exclusively for one instrument, the piano. No symphonies, operas, string quartets, not even a requiem to his credit; but where would the piano be without Chopin?

His two piano concerti employ an orchestra, of course, yet the soloist has such prominence that the other players spend more time listening than playing. But they don't mind, and neither does the audience. With this kind of breathtaking piano writing, who needs any other instruments to help?

I've chosen for our program Chopin's *Piano Concerto No. 2 in F Minor*. Lizst and Schumann liked its second movement best, but my favorite is the third. Since this is fashioned from a Polish dance, the mazurka, it seems to show us the true heart of Chopin and his love for his homeland.

Also note the interesting section where the strings play "col legno" (with the wood rather than the hairs of the bow). Rather fancy orchestration for a man who wrote almost exclusively for one instrument.

## CONCERTO PROGRAM #3
### LIZST: PIANO CONCERTO NO. 1 IN E♭ MAJOR
### BRAHMS: PIANO CONCERTO NO. 2 IN B♭ MAJOR

### FRANZ LIZST (1811-1886)

You'd expect the wildest pianist of the nineteenth century to write some wild concerti for his instrument. Actually Lizst wrote only two of them, but the first, by far the most popular, is a barnburner. *Piano Concerto No. 1 in E♭ Major* contains not only its fill of uproarious keyboard virtuosity, but also a large dose of compositional innovation.

For instance, the entire work runs in one continuous movement rather than three, the traditional number. It also has elements of a full symphony, including slow material and even a humorous "scherzo" section, as a typical symphony would contain.

This work is surely the first in history to contain a prominent orchestral solo for the triangle. Music critic Eduard Hanslick labeled the piece "The Triangle Concerto." Well, the critics always gave Lizst a difficult time. No wonder the composer is said to have quietly sung with the concerto's opening seven notes, *"Das versteht Ihr alle nicht"* ("This you cannot understand").

### JOHANNES BRAHMS (1833-1897)

Another great pianist, Johannes Brahms, also wrote two concerti for his instrument—both masterpieces. Some prefer the power and drama of his first; the animation of its last movement is certainly a tough act to follow. But Brahms's *Piano Concerto No. 2 in B♭ Major* has become one of the most frequently performed pieces in the repertoire.

This work's four extended movements make it seem more like an heroic symphony than a typical concerto. Yet after the soloist's second entrance in the first measure, you'll notice that the piano has the spotlight the rest of the evening—

notwithstanding the beautiful solo cello in the slow movement. This work is extravagant Romanticism. You may need some time to become familiar with it, but then it may become a passion for you, as it is for most of the world's concert pianists.

## CONCERTO PROGRAM #4
## TCHAIKOVSKY: PIANO CONCERTO NO. 1 IN B♭ MAJOR
## GRIEG: PIANO CONCERTO IN A MINOR

### PETER ILLYCH TCHAIKOVSKY (1840-1893)

Speaking of extravagant Romanticism, we've now reached its summit—"the Tchaikovsky," that is, his *Piano Concerto No. 1 in B♭ Major*. He wrote two others as well, but these are all but forgotten, while his first has become the concerto of concerti.

The well-known opening of this work, with commanding horns and then immense crashing piano chords, is the introduction into a world of soaring melodies and flying cadenzas. Russian virtuoso pianist Vladimir Horowitz once teamed with his father-in-law, Italian conductor Arturo Toscanini, for an historic recording of this work. Ever since then it's been hailed as the "Beethoven's Fifth" or "Handel's Messiah" of piano concerti.

If you haven't heard this classic masterpiece, don't admit it to anyone. Just slip out quietly tonight and head to the record store. You'll be glad you did.

### EDVARD GRIEG (1843-1907)

For a different type of composition with an enchanting Scandinavian flavor, try the Grieg concerto. Like the Tchaikovsky or the Schumann, it has a super-famous beginning, which piano students sometimes use to show off at parties. (Call their bluff — ask them to play the formidable cadenza of the *last* movement.)

Although the first and third movements are renowned for their tuneful themes and powerful fanfares, don't overlook the exquisite charm of the slow movement. It contains enough Norwegian beauty to make you call your travel agent.

## CONCERTO PROGRAM #5
## RACHMANINOV: PIANO CONCERTO NO. 2 IN C MINOR
## GERSHWIN: CONCERTO IN F

### SERGEI RACHMANINOV (1873-1943)

Classical performers affectionately refer to the four piano concerti of Rachmaninov (Rock-MON-i-nov) as "Rach 1, Rach 2, Rach 3 and Rach 4" (pronounced "Rock 1," etc.) All four are interesting, and the third features more fast-paced action than an Indiana Jones movie. But it's the second concerto that has acquired world prominence.

You'll find all three of its movements heavy, colorful and expansive. You may even recognize a theme from the last movement that was made later into a popular song: "Full Moon and Empty Arms."

That kind of borrowing from the classical repertoire for adaptation in the popular repertoire takes place quite often. Classical music has supplied pop songwriters with many albumfuls of great themes. Interestingly enough, the process has run the other direction as well; throughout history the great masters have often adapted folk music (and later, jazz) to their own grand style.

Now that we're listening again to music of the twentieth century, we have hundreds of piano concerti to choose from, written by thousands of composers—greats, near-greats and not-so-greats. Rather than spend the rest of the book on this swelling subject, let's choose a few of the most important examples to mention briefly. They can't all be on our program, but you should hear some of them when you can.

## BELA BARTOK (1881-1945)

Two of the most prolific modern composers for this genre are the Hungarian Bela Bartok and the Russian Sergei Prokofiev. To the uninitiated, Bartok's music seems rather wild, but there's always method to his madness. Of his three piano concerti, the third is the most historically significant; it had a major influence on composers for decades.

This piece offers a delightful mix of Hungarian folklore and contemporary idioms. Like other concerti, its outside (that is, first and last) movements are full of virtuosity. But my favorite part is the fascinating dialogue between the soloist and orchestra in the middle movement.

The composer left musicians a riddle in this work similar to that of Mozart's *Requiem*: Bartok died before completing the last page. Fortunately, the form was so far completed that to fill in the remainder was not difficult. I should say, not difficult to write down—it's outrageously demanding to play.

## SERGEI PROKOFIEV (1891-1953)

Another great Sergei from the land of many famous Sergeis is Prokofiev, who wrote five concerti for his favorite instrument. *Piano Concerto No. 2 in C* is both his most difficult and his most popular. If your only acquaintance with Prokofiev's work is *Peter and the Wolf*, then this ferocious side of the composer may shock you at first.

Yet even at his wildest, Prokofiev is never far from what's popular. The variations of the second movement will remind you of Disney's cartoon music, and you'll find the electrifying finale to be just as enjoyable the fiftieth time you hear it as it is the first.

## GEORGE GERSHWIN (1898-1937)

Let's end our feast of piano concerti with some dessert. You've had some massive musical courses to digest, and now you deserve something lighter. If Prokofiev was a

# THE COMPONENTS OF MUSICAL SOUND: DYNAMICS

"Were the notes loud or soft?" the detective asks next. After a moment's pause, he grows impatient. "The musical notes you heard right after the scream—were they LOUD?" he shouts. Then in a whisper: "Or were they *soft*?"

Being an experienced and thorough detective on the Boston streets, he checks every detail. What he's asking about now is the volume of the sounds you heard—or, as we say in music, the *dynamics*.

The best way I know to experience the full dynamic range of music is to attend a performance of a guitar concerto, especially one written in the twentieth century using a large modern orchestra. A skilled classical guitarist can, if required, play so quietly that the instrument can hardly be heard a few feet away. Such a concerto will sometimes call for the soloist to play an unaccompanied, hushed passage that may be followed by the entire orchestra at its loudest. Now that's contrast.

A scientist can measure the volume of a given sound (called the "amplitude of a given vibrating frequency") in terms of decibels. A jackhammer produces about a hundred decibels; most rock groups, a hundred and twenty decibels; and Mahler's *Symphony of a Thousand* is off the scale.

But composers don't ask performers to play a passage, for example, "at sixty-seven decibels." Instead, they write one of the following abbreviations under the line of music: pppp, ppp, pp, p, mp, mf, f, ff, fff or ffff.

Most musical terms come from the Italian language. In Italian, *piano* means to play softly, and *forte* means to play loudly. Their abbreviations are "p" and "f." Furthermore, *pianissimo* ("pp," sometimes adding even more "p's") denotes playing *very* quietly, while *fortissimo* ("ff," and so on) means to really let out some sound. Later, the more subtle mezzo-piano ("mp") and mezzo-forte ("mf") in the middle range were added. Gradual changes are indicated by such words as *crescendo* (becoming louder) and diminuendo (becoming quieter), or by placing symbols that look like long wedges under the notes.

You're probably wondering how this Italian word for soft—*piano*—came to be applied to a keyboard instrument. Before the invention of the modern piano, earlier keyboard instruments such as the harpsichord or clavichord had to play always at the same dynamic level (the same volume). But this new instrument had the advantage of giving the performer the ability to play either soft or loud, depending on how forcefully he pressed down the keys.

For that reason, they called this new instrument the "Soft-Loud," which in Italian is "pianoforte." Today, the name has been shortened to simply "piano."

Just think how dull music would be if there were no dynamic changes—the same volume over and over. In fact, one of the most frequent complaints about a mediocre performance is that "it was all played at the same level." Neither composers nor performers could express themselves fully without forte's and pianissimo's.

Neither could detectives catch their murder suspects. Before this one can ask again, you remember fully. "Loud. Every note was very loud." The detectives become agitated.

"I knew it!" one shouts. "It had to be him!" Another adds: "This time we've got enough evidence on him to send him up the river." *(To be continued.)*

master composer who dabbled in popular styles, then imagine what happens when a master songwriter tries his hand at a piano concerto. The result is Gershwin's *Concerto in F,* a work that easily fits the category "serious fun."

In the outside movements this multi-talented man—who even wrote songs for the Marx Brothers—behaved himself with "proper" dignity as he created convincing classical compositions. But when the dance and even blues sections of the second movement appear, we remember who Gershwin really is. Whether or not this work will ever vie with the Beethoven "Emperor," it's nevertheless a triumph of the fusion of styles.

If you like this piece, you'll want to hear Gershwin's *Rhapsody in Blue,* for piano and orchestra. Not exactly a concerto, it still deserves mention here, and its popularity is well deserved.

## THE VIOLIN CONCERTO

### CONCERTO PROGRAM #6
### VIVALDI: THE FOUR SEASONS

#### ANTONIO VIVALDI (1678-1741)

Now we must call the stagehands to move the piano offstage and make room for the solo violinist. Since the violin is a much older instrument than the piano, it's not surprising that we have violin concerti written decades before those for the piano. The first of lasting popularity is by the prolific composer Antonio Vivaldi, whom we will discuss at length a bit later. Even if you don't know any other works by the "red-haired priest," as he was called, you may well have heard of his magnum opus, *The Four Seasons.*

This wonderful work is actually four concerti in one—a violin concerto for each season of the year. Each concerto is a complete three-movement work, the whole being written around a four-section poem about spring, summer, fall and winter.

The marvel is that you really do *hear* the different seasons with remarkable clarity. Listen for the violin "birdcalls" of the spring; a terrific storm during the summer; the hunting hounds of autumn; and the biting wind, pizzicato rain (*pizzicato* means the strings are plucked rather than played with the bow), and light snowfall in the winter. Remember that this was written many decades before Beethoven's *Pastoral Symphony.*

*The Four Seasons* is a perennial favorite, both for the virtuoso violin soloists and for their entranced audiences.

## CONCERTO PROGRAM #7
## BEETHOVEN: VIOLIN CONCERTO IN D MAJOR
## MENDELSSOHN: VIOLIN CONCERTO IN E MINOR

### LUDWIG VAN BEETHOVEN (1770-1827)

Although beautiful concerti for the violin were written by Bach, Haydn and Mozart—never miss a chance to hear one!—this program only has room for the cream of the cream. So in the violin repertoire we move to the sublime Beethoven.

The opening four notes of his *Violin Concerto in D Major,* played by the tympani as a solo, notifies us that this work is as innovative as it is beautiful. The first movement is fully twice as long as the typical concerto of the composer's time, yet the intricate weaving of the soloist and the orchestra always keeps our interest.

The second movement is exquisitely hushed, with great tenderness and emotion. Its mature passion led one great violin teacher to insist that "no youthful violinist should be allowed to play the work." (I know many young prodegies who would disagree.)

But the boisterous third movement reminds us that Beethoven also had a sense of humor. After a ferocious cadenza, he ends the concerto with a bang.

### FELIX MENDELSSOHN (1809-1847)

Beethoven's violin concerto was first made popular at a performance by the twelve-year-old prodigy, Joseph Joachim. The concert was conducted by Felix Mendelssohn, who later composed a concerto that's played even more often than the one by Beethoven. Fortunately for students, it's a bit easier than the Beethoven, too.

Mendelssohn's *Violin Concerto in E Minor* is melody at its purest, moving from one famous theme to another. Unlike its predecessors, this piece doesn't allow the orchestra to provide either introduction or opening themes. Instead, the soloist immediately generates the first theme, and remains prominent to the end.

The first two movements contain some luscious "love story" music, while the effervescent theme of the third keeps us on the edge of our seats. This work is utterly violinistic; by that, I mean that its spirited bow strokes, soaring melodies and dramatic violin chords bring out the best of the medium. It's totally unplayable by, and unthinkable for, any other instrument.

## CONCERTO PROGRAM #8
## BRAHMS: VIOLIN CONCERTO IN D MAJOR
## TCHAIKOVSKY: VIOLIN CONCERTO IN D MAJOR

### JOHANNES BRAHMS (1833-1897)

That same twelve-year-old prodigy who made Beethoven's concerto popular, Joseph Joachim, grew up to become a musical collaborator with our old friend Brahms. Considering the masterpiece Brahms created in his *Violin Concerto in D*

*Major,* it's hard to imagine why the modest composer would write Joachim: "Of course you must correct it...if you don't think it's worth orchestrating, say so." Today, thousands of violinists and concert-goers affirm that the piece certainly was worth it.

In contrast to the boldness of Brahms's piano concerti, the violin concerto is characterized by serenity. Even the faster themes seem lyrical, especially in the first two movements. The last movement, subtitled "Hungarian," brings out the "gypsy fiddler" in every great violinist.

This work is a delight for a virtuoso, especially since Brahms elected to leave vacant the cadenza, to allow the soloist to compose his or her own. Of course, it is intimidating to compose in the shadow of one of music's great "Three B's."

## PETER ILYICH TCHAIKOVSKY (1840-1893)

If you'd like a bit of Romantic razzle-dazzle for violin and orchestra, check out the Tchaikovsky. The perfect combination of fireworks and amorous melodies, this piece brings the notion of "virtuoso" to a new level. After the obliging drama of the first movement, we take a lovely tour of Old Russia in the second, which the composer entitled "Canzonette," or "Little Song." Then the rondo (the last movement, featuring a kind of refrain) explodes with a flair that hardly can be exaggerated.

This is showmanship at its best—enough brilliant virtuosity to qualify for the musical Olympics, but written by a genius who knows how to make such technical challenges into great music.

As with the piano concerto repertoire, there's a myriad of violin concerti from the twentieth century. None has yet to achieve the level of popularity held by the works we've just examined, but many are coming close. My favorites are the Sibelius, Prokofiev's second, and the Bartok (now called Bartok's *Second* Violin Concerto, since someone discovered an earlier but less interesting one).

You'll also discover a few gems by composers such as Carl Nielson, Arnold Schoenberg, Ernest Bloch, Alban Berg, Aram Ilich Khatchaturyan, Samuel Barber and Igor Stravinsky. All attempt to find that elusive balance of beautiful music and technical mastery.

## CONCERTI FOR OTHER INSTRUMENTS

### CONCERTO PROGRAM #9
### DVORAK: CELLO CONCERTO IN B MINOR
### TCHAIKOVSKY: VARIATION ON A ROCOCO THEME

## ANTONIN DVORAK (1841-1904)

The piano and the violin have captured the lion's share of the basic concerto repertoire, but other instruments have their masterpieces as well. Since I'm married to a superb cellist we'll hear from the cello (CHEH-low) next.

This instrument—its name from days gone by is "violoncello"—has several great works in this genre. You might want to listen sometime to those by Haydn, Luigi Boccherini (whom we haven't yet heard from), Schumann, Saint-Saens and Elgar. You'll also find a number of interesting efforts from the twentieth century.

Nevertheless, the pinnacle of cello playing is the heroic *Concerto in B Minor* by Antonin Dvorak, which we've chosen for our program. Even his friend Brahms exclaimed about it: "Why on earth didn't I know that one could write a violoncello concerto like this? If I had only known, I would have written one long ago!" I wish he would have, and so does every cellist.

In any case, this concerto was written while Dvorak lived in America. It contains musical references to both Indian melodies and Negro spirituals—the same sources, you'll remember, for his *New World Symphony*. This work has everything: Romantic drama, virtuosity, an exhaustive quota of cello technique. It's a true classic.

## PETER ILLYCH TCHAIKOVSKY (1840-1893)

Let's look at a popular "concerto" that's not really a concerto. Whatever its name, Tchaikovsky's "Rococo Variations" makes a perfect showpiece for a cello virtuoso and orchestra. The lovely theme—given in the cello's opening statement—is Tchaikovsky's own, but written to sound as if it were composed a century earlier in the French Rococo movement. Its simplicity allows the composer room to manuever within his seven variations, each of which features the soloist.

A blow-by-blow description reveals an interesting buildup: Variation 1 speeds up the theme a bit, and Variation 2 even more so. Then comes the tenderness of the slow Variation 3, which ends up so high you can hardly hear it. Variation 4 moves back to the original stateliness, but adds two short cadenzas that feature chromatic scales requiring almost superhuman abilities by the cellist.

In Variation 5 the flute takes the theme while the soloist trills his or her fingers off, and ends with an even longer cadenza. Then comes Variation 6, a moving andante in a minor key. Finally, the last variation bursts upon us with the soloist's rapid interplay with the orchestra. What an ending! This is one of those pieces that tests how fast a human being actually can play.

## ANTONIO VIVALDI (1678-1741)

A chapter about the concerto would not be complete without naming the "father of the concerto," Antonio Vivaldi.

As a "father" he was quite prolific, writing more than six hundred concerti. It's true that most of them were for strings alone, and no doubt many of them sound very much alike. Nevertheless, none are harmful to your health and many are wonderful; they ought to be performed more frequently.

We already mentioned Vivaldi's famous *Four Seasons for Violin and Orchestra;*

other praiseworthy works include his *Bassoon Concerto in E Minor, Flute Concerto in E Minor, Oboe Concerto in F Major,* and even a *Concerto for Two Cellos in G Minor,* among many others.

Vivaldi has been performed by a number of players for good reason: For years, if you weren't a pianist, violinist or a cellist yet you wanted to play a concerto, he was almost the only composer who had written for your instrument. Until the proliferation of the twentieth century's "anything goes" policy among composers, Vivaldi cornered the market on such items as a mandolin concerto or piccolo concerto. The "red-haired priest of Venice" has an inexhaustible well of material in this genre, and to this day his concerti remain his principle claim to fame.

<h2 style="text-align:center">CONCERTO PROGRAM #10<br>BACH: BRANDENBURG CONCERTO NO. 2 IN F MAJOR<br>BACH: CONCERTO FOR TWO VIOLINS IN D MINOR</h2>

### JOHANN SEBASTIAN BACH (1685-1750)

Old J.S., another principle concerto composer, was as prolific at writing them as he was at everything else he wrote. He particularly liked to compose a "Concerto Grosso" (*grosso* is Italian for *big* ). Throughout the Baroque Period it was more popular to compose using this more complex form—which employs a number of different soloists in its own group alternating with the orchestra accompaniment—than to write a concerto with only one soloist, as later became the norm.

The culmination of the concerto grosso form is undoubtably Bach's magnificent *Brandenburg Concerti.* These six works represent his crowning achievement in Baroque instrumental composition, and each one is a must-hear. Fortunately, recordings of "the Brandenburgs" are always sold conveniently in a set.

The most famous is the second, for oboe, trumpet, violin and flute (originally, it was for recorder rather than flute, and sometimes the recorder is still used). I've chosen it for our program. But my personal favorite is the fourth, for two flutes and violin. Then again, there's the fifth, for harpsichord, flute and violin, and...well, get the whole set.

Although the *Brandenberg Concerto No. 2* utilizes four soloists, it's the trumpet that claims first place, especially in the last movement. This piece begins as a fugue, with each soloist entering separately: trumpet, oboe, violin, then flute. The Baroque trumpet writing is so virtuosic that the soloist is glad to have a break in the second movement. This lovely movement only involves the flute, oboe and violin—the trumpeter is probably off-stage getting a drink of water or lying on the floor resting up for the Herculean third movement.

Although Bach also wrote great concerti for solo violin and solo harpsichord, he always seemed to gravitate toward multiple soloists. I've selected the powerful *Concerto for Two Violins in D Minor* for our program, with its gorgeous slow movement.

The outside movements are both powerful, but they're so rhythmically complex that the themes all seem to run together. It's the slow movement that forms the pinnacle of the work: The two violin lines delicately interplay, often with one of them sustaining long notes while the other keeps moving—then the parts reverse. This is Bach at his loveliest.

Bach also wrote concerti for two harpsichords and even *four* harpsichords. The latter is a wonderful piece, but it's not performed often. Just imagine the challenge: First, locate four of these rare instruments, then cram them all on one stage, and finally tune them to one another.

## CONCERTO PROGRAM #11
## MOZART: CLARINET CONCERTO IN A MAJOR
## MOZART: FLUTE CONCERTO IN G MAJOR

### WOLFGANG AMADEUS MOZART (1756-1791)

The third exceptional composer in the concerto category was our friend Wolfgang, who was exceptional in every other category as well. But the concerto was especially suited for this combination performer/composer genius. Once, when he was performing a piano concerto for Joseph II, emperor of the Holy Roman Empire, the sovereign noticed that every member of the orchestra had Mozart's manuscripts before him, yet the composer had nothing.

"Where's your part?" Joseph asked.

Mozart tapped his forehead. "Here."

After you've enjoyed his twenty-seven piano concerti, and half a dozen or so violin concerti, the fun really begins. Among the pieces for the woodwind family, Mozart's excellent *Clarinet Concerto in A Major*, chosen for this program, is still the best in the repertoire. Notice how Mozart makes great use of the extended range of the clarinet. Not only does the soloist have wide arpeggios (chords whose notes are performed one after another rather than all together), but there are wide skips in the melody as well—that is, low pitches often are abruptly succeeded by very high ones, and vice-versa. Nevertheless, Mozart's innate gift for melody holds the work together, and all three movements are noted for their singable melodies.

Mozart's two flute concerti are equally splendid; one of them he rewrote for the oboe. The composition works well for either instrument, and they are both very popular. But his other flute concerto, in G major, is every flutist's favorite—the last

## THE COMPONENTS OF MUSICAL SOUND: TIMBRE

Once more we find ourselves talking to detectives of the Boston police department as they try to solve the murder that took place in your apartment building.

"Now comes the critical point," they tell you. "We need to identify the musical instrument you heard play right after the scream. What type of sound was it?"

A good question. How can you answer? You didn't see the instrument; you only heard it. Have you ever wondered how you can immediately tell the difference between an oboe playing a melody and a flute playing that same melody?

It has to do with a fascinating element of musical acoustics we call *timbre* or *tone quality.* When an instrument such as an oboe is played, it seems to produce only one sound at a time. But actually, with every note played a number of other pitches, called "overtones," are being produced as well. These sub-audible pitches are characteristic of the instrument's specific shape and construction. Some overtones will be stronger than others, and their combinations tell our ears which instrument we are hearing. There are also other attributes which our ears can discriminate, such as the subtle sounds of bow hair on strings, breath indications in the winds, and different levels of the sounds' "attack and delay," especially notable in the percussion section.

Music lovers are no more consciously aware of the overtone series as we are of the music's scientifically-measured decibel level. Instead, we speak of the rich sound of a pipe organ, the dark sound of a bassoon, the mysterious sound of a clarinet in its lowest register, and the bright sound of open strings. Certainly this is all somewhat arbitrary, but these descriptive adjectives show that the nebulous world of musical sounds has a distinct effect on our equally-nebulous feelings.

Nevertheless, these detectives don't want nebulous answers; they want to know the facts of the case. "What instrument was it you heard?"

"Strings!" you say. "It sounded like a stringed instrument, a low one."

The detectives shake hands. "That confirms it. It's him all right, the infamous 'Boston Stringler.' That villain always strangles his victims with a double bass string, then plays the opening to Beethoven's *Fifth Symphony* before he leaves the scene of the crime with his instrument. Get a warrant for his arrest and head down to symphony hall."

great concerto written for their instrument until the twentieth century.

This one has plenty of Mozartian charm but also plenty of flash, with rapid runs throughout every register of the instrument. From the martial opening theme until the joyous rondo finale, the composer always keeps his soloist in the spotlight.

## CONCERTO PROGRAM #12
## MOZART: HORN CONCERTO NO. 3 IN E♭ MAJOR
## MOZART: CONCERTO FOR FLUTE AND HARP

Next are Mozart's amazing horn concerti. All four have a distinct place in the standard repertoire, and you'll always be glad to hear one played by a sensitive musician. The horn player for which Mozart wrote them must have been quite a performer, since the horns of his day were much more difficult to play than our modern versions.

Don't ask me how those players produce all those fast high notes merely by moving their facial muscles fractions of inches. Simply close your eyes and enjoy it.

*Horn Concerto No. 3 in E♭ Major,* chosen for this program, is one of four that we still have by this prolific composer; two others have been lost. All three movements are well-known; the second is so familiar that I recently heard its lovely theme played in the background of a television commercial. But it's the finale that gets our attention. The rapid-fire, repeated notes give the impression of a musical machine gun. This is an amazing piece in the hands of a virtuoso soloist.

Mozart also wrote a number of celebrated concerti for two instruments, including works for two pianos and for two violins. But my favorites are his *Sinfonia Concertante for Violin and Viola* and the *Concerto for Flute and Harp,* selected for our program. This latter piece was written for a father-daughter act. They must have had to work hard on that double cadenza in the first movement. You'll find the whole work resplendent in delightful melody, especially in the second movement.

### A FEW MORE GREAT CONCERTI

We've looked at the principle concerti for piano, violin and cello, plus the concerto works of the master composers Vivaldi, Bach and Mozart. Yet a few great works by other composers for other instruments (or combinations of instruments) are simply too good to miss. Let's examine a quick potpourri of pieces for orchestra and assorted soloists.

## CONCERTO PROGRAM #13
## BRAHMS: CONCERTO FOR VIOLIN AND CELLO IN A MINOR
## HAYDN: TRUMPET CONCERTO IN E♭ MAJOR

You may remember the Brahms violin concerto, and how he wished he had written a cello concerto. Well, he finally did—almost. Actually, Brahms wrote an interesting combination, the *Concerto for Violin and Cello in A Minor.* Can you imagine? Two virtuoso soloists on the same stage.

Perhaps Brahms knew enough about temperamental soloists not to have them compete for the flashiest themes. Rather than the typical virtuostic acrobatics of many concerti, the composer simply gave the soloists beautiful music, and plenty of it. Each movement is a gem, and the third—with its Native American rhythm and Romantic duets—provides a splendid finale.

How about *three* soloists? Beethoven's *Concerto for Violin, Cello and Piano in C Major* (not on this program) almost looks like a reversion to the "concerto grosso" idea of the Baroque era. But this piece sounds as Romantically Beethovenesque as the *Fifth Symphony.*

You might consider this a concerto for a piano trio (that is, piano, violin and cello), for not only do the standard three instruments play, but they also function throughout as a team. Beethoven entitled the third movement "Alla Polacca"—that is, "in the Polish style," like a Polish dance. It's yet another marvelous example of the cheerful, humorous side of the otherwise stormy Beethoven.

How about a concerto with the king of the brass? I've selected for our program perhaps the best known of them, Haydn's *Trumpet Concerto in E♭ Major.* This is an interesting and enjoyable work. The second movement is simple enough to be played by students, yet the last movement is difficult enough to trip up professionals.

This is vintage Haydn, the composer who spent years at the Esterhazy Castle, "cut off from the world," as he put it. Haydn later recalled of his time there: "There was no one to confuse or torment me, and I was forced to become original."

Like the Mozart horn concerti, this work was written for an older instrument in a day when keys and valves were rather newfangled. It makes you appreciate technical progress to hear it played on a modern trumpet today; no doubt Haydn would have loved it all the more.

After referring to so many piano and harpsichord works, we can't forget the other principle keyboard instrument, the organ, though we don't have room to include it in our program. Since pipe organs can't come to the orchestra, the orchestra has to go to the pipe organ. This can be a problem, so the organ concerto repertoire is a little thinner than we would like.

Fortunately, Handel wrote a number of fine works in this genre. An outstanding organist himself, he knew what he was doing. My favorite is his *Organ Concerto in B♭ Major.* Organ and orchestra make such a nice combination that you'll wish Bach had written a few of them too.

That's the one trouble with the concerto repertoire: You always find yourself wishing more had been written for your favorite instrument, especially if you're not a pianist or a violinist. For instance, all cellists wish that Beethoven or Mozart had written a cello concerto; all clarinetists wish that Brahms had written a clarinet concerto; all hornists wish that Mahler had written a horn concerto. And all percussionists wish that *any* of the great composers had written them a concerto!

Even so, there are hundreds of great concerti out there, with something for everyone. I'd love for you to hear the Strauss *Horn Concerto in E Flat Major*, Berlioz's *Harold in Italy*, for viola and orchestra; the *Dances Sacrees et Profanes* of Debussy, for harp and orchestra; Alexander Glazunov's *Alto Saxophone Concerto*; even the classical guitarists' delight, Joaquin Rodrigo's *Concierto de Aranjuez*. As I said, this book can only be so long—but your discovery and enjoyment of great musical works can last a lifetime.

Let's conclude this genre with a fun, if somewhat arbitrary, list of its best works. We noted earlier that every instrument has its concerto, and most have many, though of course they're not all written by famous composers. Still, they're loved and performed by many, so I'll at least give you one of the best for each of the principle instruments. This way, if you want to strike up a conversation with an interesting person who's carrying a saxophone case, you can always say, "Hi! How's your Ibert?"

## EVERY INSTRUMENT'S FAVORITE CONCERTO

| INSTRUMENT | COMPOSER | TITLE |
| --- | --- | --- |
| Piano | Tchaikovsky | Piano Concerto No. 1 in B♭ Major |
| Organ | Handel | Organ Concerto in B♭ Major |
| Harpsichord | Bach | Brandenburg Concerto No. 5 in D Major |
| Violin | Beethoven | Violin Concerto in D Major |
| Viola | Walton | Concerto for Viola |
| Cello | Dvorak | Cello Concerto in B Minor |
| Bass | Dittersdorf | Concerto for Double Bass in E♭ Major |
| Flute | Mozart | Flute Concerto in G Major |
| Piccolo | Vivaldi | Concerto for Piccolo in C Major |
| Oboe | Mozart | Oboe Concerto in D Major |
| English Horn | Donizetti | Concertino in G Major |
| Clarinet | Mozart | Clarinet Concerto in A Major |
| Bassoon | Weber | Bassoon Concerto in F Major |
| Saxophone | Ibert | Concertino da Camera |
| Trumpet | Haydn | Trumpet Concerto in E♭ Major |
| Horn | Strauss | Horn Concerto No. 2 in E♭ Major |
| Trombone | Creston | Concerto for Trombone |
| Tuba | Vaughan Williams | Concerto for Tuba |
| Harp | Handel | Concerto for Harp in B♭ Major |
| Percussion | Milhaud | Concerto for Percussion and Small Orchestra |
| Guitar | Rodrigo | Concierto de Aranjuez |

# CONCERTO REPERTOIRE

Note: Where the solo instrument isn't mentioned in the title itself, it's given in parentheses.

## THE TOP 15

Bach
  Brandenburg Concerto No. 2 in F Major (flute, trumpet and violin)
Beethoven
  Piano Concerto No. 5 in E♭ Major, "Emperor"
  Violin Concerto in D Major
Brahms
  Piano Concerto No. 1 in D Minor
  Violin Concerto in D Major
Dvorak
  Cello Concerto in B Minor
Grieg
  Piano Concerto in A Minor
Lizst
  Piano Concerto No. 1
Mendelssohn
  Violin Concerto in E Minor
Mozart
  Clarinet Concerto in A Major
Rachmaninov
  Piano Concerto No. 2 in C Minor
Schumann
  Piano Concerto in A Minor
Tchaikovsky
  Piano Concerto No. 1 in B♭ Major
  Violin Concerto in D Major
Vivaldi
  The Four Seasons (violin)

## THE TOP 50

Bach
  Brandenburg Concerto No. 2 in F Major (flute, oboe, trumpet and violin)
  Brandenburg Concerto No. 4 in G Major (two flutes and violin)
  Brandenburg Concerto No. 5 in D Major (harpsichord)
  Violin Concerto No. 1 in A Minor
  Violin Concerto No. 2 in E Major
  Concerto for Two Violins in D Minor
Bartok
  Piano Concerto No. 3
Beethoven
  Piano Concerto No. 4 in G Major
  Piano Concerto No. 5 in E♭ Major, "Emperor"
  Violin Concerto in D Major
  Concerto for Violin, Cello and Piano in C Major
Berlioz
  Harold in Italy, for Viola and Orchestra
Brahms
  Piano Concerto No. 1 in D Minor
  Violin Concerto in D Major
  Concerto for Violin and Cello in A Minor
Bruch
  Scottish Fantasy for Violin and Orchestra
Chopin
  Piano Concerto No. 2 in F Minor
Dvorak
  Cello Concerto in B Minor
Gershwin
  Concerto in F, for Piano and Orchestra
Grieg
  Piano Concerto in A Minor
Haydn
  Cello Concerto No. 2 in D Major
  Trumpet Concerto in E♭ Major
Liszt
  Piano Concerto No. 1 in E♭ Major
Mendelssohn
  Piano Concerto No. 1 in G Minor
  Violin Concerto in E Minor
Mozart
  Piano Concerto No. 20 in D Minor
  Piano Concerto No. 21 in C Major, "Elvira Madigan"
  Piano Concerto No. 23 in A Major
  Piano Concerto No. 27 in B♭ Major
  Violin Concerto No. 4 in D Major
  Violin Concerto No. 5 in A Major
  Clarinet Concerto in A Major
  Horn Concerto No. 4 in E♭ Major
  Concerto for Flute and Harp in C Major
  Sinfonia Concertante for Violin and Viola in E♭ Major
Prokofiev
  Piano Concerto No. 5 in G Major
Rachmaninov
  Piano Concerto No. 2 in C Minor
  Piano Concerto No. 3 in D Minor
  Rhapsody on a Theme of Paganini, for Piano and Orchestra
Debussy
  Dances Sacrees et Profanes, for Harp and Orchestra
Ravel
  Piano Concerto in G Major
  Piano Concerto in D Major for the Left Hand
Schumann
  Piano Concerto in A Minor
  Cello Concerto in A Minor
Sibelius
  Violin Concerto in D Minor
Stravinsky
  Violin Concerto in D Major
Tchaikovsky
  Piano Concerto No. 1 in B♭ Major
  Violin Concerto in D Major
  Variations on a Rococo Theme, for Cello and Orchestra
Vivaldi
  The Four Seasons (for violin)

*The "smiling" portrait of Antonio Vivaldi.
Because of his hair and his ministry,
he was called "the red priest."*

*Frederick the Great (1712–1786) playing the flute. Music at court in the 18th century. The soloist is Frederick the Great, who practiced his flute between battles of the Seven Years War.*

# OPERA

*Opera to me comes before everything else.*

—Wolfgang Amadeus Mozart

"Opera at last!" some of you may be saying. "Oh, no!" others may be moaning. In either case, I believe you're in for some fun. After all, you're reading this book because you love great music, and you probably love great theater, too. Put them together, and what do you get? Opera—the world's most all-encompassing, colorful, expensive, prima-donna-ridden, lovable art form.

Then why all the bad press and bad jokes about opera? Why does it conjure up visions of weighty women when seldom that is the case? Why does it elicit comments like the one I found in Samuel Johnson's 1755 dictionary: "Opera: an exotic and irrational entertainment"? Or as the American humorist Richard Benchley said it: "Opera is where a guy gets stabbed in the back, and instead of dying, he sings."

At least two reasons strike me for these witticisms and misunderstandings. First, opera is by its nature the ultimate in "non-reality." No one goes about daily life singing to everyone and listening to their responses in song. Yet that happens in opera (as well as in Broadway musicals, I might add). People sing through love, hate, marriages, murders, wars and rumors of wars, and they keep on singing. Of course, that might not be so bad an idea; life could be happier for everyone.

In fact, opera gives a singing version of all history, which can be confusing at first. Opera characters include kings, queens, presidents, mermaids, farmers, soldiers, cooks, priests and pickpockets, to name only a few. All of them sing to each other about everything. But after all, those who want only tangible, verifiable (and boring) "reality" should be reading almanacs instead of books about music.

The second reason opera is sometimes under-appreciated has to do with the preparation involved in fully understanding and enjoying it. Opera is an all-encompassing, complex art form, so you can't just sit down to a performance of *Boris Godounov* and expect to take it all in with no effort exerted beforehand.

"Ay, there's the rub," as Hamlet would say. Many of us raised on fast food and push-button lawnmowers don't relish the idea of *working* to enjoy something. But in this case, the labor is well worth it, since the amount of preparation is modest and the rewards are fantastic.

Consider how different the outcome might be for each of four people in a typical opera house audience—let's say the show is Puccini's *Madame Butterfly*. They've all paid the same hard-earned cash for the tickets, but they've come with varying levels of interest and preparedness. Not surprisingly, the rewards of the experience vary accordingly.

One man was brought kicking and screaming to the opera by his wife, and he falls asleep; his wife will "reward" him all the way home. Another is a retired lieutenant who once visited Nagasaki (the setting for the opera); he's interested and amused by the plot—when he can follow it. A third person has read the libretto (the text of the opera); she's begun to develop a genuine appreciation for the beautiful melodies of the different arias (songs).

The fourth person has listened to a recording or two of this particular opera and also saw it in a different production the year before. He's enraptured by what he sees and hears on stage.

Which one of these people are you today? Which will you be next year? No one can say for sure how your musical tastes will develop, but I can tell you this: Opera can be habit-forming, nearly addictive, even for those we might have least expected would enjoy it.

I've known people with a great love for the symphony, but their passion can't be compared to the intense devotion I've seen in many opera lovers. You may need a little more time to get acquainted with opera than you will with the symphony, but once you take the plunge, you may never go back—there's so much about opera to love.

Many operas are performed today in English translation, making them more accessible to audiences. Some translate better than others, of course, but beginners can certainly get their feet wet painlessly when a production is in their own language. In addition, many televised operas provide translated subtitles, and even many opera houses are being equipped with supertitle projectors. With that innovation, you can keep your eyes on the action and still understand the words!

Admittedly, opera tickets generally cost more than orchestra or chamber music tickets. But there's a good reason: Opera is a rather costly venture to undertake. Just think of all the expenses: top soloists in extravagant costumes, huge sets, backdrops, lights, a technical crew, a paid orchestra, often a paid chorus—and more rehearsals than any orchestra ever dreamed of having.

You're buying a lot with that little ticket. In fact, I can assure you that the opera company is hardly breaking even, if at all. If they didn't love it, they wouldn't be in it. I heard a great quote recently by Rudolf Bing, who ran the Metropolitan Opera in New York for years: "The opera always loses money. That's as it should be. Opera has no business making money."

Since opera has more aspects to appreciate than a symphony, our approach in this chapter will differ from those in earlier chapters. Up till now we've reviewed dozens of works in various genres, but in this chapter we'll focus on only a few key operas, spending more time on each one. But first we need a little background on the various ingredients you'll find throughout the repertoire.

## HOW TO COOK UP AN OPERA

An opera is much like a play. There are comic and tragic operas just as there are comic and tragic plays. The structure is similar as well: usually three or four acts, with each act containing several scenes. But within the scenes of an opera lie a variety of dramatic and musical possibilities.

Composers of opera employ two basic building materials: (1) the *principal songs*, which are usually called "arias" (ARE-ee-as)—the Italian word for "airs"; and (2) *everything else,* that is, the music between the principal songs that links them all together and keeps the storyline going. Though great arias are beautiful and we all applaud for them, they seldom advance the plot. So composers provide music in between them—the bulk of the opera—to actually tell the story.

In the earlier operas, this "everything else" music often was considered so unimportant that patrons would even excuse themselves, go outside and wait until time for their favorite aria. Throughout much of the seventeenth and eighteenth centuries, composers employed a declamatory technique known as "recitative," in which the singer would quickly sing—often on the same note with little accompaniment—line after line of the story. But from Mozart to the present, composers have attempted to write their operas so that all the in-between music sounds as nice as the arias.

These principal songs, like the singers who sing them, come in all shapes and sizes. Typically, an aria is for a solo singer, often singing to himself or herself in a kind of open-diary meditation. But some of opera's greatest moments are in ensemble songs—duets, trios, quartets and larger groups.

As you might expect, many great operas have at least one love duet between the hero and heroine. A number of works, especially comic ones, have wonderful

## THE ELEMENTS OF MUSIC COMPOSITION: MELODY

For chefs to create a banquet, they need certain ingredients as well as the directions for each recipe. Composers need much the same to create a musical masterpiece. The basic ingredients for composition are the four components of musical sound we discussed while solving a murder mystery. The recipe—that is, how the composer puts these components together—include such musical elements as melody, harmony, rhythm and form.

A melody is simply a succession of musical tones. Some may be longer than the others, some shorter; some will surely be higher or lower than others, but the listener takes in these "tunes" as a whole. They're no longer individual notes. They work together and we remember them together.

Melodies come in all shapes and sizes. They may have one-step runs like a musical scale or make wide skips in pitch. They may be simple and repetitive or rhythmically complex, long or short, rising or falling—or probably both.

The four-note opening to Beethoven's *Fifth Symphony* is a melody, as is the expansive love-theme of Tchaikovsky's *Romeo and Juliet Overture*. Sometimes they're called "themes," and the shorter ones are called "motifs," but they all reside within the world of melody.

We give the notes, or pitches, in which melodies are constructed letter names. You may have heard of "middle C," but do you know its friends A, B, D, E, F and G? You won't find any *Symphony in J Major* or *Sonata in Q Minor*. Once you get past the letter G, the notes begin with A again. So the musical alphabet is only seven letters long.

There are also sharps and flats, which slightly raise or lower the pitch of a note. Look at a piano keyboard sometime. Adjacent keys (with no others in between) on the keyboard are said to be a "half step" apart. Those with one key in between are said to be a "whole step" apart. For example, A and B are a whole-step apart, while A and B♭ (B-flat) are only a half-step apart.

It may seem strange that, with a huge orchestra capable of a myriad of notes at our disposal, such a principle element of music would consist of one little note at a time. Yet it's the tune that we come away whistling after the concert. You simply cannot create great music without a great concept of melody. As the composer Charles Francois Gounod said: "Melody, always melody...that is the sole, the unique secret of our art."

ensemble finales, in which all the characters are on stage for a climatic flourish, guaranteed to bring down the house.

But we're getting ahead of ourselves. Most operas start with an overture, in which the orchestra plays a medley of the principle themes of the opera. Many of these overtures are famous in their own right, and some are performed today while the operas they once introduced have long since fallen into obscurity.

For that reason, you can find opera outside the opera house. Orchestras play the overtures in purely instrumental concerts. Singers fill their recital programs with their favorite arias, usually with a piano version of the orchestral accompaniment.

What about the texts, or more properly, the libretti? What are the stories we find in operas about? Actually, you can find almost any subject matter here: operas about politics, about historical figures, about the conflict of heaven and hell. But you probably won't be surprised to learn that the most common subject is romantic love.

In opera you'll hear of tenors chasing after sopranos and hundreds of altos wooing basses. As with Shakespeare's drama, interesting complications often arise in the plot that frustrate the efforts of couples trying to get together. But the sweethearts are usually united in the finale: In the happy ones, they get married; in the tragedies, they exterminate one another, or maybe die of consumption (an opera favorite).

But don't worry. It's always done artistically. In fact, they never stop singing, right up until their last croak. That's opera!

Now that we've noted the ingredients, let's sample the wares of a few master "chefs" of opera. I've selected a number of very different works, which also happen to be some of the most popular operas of all time. We'll examine the story, the overture, the principal arias and the music that holds them all together. This may be a bit more involved than some of the simpler musical forms, but it's worth the extra effort to understand.

## OPERA PROGRAM #1
## MOZART: THE MARRIAGE OF FIGARO

Figaro. You've no doubt heard of this guy; now what's he all about? Not surprisingly, the opera tells a love story in which a soprano (Susanna) and a bass (Figaro) try to get together. Unfortunately, a baritone (Count Almaviva) also wants the soprano, and a contralto (Marcellina) also wants the bass. Then there's the baritone's wife (Countess Rosina), another soprano who's exasperated with her husband because of his flirting with another soprano (Barbarina), who is also loved by....Need I go on? The amazing thing is that somehow it all works out and Mozart gets everyone happily married to the right singer, including Figaro.

All these loony romances form the seemingly superficial plot that amused the nobles of Mozart's day. But the real message is a mockery of the class-system injustice that soon lead to the French Revolution. The "good guy" is the clever servant Figaro who outfoxes his "bad guy" employer, the licentious Count. That was an uncomfortable plot for the nervous aristocracy, who were used to having their way.

When the Emperor heard the opera in Vienna, he dismissed it: "Too many notes, my dear Mozart, too many notes."

Undaunted, the little genius replied: "But not one more than necessary, Your Highness."

What about the music itself? Dazzling! Mozart at his lyrical zenith. The overture grabs you immediately with its lightning woodwinds and brilliant climaxes.

When the singing begins, we become entranced. Song after resplendent song, this is the perfect example of Mozart's unlimited supply of beautiful melody. You'll hear many celebrated arias—in particular, Figaro's famous marching song at the end of the first act, *Non Piu Andrai,* as well as the lovely *Voi Che Sapete.* You'll also be thrilled by some of the greatest ensemble singing in the entire opera repertoire.

In many ways, *The Marriage of Figaro* is a landmark, the first of the truly great operas ever written and an excellent introduction to the genre. Don't just listen to a recording of it; you'll miss the costumes and sets. Catch it the next time it is in town.

## OPERA PROGRAM #2
### VERDI: AIDA

On to ancient Egypt and Verdi's popular *Aida* ("eye-E-duh"). Verdi was the Italian master of opera at the same time that Wagner was turning German opera upside down. This is one of those works for whom the word *grandiose* was coined. Aida is so big that it's often performed outside on huge stages, with a cast that includes live elephants and almost everything else in ancient Egypt but the pyramids.

The libretto is of the "Romeo and Juliet" type, with two lovers from warring countries, Egypt and Ethiopia. The Egyptian captain Radames (tenor, of course) loves a slave-girl Aida (soprano, of course), who happens to be the captured daughter of the big, bad Ethiopian king Amonasro (baritone, of course). Aida loves both her people and the Egyptian Radames, and the plot is further complicated since she's the slave of the jealous Princess Amneris (mezzo-soprano, of course), who also loves Radames. Everyone loves a tenor.

Unfortunately, things don't work out quite as congenially as in *The Marriage of Figaro.* In fact, when the spurned Princess discovers that Aida and her dad are urging Radames to cross party lines and work for the Ethiopians, she spitefully tells the Egyptian high priest Ramfis (bass, of course). His sentence is perfect for opera fans: Radames is to be buried alive—remember, he has to keep singing. A la Shakespeare, as the last stone to his tomb is placed, Radames discovers his girlfriend Aida hiding with him, so he can die with a duet instead of a solo.

As always, it's the glorious music that makes this tragic plot a masterpiece. Verdi is the virtuoso of Italian melody; hundreds of recitals program such illustrious arias as Radames's "Celeste Aida," and the duets and choruses are equally renowned. You almost certainly already know many of these tunes, since numerous melodies from *Aida* have been used in popular ditties and movies.

This is another excellent work for getting acquainted with opera. The grandeur will overwhelm you, and you'll be delighted to find some familiar melodies.

## OPERA PROGRAM #3
### BIZET: CARMEN

Here's a surprise: The world's most popular opera is not about kings, queens or the aristocracy. It's about the poor—about workers, gypsies and common soldiers.

The heroine is not your typical lovely soprano, but a mezzo, with a darker, gutsier voice. Yet Carmen conquers all. On occasion, snobby royalty reluctantly attended, and though expected to poo-poo such vulgar entertainment, come out humming its irresistible tunes. Tchaikovsky, among others, considered it "the perfect opera" and spent hours memorizing its every note.

The libretto is melancholy but poignant. There are no unblemished heroes—even Carmen turns fickle and drops her boyfriend, who in turn kills her. Yet we all sympathize with them somehow as characters trapped by the impoverished system that surrounds them.

At any rate, soldier Don Jose (tenor) meets gypsy Carmen (mezzo), and she captivates him like she does every other fellow in the opera. Much like the Popeye and Olive Oyl dynamic of the old cartoons, the plot soon introduces a Brutus-like character in the bullfighter Escarmillo (baritone), who attracts Carmen with his famous "Toreador Song."

She falls for him and, after escapades with smugglers and gypsies, promises her love to him if he wins his next bullfight. When soldier Don Jose finds out about his rejection, he doesn't quite have Popeye's standards of chivalry, and stabs Olive Oyl, I mean Carmen, just in time for the bullfighter's victory. We all cry, and when Carmen later appears for her curtain call, we cheer uncontrollably.

Those who have never heard this work may wonder how this cartoon plot got to be the world's favorite opera. The answer is simple—melody. Every aria in this work is a must-hear.

As soon as Carmen sings her well-known "Habanera" (usually translated, "Love is a bird," or better yet, "Love is for the birds"), you know you're in for a fun evening. The composer, Alexandre-Cesar-Leopold Bizet (bee-ZAY, 1838-1875) put everything he had into this work, but he died at the age of thirty-six, soon after Carmen's premiere. What a shame he didn't live to savor his triumph and compose a few more masterpieces.

## OPERA PROGRAMS #4, #5, #6 AND #7!
## WAGNER: THE RING OF THE NIBELUNGS

"Irresistible as the sea," wrote Claude Debussy about Wagner's *The Ring of the Nibelungs*. Others felt differently. Rossini, for example, once said that "Wagner has lovely moments but awful quarters of an hour."

You may love him, you may hate him, but you can't ignore Wagner or his nineteen-hour monument. Although he still has his critics, he's influenced every composer for a century and captured such diverse literary devotees as George Bernard Shaw and C.S. Lewis.

*The Ring* is actually four operas put together: *Das Rheingold, Die Walkure, Siegfried* and *Gotterdammerung*, a colossal accomplishment.

Wagner's own words about the work, for which he wrote both the text and the music, left modesty far behind: "The whole will become—out with it! I am not ashamed to say so—the greatest work of poetry ever written."

This and a hundred other strange anecdotes illustrating Wagner's personal excesses often frighten people away from him. But those who flee Wagner miss a world of great music. It's a rather different world than ours, of course, filled with giants, mermaids, dwarfs, women warriors and very few normal people—sort of a cross between Norse mythology and *Star Wars*. But the music is so powerful, so gripping, that it's difficult to resist.

One of the principle features of Wagner's opera is a technique called the *leitmotif*, which Wagner perfected. The idea is simple: A musical theme is given to each character. That theme is played by the orchestra whenever that character appears or is mentioned.

The leitmotif helps the audience keep the singers straight. It is sort of a musical scorecard. Not only the cast but even an inanimate object can rate its own leitmotif, such as the "sword theme" that rings out when Siegmund manages to pull it out of the ash tree.

Frankly, the opera's text (340 pages in my edition) is a little weird. I'm no expert in Norse mythology, but if it was half as strange as the Wagnerian version, I can see why the early Christian missionaries found the Northern Europeans quite happy to convert to Christianity. *The Ring* has a cast of gods and goddesses who are weak and selfish, gnomes who are greedy and banal, and giants with the combined intelligence of the Three Stooges. Next to these characters, the few humans involved seem quite heroic.

The plot revolves around some beautiful gold from the Rhine river and a magic ring that gives the bearer great power—and is therefore coveted by everyone. The

## THE ELEMENTS OF MUSIC COMPOSITION: HARMONY

Harmony is the art of using notes simultaneously. If melody is a horizontal series of one note at a time in sequence, harmony is the vertical occurrence of many notes. Often a composer will take a given melody and "harmonize" it, that is, he or she will choose various combinations of notes to blend with the notes of the melody. These harmonies can be very simple or overwhelmingly complicated, depending on the composer's desire and genius.

Let's begin with the simple. If you have two notes played simultaneously, the measurement of distance between the two notes is called an *interval.* If you have three or more notes, the group is called a chord.

Suppose you sit down at the piano and play two notes, say A and C. This interval is called a "third." Why a third? To find out, just count. Call A one, and count up A, B, C, or 1, 2, 3. The distance between the outermost parts of this interval is thus a third.

Try another. What's the interval called between B and G? Count B, C, D, E, F, G, or 1, 2, 3, 4, 5, 6. The interval between B and G is a sixth.

Things get complicated after this, and we find oddities like minor thirds, diminished fourths and augmented fifths. We don't have space to examine all those, but by now you should at least be able to see that the science of music is akin to that of mathematics. Harmony throughout the centuries has changed and transformed into amazing complexities, but it's ultimately a numbers game. Perhaps that's why so many scientists love music.

At any rate, a good melody is nice, but without the world of harmony there would be no orchestras or choirs or even pianos. You may leave the concert hall whistling the melody, but without its harmony, you wouldn't have stayed awake through the concert in the first place. I like composer Edvard Grieg's comment: "The realm of harmonies was always my dream world."

---

worst culprit is probably Woten, king of the gods (bass), who is henpecked by his goddess wife, Fricka (soprano). Like many kings of old, Woten has no scruples in begetting children through other females, mortal and immortal, and his shenanigans complicate the plot immeasurably.

Wotan's offspring include a number of warrior women, the Valkyries, whose leader Brunnhilda (soprano in armor) has inspired a popular comic strip, as well as lots of jokes about fat ladies in opera. In fact, *The Ring* finally ends with Brunnhilda riding her steed into a burning funeral pyre (while singing, of course) as the gods meet their doom.

Since few people on the planet will ever see *The Ring* in its entirety in one production, just how *does* someone go about experiencing this work? Perhaps the best answer is simply, in little pieces. You'll find some excellent excerpt albums available.

The excerpt called "The Ride of the Valkyries" alone is worth the cost of a new CD. Better yet, if you can work your way through a synopsis of the entire *Ring*, you'll be better prepared to enjoy a typical production of *Das Rhinegold* or *Gotterdammerung*, knowing where each fits in the context of the whole work. Check your local library for more information. The libretto may be rather bewildering at times, but the music itself will lift you right out of your seat.

## OPERA PROGRAM #8
## PUCCINI: LA BOHEME

Ah, Puccini. Get ready for the world's most romantic piece of music. When you've found an attractive someone you want to impress, take him or her to *La Boheme*. The romance between the poor poet Rodolfo (tenor) and the pretty soprano Mimi is irresistible. From their opening arias, "Che Gelida Manina" and "Mi Chiamano Mimi," the audience is in love with them both.

Like *Carmen*, this plot is not about the rich, but rather the penniless Bohemians of Paris. Also like Carmen (and dozens of other operas), the work's heroine dies at the end. But at least this time she isn't stabbed.

At the heart of the story are four artistic friends who, like the "beatniks" of a later time, live in poverty but relative contentment. Two of them, Rodolfo and Marcello, have the good fortune to have soprano girlfriends, Mimi and Musetta, an arrangement that provides us with some great ensemble singing. Unfortunately, Mimi is dying from consumption, and after some carefree interludes together, Musetta prays for her friend's healing, Mimi finally dies, Rodolfo cries—and so does the audience. Thank goodness for curtain calls, where dead singers always revive to take a bow.

You might ask how this simple story became one of the world's most beloved operas. The answer is the music itself. It's from the late Romantic period, exquisitely orchestrated, and it seems to move from one love theme to another, each superior to the one before.

Not only are there love duets — when friends Rodolfo and Marcello sing together in their cold apartment about their lovers ("O Mimi, tu piu non torni"), the audience is smiling through their tears. *La Boheme* is an opera that overflows with feeling, and its success stems from its ability to involve the listener deeply in its wide range of emotions.

## THE PRINCIPAL OPERA COMPOSERS

Remember Vivaldi, the Baroque composer who wrote hundreds of concerti but almost nothing else? Or how about Chopin, who composed some of the greatest piano music in history but almost nothing else? This phenomenon of the one-genre composer is not uncommon, and it occurs frequently in the opera world.

Puccini once put it this way: "God touched me with His little finger and said, Write for the theater, only for the theater." There simply aren't many Mozarts around who can compose equally well for every genre. So let's hear now from those masters who spent their lives specializing in the opera form.

## OPERA PROGRAM #9
### ROSSINI: THE BARBER OF SEVILLE

### GIOACCHINO ROSSINI (1792-1868)

Everyone who knows about *The Lone Ranger* television program has heard its famous theme from the *William Tell Overture*. Gioacchino Rossini wrote this piece, the opera *William Tell* (complete with an apple on a *soprano's* head, since the part of William Tell's little son is sung by a soprano), and over forty other operas.

I've chosen Rossini's most popular work, *The Barber of Seville,* for our program. This opera was written in thirteen days "without even stopping to shave," as Rossini put it—no pun intended.

The libretto is taken from the same goofy play that gave us Mozart's *Marriage of Figaro.* Yes, Figaro is in this opera too, except now he's moved up from the bass to the baritone and works as the town barber. Again, the object of the game is to get the right couple together (Rosina and Count Almaviva, soprano and tenor as always) by thwarting Dr. Bartholo, the bad, bad bass. It's the same old plot but with some fabulous music; my favorite part is the clever ensemble singing in the music room (second act). Pass the pasta.

Rossini could compose for every occasion. Once a friend found him working with music paper and asked what he was creating. He answered in complete earnestness: "It's my dog's birthday, and I write a little piece for him every year." An amazingly creative man, Rossini once proclaimed, "Give me a laundry list and I will set it to music."

Perhaps he should have. No doubt the result would have sounded marvelous, and we all would have happily bought tickets to hear it.

## OPERA PROGRAM #10
### DONIZETTI: THE ELIXIR OF LOVE

### GAETANO DONIZETTI (1797-1848)

You don't have to be Italian to write great opera, but it helps. Donizetti composed seventy of them, including several must-hear works: *The Elixir of Love, Lucia di*

*Lammermoor, The Daughter of the Regiment* and *Don Pasquale. Don* basically means a "gentleman" or a "lord," or someone who would like to be, so it's a common title and appears in an immeasurable list of operas: *Don Carlos, Don Giovanni, Don Quixote, Don Juan, Don Rodrigo,* and so on.

The plot to *The Elixir of Love* is vintage opera. Two men (tenor Nemorino, a peasant, and baritone Belcore, a sergeant) each vie for the same rich and pretty soprano, Adino. When a quack arrives in town selling a potion guaranteed to create love, Nemorino buys a bottle and downs the contents. It is actually a bottle of wine, and his drunken response so shocks Adino that she decides to marry Belcore, the sergeant.

Then news arrives that an inheritance has just made our peasant tenor, Nemorino, rich. Now all the peasant girls flirt with him, and he credits this to the love potion in the hilarious quartet, "The dose has done me good."

Fortunately, Adino has a change of heart so the tenor and the soprano get together as we knew they would. The observing peasants come to believe in the potency of the love potion, and the opera ends with them all buying liberally from the quack's stock of bottles.

Donizetti and his fellow Italian Vincenzo Bellini (composer of *Norma* and *I Puritani)* are called the great masters of "bel canto" ("beautiful song"). When you hear their operas, you'll understand why. These works are perfect material for a romantic date.

## OPERA PROGRAM #11
## WAGNER: TANNHAUSER

### RICHARD WAGNER (1813-1883)

Now what's this German iconoclast doing in this list of Italian romance-makers? Breaking the rules, of course, but also creating romantic opera, German style. Forget the pasta. Grab some knockwurst and find tickets to *Lohengrin* or *Tannhauser* or *The Flying Dutchman* or the ultra-romantic *Tristan und Isolde.*

Wagner loved the opera form, although he liked to call his own operas "music-dramas." Once he confided to a friend: "How I love Rossini! But don't tell my Wagnerians—they would never forgive me."

In addition to *The Ring of the Nibelungs,* which we've already heard, Wagner composed a number of other works. These others are usually more accessible, since they all have the same expertise and power that characterize Wagner yet use libretti that are a little more down-to-earth than *The Ring.* Wagner even wrote a comic (sort of) opera, *Die Meistersinger,* and a religious (sort of) opera, *Parsifal.*

*Tannhauser* itself has many religious themes, but these are rather strangely woven together. The story takes place in the thirteenth century. Our moody hero, Tannhauser (a tenor), has fallen in love with both a lovely girl, Elizabeth, and a lovely goddess, Venus. On entering a singing contest for the hand of Elizabeth, he makes a bad move by singing about his love for Venus.

A group of medieval knights almost eliminate him with drawn swords, but he repents. He's so penitent, in fact, that he insists on traveling to Rome to seek the Pope's pardon, which he never gets. The long-suffering Elizabeth wasn't angry with him anyway, and after she dies at the end, Tannhauser soon gets to join her in death.

It's a weird tale, but it has many musical hits, including a fantastic overture, the beautiful "Pilgrim's Chorus," and every Wagnerite's favorite baritone solo, the "Song of the Evening Star." This last piece is sung by Wolfram, another singer who's in love with Elizabeth—but then again, who isn't?

Be brave, check out this wild performance, and hold onto your seat.

## OPERA PROGRAM #12
### VERDI: LA TRAVIATA

### GIUSEPPE VERDI (1813-1901)

Now we go back to Italy to meet the king of opera, Giuseppe Verdi. When the Marx Brothers wanted to have some fun in their classic film *A Night at the Opera*, they knew where to look. Verdi can conjure up a love scene like no one else, and that's just for starters.

His early works are seldom performed, as he was late to master his art; Verdi himself later referred to these years as his "galley period." But after the appearance in 1851 of the great *Rigoletto* (with a vocal quartet you simply must hear), Verdi careened from hit to hit. We've already heard *Aida;* perhaps you're also familiar with *La Traviata, La Forza del Destino, Don Carlo,* or even the "anvil chorus" from *Il Trovatore.*

*La Traviata* (roughly translated, "The Lost One"), is a classic Italian love story. Love (between soprano and tenor—who else?) is found, lost, and then found again, just before the soprano dies of consumption (what else?). After years of a glamorous Parisian lifestyle, Violetta settles down with Alfredo, a young man from a well-to-do family. Alfredo's dad soon breaks up the match, and all is sad until the last scene. As Violetta lies on her deathbed, Alfredo returns, and the two reaffirm their mutual love in the love-duet of love-duets, "Parigi, O Cara."

After *Aida,* Verdi was curiously silent for sixteen years before the premieres of his last two masterpieces, *Otello* and *Falstaff.* It was worth the wait; they are both wonderful!

## OPERA PROGRAM #13
### PUCCINI: MADAME BUTTERFLY

### GIACOMO PUCCINI (1858-1924)

We begin and end our list with Italians, as is operatically appropriate. Puccini continued the Verdi tradition but added a little more elegance, bringing opera well into the twentieth century. His soaring melodies and love duets are legendary, although his writing for the theater tends to kill off his leading ladies before the opera ends. Bring tissues if you cry easily—or at all.

*Madame Butterfly's* popularity with American audiences probably is due to the inclusion in the principle cast of an American character, Lieutenant Pinkerton, U.S. Navy. But this unfaithful tenor will never be featured on a Navy recruiting poster.

While stationed in Nagasaki, the Lieutenant conveniently marries a local soprano, Cho Cho San (Madame Butterfly). After he returns to the United States, she remains faithful to him, despite the protests of family and friends. Butterfly reveals her fair-haired child just before cannons announce the arrival of a Navy ship. It contains—alas!—the Lieutenant and Mrs. Kate Pinkerton, his American wife. Butterfly takes the news heroically, that is, if you consider suicide heroic. Left alone with her little son, she blindfolds him, gives him an American flag to wave, and falls on her father's sword—which is inscribed, "To die with honor, when one can no longer live with honor."

Only in an opera!

Puccini's list of successes is impressive: Besides *La Boheme* (which we've already heard), he wrote *Tosca, Gianni Schicchi, La Fanciulla del West, Manon Lescaut, Suor Angelica, Turandot* and of course *Madame Butterfly.* This last work initially was a failure. But Puccini knew better. "It is I who am right!" he insisted. "You shall see!" We do, Giacomo, we do.

### OTHER OUTSTANDING OPERAS

Before we leave the operatic world behind, taste a few more ever-popular classics. These don't always fit the mold, but opera molds were made to be broken.

## OPERA PROGRAM #14
### BEETHOVEN: FIDELIO

The king of the three B's wrote only one opera, but it's vintage Beethoven: dramatic music; heroic, sacrificial love; a revolutionary spirit—all this and more is *Fidelio.* As usual, the composer worked years on this effort (originally titled *Leonore),* writing and rewriting and giving us a number of overtures that are still performed today on orchestra programs.

This opera is a masterpiece whose themes declare the triumph of good over evil, of noble, selfless character over corruption. Beethoven called it "my crown of martyrdom."

The plot is intriguing. Good-guy Florestan (tenor) incurs the wrath of bad-guy Don Pizarro (baritone), who throws Florestan into prison. Enter the wonderful Leonore (soprano), opera's most faithful wife. She has all the sterling qualities that the bachelor Beethoven always wanted, but never found, in a mate.

To save her husband, Leonore disguises herself as a boy named Fidelio, gets a job at the jail and tolerates the lecherous advances of the jailer's daughter. When the vile Don Pizarro is about to murder her husband, Leonore hurls herself between them crying, "First kill his wife!" Her identity and her pistol are revealed, the bad guy is incarcerated, and the loving couple sing each other's praises—as we do too. Leonore is a spunky gal; what a shame that Beethoven never found her in real life.

## OPERA PROGRAM #15
### GOUNOD: FAUST

The Faust legend has captivated readers and audiences for centuries. Its most celebrated opera rendition (there are many) is by Gounod. In it Faust (tenor) is enticed by the devil, that is, Mephistopheles (bass) to sell his soul for the pleasures of youth.

Between various other adventures, Faust meets the lovely Marguerite (soprano) in time for a lovely duet, and it looks for a while like a typical romantic opera. But Mephistopheles can't leave well enough alone. He helps kill Marguerite's brother, and she almost goes crazy with grief and remorse.

In the last scene, Mephistopheles reveals his truly devilish nature. Faust realizes the consequences of his self-indulgent actions, but it's too late. He's dragged down to hell, while the penitent Marguerite is escorted by angels to heaven.

This is a far cry from the romance of *The Barber of Seville*. But opera is more than amorous tales of infatuation. In many, a few morals are presented and some lessons learned.

Besides, as we've seen before, it's the *music* far more than the plot that packs opera houses. Gounod has a splendid gift for melody, and he brings out the supernatural conflicts with style. He once claimed, "Musical ideas sprang to my mind like a flight of butterflies, and all I had to do was stretch out my hand to catch them."

There are other Faust operas—in fact, the theology makes a bit more sense in Arrigo Boito's *Mefistofele*—but none has had the impact of the Gounod rendition.

## OPERA PROGRAM #16
## MUSSORGSKY: BORIS GODOUNOV

**MODEST MUSSORGSKY (1839-1881)**

Let's break out of the Italian-German circuit. How about a Russian opera with a czar for the star? The time-honored model is Modest Mussorgsky's *Boris Godounov.* (It's pronounced GOOD-o-nof; in the old Rocky and Bullwinkle cartoons, the name of the bad guy spoofed this title; they called him "Boris *Bad*ounov").

In this dramatic work, the composer takes a text from the Russian poet Alexander Pushkin and weaves it into a pageant of old Russia. In a play for power, Boris (bass) secretly murders the heir to the throne and soon gets the top job himself. Filled with guilt and remorse, he survives an assortment of revolts and intrigues before he's finally confronted with his misdeeds.

As opera would have it, Boris gets his chance to die theatrically (tumbling off his throne and down the stairs), but not before he appeals to his wise son to rule justly—sort of a Russian happy ending. For sheer intensity and emotion, this opera is hard to beat.

## OPERA PROGRAM #17
## DEBUSSY: PELLEAS ET MELISANDE

How about a very French opera? My favorite is Debussy's impressionistic work, *Pelleas et Melisande,* his sole creation in the opera department. It's an exotically beautiful piece and unique in that it has no arias, no duets and no choruses.

Instead, the work is "through-composed," expressing various moods and impressions that unite the music and the mystical text. With a kind of French Wagnerian atmosphere, the action takes place in "antiquity." A lovely maiden Melisande (soprano) is loved by two brothers, Pelleas (tenor) and Golaud (baritone). The brothers quarrel and Golaud kills Pelleas. But of course this is opera, so Melisande is going to die at the end anyway. The sibling rivalry plot may not interest you, but Debussy's music is so gorgeous you don't mind.

This great Frenchman worked many years on his only opera, and after its success, he was approached by a publisher who wanted the rights to opera number two. When the surprised composer asked the publisher how soon he would want this proposed composition, he was told that his company could easily wait "three or four months."

"Three or four months!" the fastidious Debussy roared. "I take that long just to decide between two chords!" Opera had come a long way from Rossini's "laundry list."

## OPERA PROGRAMS #18 AND #19
## MASCAGNI: CAVALLERIA RUSTICANA
## LEONCAVALLO: I PAGLIACCI

## PIETRO MASCAGNI (1863-1945)
## RUGGERO LEONCAVALLO (1858-1919)

Before we go to England again for the finale, I must tell you about opera's popular Siamese twins: Pietro Mascagni's *Cavalleria Rusticana* ("Rustic Chivalry") and Ruggero Leoncavallo's *I Pagliacci* ("The Clowns"). Professional musicians call them "Cav and Pag," and they're nearly always performed together. Though they're not by the same composer, and they're not of the same libretto, they're similar in style. You'll hear them classified as "verismo" operas (roughly meaning "realistic" operas), but forget the terminology and just enjoy the marvelous music.

This is real Italian singing, the stuff that tenors warble in fancy Italian restaurants—the music that made Italian opera famous. You can already guess the plots of the libretti: This guy loves this girl, but that girl loves another guy, but this other girl loves the first guy...

Just find some good spaghetti, get yourself comfortable, and enjoy the scrumptious singing.

## OPERA PROGRAM #20
## BRITTEN: MIDSUMMER NIGHT'S DREAM

We'll end this chapter with an opera in English, lest you think that there aren't any. Actually, Handel was writing English opera centuries ago, but the best ones for my money are being composed in our own century on both sides of the Atlantic. Some of the finest are by Benjamin Britten, and perhaps the summit is his Shakespearean comedy, *Midsummer Night's Dream*. Here's Shakespeare again, showing up everywhere in music. From Gounod's *Romeo and Juliet* to Verdi's *Otello*, he's in the opera house too.

It's great to hear Shakespeare sung in the original language, especially when set to music by a master of vocal writing like Britten. What a pleasure, too, to be able to laugh out loud in the middle of an opera without having to resort to a translation of the libretto to catch the humor. *Midsummer Night's Dream* is a great opera, a fun opera and a grand climax for this chapter.

By now I hope you see that opera is such wonderful fun you should have tried it years ago. Of course it can be quite serious as well, but even at its most tragic, opera is so overwhelming, so inspiring, that you leave the performance uplifted. Take my challenge: Find a good opera, do a little preparation, and go expecting to have a fabulous time. You will!

# OPERA REPERTOIRE

## THE TOP 15

Bizet
   Carmen
Donizetti
   The Elixir of Love
Gounod
   Faust
Mozart
   Don Giovanni
   The Magic Flute
   The Marriage of Figaro
Puccini
   La Boheme
   Madame Butterfly
   Tosca
Rossini
   The Barber of Seville
Verdi
   Aida
   La Traviata
   Rigoletto
   Otello
Wagner
   The Ring of the Nibelung
   (four-opera series):
      Das Rheingold
      Die Walkure
      Siegfried
      Gotterdammerung

## THE TOP 50

Beethoven
   Fidelio
Bellini
   Norma
Bizet
   Carmen

Britten
   Midsummer Night's Dream
Debussy
   Pelleas et Melisande
Donizetti
   Don Pasquale
   La Fille du Regiment
   Lucia di Lammermoor
   The Elixir of Love
Giordano
   Andrea Chenier
Gounod
   Faust
   Romeo and Juliet
Humperdinck
   Hansel und Gretel
Leoncavallo
   Pagliacci
Mascagni
   Cavalleria Rusticana
Massenet
   Manon
   Werther
Menotti
   Amahl and the Night Visitors
Mozart
   Don Giovanni
   Cosi Fan Tutti
   The Magic Flute
   The Marriage of Figaro
Mussorgsky
   Boris Godounov
Offenbach
   The Tales of Hoffmann
Ponchielli
   La Gioconda
Puccini
   La Boheme

   Madame Butterfly
   Turandot
   Tosca
Rossini
   The Barber of Seville
Saint-Saens
   Samson et Dalila
Strauss, R.
   Der Rosenkavalier
Strauss, J.
   Die Fledermaus
Tchaikovsky
   Eugene Onegin
Verdi
   Aida
   Don Carlo
   Falstaff
   Il Trovatore
   La Forza del Destino
   La Traviata
   Rigoletto
   Otello
Wagner
   The Ring of the Nibelungs
   (four-opera series):
      Das Rheingold
      Die Walkure
      Siegfried
      Goetterdaemmerung
   Die Meistersinger
   Lohengrin
   Parsifal
   Tannhauser
   The Flying Dutchman
   Tristan und Isolde
Weber
   Der Freischutz

*(Above) Verdi, King of Italian opera, bears a striking resemblance to General Robert E. Lee.*

*(Left) He may look like a bullfighter, but he actually is Enrico Caruso—perhaps the most celebrated singer in history. One of his early gramophone recordings went "solid gold," selling over 1 million albums— the first time a recording artist ever pulled off that difficult feat.*

# 6

# CHAMBER MUSIC

*(On being chided about the complex sophistication of his string quartets),*
*"Oh, they are not for you. They are for another age."*

—Ludwig Van Beethoven

Ludwig, that age has come. Today, Beethoven string quartets are loved by millions.

Originally, chamber music took its name from the private chambers of rich patrons for whom it was performed. But today it's a much more public affair—chamber music is the rage from Vienna to San Francisco, and major cities have dozens of chamber groups that perform on stages from Carnegie Hall to classy restaurants. Those who have fallen in love with this intimate manner of music-making never seem to exhaust all the reasons to appreciate it.

And no wonder, considering the vast variety of the genre. For example, a glance at the concerts recently listed in my local newspaper gave me a choice of two string quartets, a piano trio, a woodwind quintet, a guitar trio and a tuba ensemble—many of them with free admission.

This music for small groups is a hit, not just with audiences, but with the performers themselves. Musicians often bring their instruments to informal "chamber music parties" to play through some of the finest repertoire imaginable. Since it's purely for pleasure and there's usually no audience around, who cares whether all the parts are covered by the right instruments? At our house we once read through a Beethoven string quartet with a flute, alto saxophone, guitar and double bass. Our apologies to Ludwig—but it was great fun.

Nor are all chamber players professional musicians. Take Albert Einstein, for example, the genius mathematician, physicist and amateur violinist. Once when he was in New York he called the distinguished Julliard School to ask whether anyone might like to play chamber music with him. So a handful of musicians agreed to read string quartets and quintets with him that evening.

The next day, Julliard's dean asked one of the musicians how well Einstein played his violin. "Einstein has a pretty good sound," said one of the musicians, "but that guy just can't *count!*"

Why the persistent popularity of chamber music? For one thing, it's easier to fit a string trio into your living room than a symphony orchestra. It's cheaper too. Since it's simpler to get a few friends together to perform than it is to produce a concert of Wagner's *Ring*, there are many more string quartets in existence than huge opera companies. Consequently, there are more concerts, they cost less to produce, and *voila!* tickets are more affordable for everyone.

But the principle reason for the prominence of chamber music is the music itself. Composers through the centuries have outdone themselves in this category, especially in music for the string quartet. Since many of the masters loved to play chamber music themselves, they lavishly wrote music for their own enjoyment.

For example, Haydn wrote over seventy string quartets as well as hundreds of other small pieces—and enjoyed being included in the performance of many of them. Once, when his distinguished reputation as a composer intimidated a child violinist, Haydn assured him: "No need to be scared of me, my boy, I'm a bad player myself."

Chamber music comes in various sizes, depending on the number and type of instruments needed. For instance, you'll find woodwind quintets, string quintets, brass quintets and piano quintets. They all use five players, but each quintet is scored for five different instruments. This means that a piano quintet doesn't call for five pianos—what a relief!

So that you'll know the lingo for concerts and repertoire, take a look at this list of the most common forms of music for three to nine players:

Piano trio: piano, violin, cello

Piano quartet: piano, violin, viola, cello

Piano quintet: piano, two violins, viola, cello

Woodwind trio: flute, oboe or clarinet, bassoon

Woodwind quartet: flute, oboe, clarinet, bassoon

Woodwind quintet: flute, oboe, clarinet, bassoon, horn

Brass trio: trumpet, horn, trombone

Brass quartet: two trumpets, horn, trombone

Brass quintet: two trumpets, horn, trombone, tuba

String trio: violin, viola, cello

String quartet: two violins, viola, cello

String quintet: two violins and either two violas and one cello, or one viola and
two cellos

String sextet: usually two violins, two violas, two cellos

String septet: seven string players; take your pick!

String octet: eight string players; usually four violins, two violas, two cellos
(a double string quartet)

String nonet: nine string players; whatever you can get

We're getting close to the so-called "chamber orchestra" size, so we'll stop at nine players.

Of the forms we've mentioned, four are most common. The most popular is the string quartet, which accounts for probably eighty percent of all chamber music. Next is the piano trio, the favorite of the groupings that involve a piano.

Then comes the woodwind quintet. It may look like a peculiar combination of instruments—after all, the horn is not a woodwind—but this group blends together beautifully. Finally is the brass quintet, the most majestic of chamber ensembles. You need a rather big "chamber" for them, because they make quite a sound.

You should be familiar with several other types as well. Any instrument added to a string trio or quartet uses its name: an oboe quartet, for example, has an oboe, violin, viola and cello. A clarinet quintet has a clarinet, two violins, viola and cello.

There are also various homogeneous groups such as guitar trios (three guitars), saxophone quartets (four saxophones of various sizes), flute ensembles (a whole room of flutes) and so on. Never miss a chance to hear a percussion ensemble; with xylophones, gongs, temple blocks, kettledrums and whistles, it's a rare assembly of sounds you'll never forget.

Twentieth-century composers have had a field day blending every conceivable combination to produce some fascinating results. For example, Stravinsky's celebrated *L'Histoire du Soldat* ("The Soldier's Tale") is a septet scored for clarinet, bassoon, trumpet, trombone, violin, double bass and percussion. George Crumb's *Ancient Voices of Children* calls for such uncommon instruments as a toy piano, harmonica, mandolin, electric piano and musical saw.

I'm aware that modern music—that is, contemporary classical music—sounds rather bizarre on first hearing (and often, after repeated hearings as well). But composers have always been ahead of their time and it usually takes audiences years to catch up with them. Beethoven declared, "Art demands of us that we shall not stand still," and his music, now extremely popular and universally accepted, sounded outlandish to his contemporaries.

Sometimes composers themselves are perplexed about their position in history. Once, when asked if he was indeed Schoenberg the controversial composer, the man answered, "I have to admit that I am. But it's like this—someone had to be, and nobody else wanted to, so I took it on myself."

It's not easy waiting decades for an appreciative audience. The composer Arthur Honneger summed it all up in 1951 when he wrote, "It is clear that the first specification for a composer is to be dead."

## THE STRING QUARTET

In the standard repertoire, the king of chamber music is unquestionably the string quartet. Everyone seems to have written for this medium, even vocal composers Giuseppe Verdi and Hugo Wolf. The ensembles that perform string quartets are multitudinous. They've been named for cities (such as the Cleveland String Quartet), famous people (the Emerson String Quartet), countries (Quartetto Italiano), composers (the Haydn String Quartet) and nearly everything else (even the WQXR String Quartet).

Since there are so many marvelous works in this genre, let's focus on the foremost string quartets in the repertoire. Because of the sheer quantity of their chamber music output, you'll again notice an emphasis on Haydn, Mozart, Beethoven and Schubert.

## CHAMBER MUSIC PROGRAM #1
### HAYDN: STRING QUARTET IN C MAJOR ("THE EMPEROR")
### MOZART: STRING QUARTET IN C MAJOR ("THE DISSONANT")

## FRANZ JOSEPH HAYDN (1732-1809)

Not surprisingly, Haydn claims the title of "father of the string quartet" along with all his other "father of..." titles. As with the symphony, he didn't exactly invent the first one, but he was the first major composer to create great quartets by the dozen.

So how do you get to know all those Haydn string quartets? One simple approach is to "go with the names," that is, listen first to the string quartets that have programmatic titles. Like his symphonies, many of Haydn's best quartets have rather imaginative designations.

I've selected for our program the "Emperor" (*String Quartet in C Major*, Opus 76, No. 3), whose second movement features the Austrian national anthem (also familiar as the setting of the hymn by John Newton, "Glorious Things of Thee Are Spoken"). Unfortunately, in World War II this melody was so often heard as the *German* national anthem as well, so the tune may bring back terrible memories to those who remember it being played by the Nazis.

But that isn't Haydn's fault. So when you hear this movement, forget Hitler and enjoy the lovely variations the composer builds around this notable melody.

Other string quartets by Haydn with interesting titles (but not in our program) include the "Joke" (in E♭ Major, Op. 33, No. 2), whose final movement abruptly ends without resolution; the "Frog" (in D Major, Op. 50, No. 6), with its croaking finale; and the "Razor" (Op. 55, No. 2), so-called not because of any musical element, but because Haydn wrote the piece as a thank-you note for a gift of two English razors he'd received.

## WOLFGANG AMADEUS MOZART (1756-1791)

Haydn once was sent another gift that, though it didn't help him shave, gave him great delight. His friend Mozart sent six string quartets dedicated to him with a note attached that read, "I send my six sons to you." These so-called "Haydn Quartets" contain some of Mozart's finest music. Two of the best also have programmatic titles, "The Hunt" (No. 17, with its fox-chase first movement) and "The Dissonant" (No. 19, chosen for this program).

The introduction of this latter work gives the piece its title. It's so harmonically complex that it irked Mozart's contemporaries. Today, we consider it a gem, a choice example of the classic string quartet.

## CHAMBER MUSIC PROGRAM #2
BEETHOVEN: STRING QUARTET NO. 10 IN E♭ MAJOR ("HARP")
BEETHOVEN: STRING QUARTET NO. 14 IN C# MINOR

## LUDWIG VAN BEETHOVEN (1770-1827)

It seems curious that the powerful music of Beethoven could be contained in the intimate tones of four stringed instruments. Yet he considered it the perfect medium of expression, and all sixteen of his efforts are in the standard repertoire today. Since Beethoven's music is often classified in three divisions—his "early," "middle" and "late" periods—we'll examine his string quartets within these categories.

Beethoven's six early period quartets are lighter and more Haydn-like than his later works, but many already contain the dramatic flair that soon characterized his work, especially No. 4 in C Minor. The "middle" quartets include the beautiful piece known as the "Harp," chosen for our program.

No, this work isn't scored for harp and string quartet. Its nickname comes from the first movement, which extensively uses pizzicato arpeggios. These are first heard soon after the slow introduction is replaced by the joyful faster tempo. The last time these arpeggios appear is in the movement's dramatic ending, superimposed onto a long and exhausting virtuoso violin passage.

As you consider listening to Beethoven's other quartets, don't be fooled by such colorless names as String Quartet No. 9 in C Major. Even an imaginative title could never capture the overwhelming beauty and emotion found in these portentous works.

Then there are the six late Beethoven quartets. Perhaps no other compositions in music history deserve so well the over-used phrase *ahead of their time*. These sublime works, written after the composer became utterly deaf, contain both beauties and innovations that the composer might not have dared if he could have physically heard them.

*String Quartet No. 14 in C# Minor,* with its multiple movements and novel effects, is considered by many to be the most important chamber music ever written. Abandoning the typical four-movement format, Beethoven produced seven movements, many of which are attached to one another. The overall effect is one of continual drama, with great contrasts in mood.

The serious, slow fugue of the first movement melts into the exuberance of the second. Later on, the energy and humor of the scherzo (fifth movement) is followed by a brief movement of grief. This quartet has everything. It's as if the composer wrote a tenth symphony and scored it for four players.

Beethoven's *Grosse Fuge* ("Big Fugue"; not on our program) is astonishing. Never miss a chance to hear this magnum opus. When you do, you'll think you're listening to the fireworks of some twentieth-century quartet.

## CHAMBER MUSIC PROGRAM #3
## SCHUBERT: STRING QUARTET IN D MINOR
### ("DEATH AND THE MAIDEN")
## DVORAK: STRING QUARTET IN F ("AMERICAN")

### FRANZ SCHUBERT (1797-1828)

Beethoven's young fan Schubert wrote fifteen string quartets, and they show him at his lyrical best. The three most important are the passionate one-movement *Quartetsatz in C Minor,* the mysterious *Quartet #12 in A Minor,* and the ever-popular "Death and the Maiden" (*String Quartet #14 in D Minor*), selected for our program.

The title of this last work comes from a Schubert song of the same name that lends its theme to the quartet's beautiful second movement. Every movement of this masterpiece is commanding, with the strength of a great symphony rather than what you'd expect from four players. The last movement is the best horse race in classical music, with a climax more thrilling than the Kentucky Derby.

Since nearly every composer we've met wrote string quartets, we can't even begin to describe them all. For those of you with Romantic tastes, I recommend the quartets by Mendelssohn, Schumann, Brahms and Dvorak. All of these wrote their own particular style into this media, and after listening a few times you'll be able to tell the difference between a Mendelssohn and a Brahms. With enough experience,

# THE ELEMENTS OF MUSIC COMPOSITION: RHYTHM

Rhythm is critical to composers. Composer Igor Stravinsky once said, "Rhythm and motion, not the element of feeling, are the foundations of musical art," and Duke Ellington added, "It don't mean a thing, if it ain't got that swing!"

They both were right. Without rhythm, music doesn't go anywhere. In fact, it hardly exists at all. As soon as two or three notes follow one another in a melody, rhythm is born.

Rhythm is the art of organizing musical ideas within recurrent periods of time. Think of all time as being divided into very small pieces or "pulses." During the second episode of our murder mystery (page 86), I said that combinations of notes with varied duration form rhythm. Those notes of varied duration are all based on regular pulses of time, which we divide into whole notes, half notes, quarter notes and so on, like cutting up a pie.

In music, however, we have various sizes of pies. That's where the notion of meter comes in. Many musical compositions naturally produce an accent once every three beats, while others produce their accent once every four beats. Since we usually consider the quarter note to equal one beat, a full measure of music becomes either three beats long, four beats long, or sometimes other lengths.

As an example, count along with the Christmas carol "We Wish You a Merry Christmas" and you'll find yourself naturally counting in groups of three, with accents on these syllables: "We *wish* you a merry *Christ*-mas. . . ." On the other hand, count along with "Angels We Have Heard on High," and you'll be counting in groups of four, with accents like this: "*An*-gels *we* have *heard* on *high*.

Concerning the meter—that is, the size of the measures—we say that the first example is in "3/4 time" ("three-four time"), having three quarter notes per measure. The second example is in "4/4 time" ("four-four time"), with four quarter notes per measure, often called "common time."

These numbers—3/4 or 4/4—are called the time signature of a composition. There are other types of time signatures as well, but the majority of music is based on either three or four beats per measure.

As you might expect in their writing of melodies, composers have always liked to mix things up a bit. So they might create one piece in which the duration of the successive pitches are all different. They might start, for example, with a half note, then two eighth notes, a half note, a whole note and four quarters.

Sometimes it gets quite complicated, and some of the notes won't fit into the measure; instead, some of their time values spill over into the next one called "syncopation."

Once a man went to his doctor for a chronic condition. His doctor, who suspected the real cause of the problem was behavioral rather than medical, said that the patient suffered from syncopation and sent him on his way.

The befuddled patient later found a dictionary and looked up this peculiar ailment. It read: "Syncopation: irregular movement from bar to bar."

you can even tell the difference between an early Mendelssohn work and a late one.

Of Dvorak's many string quartets, one rates special mention because of its well-deserved popularity. Remember how we said this rural Czech composer found himself working in New York and wrote the *New World Symphony*? That's not all he composed while in the New World. His marvelous *String Quartet in F*, chosen for our program, is subtitled "American."

This piece has always been a hit on both sides of the Atlantic. In it you'll hear more than a few melodies with a Native American flavor, and both the scherzo and the finale contain enough jazzy rhythm to make it in New Orleans.

## CHAMBER MUSIC PROGRAM #4
### DEBUSSY: STRING QUARTET IN G MINOR, OP. 10
### RAVEL: STRING QUARTET IN F MAJOR

### CLAUSE DEBUSSY (1862-1918) AND MAURICE RAVEL (1875-1937)

Connoisseurs of French cuisine will adore the Impressionist quartets of Debussy and Ravel. These two composers are often grouped together, and since they each wrote only one quartet, you'll seldom find a CD that has one without the other. The Debussy is an early work of the composer, but it offers many snatches of genius—especially in the second movement, with its innovative use of ensemble pizzicato.

When Debussy heard Ravel's work of this genre, he told him: "In the name of God, I implore you not to change a note of your quartet." When you hear it, you'll know why. The work is a gem of great contrasts, from the sweetness of the opening to its ferocious finale in 5/4 time.

### BELA BARTOK (1881-1945)

Those adventurous souls who like to brave the dissonance of the twentieth century should sample the power of the Bartok string quartets, especially his last three. Perhaps this is an acquired taste, but these works have had a major impact on thousands of modern composers. Many consider the Bartok six quartets to be the greatest chamber music of this century.

Like the late quartets of Beethoven, Bartok's seem "ahead of their time." But Bartok always had a method to his madness; after repeated listenings, the incredible genius behind these works is startlingly revealed.

## OTHER MASTERPIECES FOR STRINGS ALONE

### CHAMBER MUSIC PROGRAM #5
### SCHUBERT: STRING QUINTET IN C
### MENDELSSOHN: STRING OCTET IN E♭

As with the quartets, you'll find a vast number of pieces in this category (trios, quintets, sextets and more), especially by our friends Haydn, Mozart, Beethoven, Schubert, Mendelssohn, Brahms and Dvorak. But to get you started, let's look at the three most notable works of this type.

The first is the Schubert *String Quintet in C.* Unlike the typical string quintet for string quartet plus another viola, Schubert scores this massive work for string quartet with an extra cello. Each movement here is a classic, but the second movement is the most perfectly Schubertian. Inside its calm lyricism hides an explosive storm rivaling the tempest of Beethoven's *Sixth Symphony.* This is an opera of great drama played by a mere five performers.

When Mendelssohn was still in his teens, he wrote one of his best-loved pieces, the *String Octet in E♭.* The actual scoring is for a "double string quartet"—that is, four violins, two violas and two celli. Mendelssohn's youthful vivacity dominates the work, and the third movement is one of history's most popular scherzos.

In fact, the composer liked it so much that he later arranged it for orchestra. In doing so he created another great musical argument: Which arrangement is best? Wind players love the orchestrated version, but most string players will always contend that it sounds best in the original. Decide for yourself.

Ever been to Florence, Italy? I haven't, but I'm glad Tchaikovsky went, for his visit became the inspiration for the *String Sextet,* entitled *Souvenir de Florence* (not on our program). This "Souvenir" sounds very orchestral in parts, almost like one of his great symphonies.

It's one of those rare works that starts off fine and then gets better with every movement. By the time the finale begins, you're ready to burst into applause.

## CHAMBER MUSIC WITH PIANO

### CHAMBER MUSIC PROGRAM #6
### BEETHOVEN: PIANO TRIO IN B♭ ("ARCHDUKE")
### SCHUBERT: PIANO TRIO IN B♭

Many people grew up with piano lessons yet never had the opportunity to play piano with other instruments—especially since only the top virtuoso pianists ever get to perform a concerto with an orchestra. In the last chapter, we'll look at the

# THE ELEMENTS OF MUSIC COMPOSITION: FORM

Earlier we compared musical composition to creating a banquet. In considering the different forms found in music, we'll complete the analogy. The chef not only has to cook everything, but also has to serve each course in the correct order and in its proper dish. In a similar way, the composer has to integrate melodies, harmonies and rhythms into a larger, comprehensive presentation.

Usually composers don't sit down to write a melody. Their plan is to compose a symphony, a complete song, maybe a string quartet, or an entire opera. They first see the bigger picture, then gradually partition it into sections and subsections, each of which will need its own melodies, harmonies and rhythms. "Form" is that organization they plan, the design or arrangement of all the smaller parts to make the whole.

Just as there are an infinite number of melodies, harmonies and rhythms, there are an infinite number of ways these parts can be put together. Nevertheless, several rudimentary forms have been used by composers for many years. They serve as a skeleton on which the flesh of the music is overlaid.

The most important of these common forms are the sonata form, the ABA form, the rondo form, and the theme with variations. The sonata is of such historical significance that we'll deal with it as a separate topic. As for the others, we'll note a few characteristics of each.

*ABA form.* It's always been natural for a composer to start somewhere (present a certain theme), go somewhere else (use a different theme), and return to the original place (go back to the first theme). This is the basis of "ABA" form, with the three different letters representing the three musical sections we've just noted.

*Rondo form.* An important variation of the ABA is called the rondo, which became the standard fourth movement in a Classical symphony or sonata. After a typical ABA is played, the music continues into a new section before returning to the original music; then another new section and a return to the beginning, and so forth. These rondos can be charted out by section: ABACADA, and so on.

Some are found in "arch form," creating such symmetrical architectural designs as ABACADACABA. Even the standard chorus-verse popular song uses this technique. After every new verse, the song always comes back to the same chorus.

*Theme with variations.* Here's an easy form to which we can all relate. Every parent has heard from a child a thousand variations on the theme "Why I didn't get around to cleaning up my room." The same concept works in musical themes as well.

A composer writes a good theme and then starts doodling with it. He or she writes a section where the theme is elongated, another where it's shortened, and others where the theme may be so mutated you can hardly recognize it. Some of the greatest examples of this technique result when composers write variations on the themes of other composers, such as Brahms's *Variations on a Theme of Haydn* or Beethoven's *Thirty-Three Variations on a Theme by Diabelli.*

piano as a solo instrument as well as an indispensable accompanist of all those other grateful instruments. But in chamber music, the piano is neither an accompanist nor a soloist. Instead, it's an integrated member of a working ensemble.

The principle chamber music setting with the keyboard is the piano trio. Like the string quartet, the piano trio is both the name of a musical form and the ensemble that performs the works of that form. Unlike the string quartet, the names of these ensembles are usually not so imaginative. Many are simply the names of the players, like the renowned Stern, Rose, Istomin Trio. It's a good thing orchestras don't use that naming system.

As you may have guessed, both Haydn and Mozart wrote some lovely piano trios, but the first true masterpieces in this genre are by Beethoven. He wrote seven such works, and his two most popular help us by having programmatic titles. They're the "Archduke" *(Piano Trio in B♭)*, dedicated to his friend, Archduke Rudolph; and the "Ghost" *(Piano Trio in D Major),* so named because of a spooky theme in the second movement.

The "Archduke" is a late Beethoven colossus, the piano trio answer to the *Ninth Symphony.* Which movement is the greatest—the majestic first, the exuberant second, the peaceful third or the brilliant fourth? Most people choose the slow movement (third), with its lovely theme and four interesting variations. I gravitate toward the scherzo, whose trio section is so chromatic that it came far before its time. You can't tell whether it was composed in the twentieth or the twenty-*first* century.

The 1800s were the century of the piano trio, and most every composer created at least one. Schubert and Mendelssohn each wrote two, Schumann three, Dvorak four and Brahms five. Some are performed more than others, but all are worth hearing.

For our program I've chosen the Schubert *Piano Trio in B♭ Major.* The opening theme of the slow movement is so beautiful that to hear it is worth any ticket price. You'll enjoy the rest of the trio as well, but, oh that theme!

## CHAMBER MUSIC PROGRAM #7
## MENDELSSOHN: PIANO TRIO IN D MINOR
## DVORAK: PIANO TRIO IN E MINOR ("DUMKY")

Mendelssohn was a virtuoso pianist. If you can find a performer good enough to toil through all the notes in his *Piano Trio in D Minor,* go hear the performance. This is Mendelssohn at his classiest, and he can be *classy.*

All cellists love the drama of the opening theme, and each movement has its share of the dramatic. But the vintage Mendelssohn movement is the third. The lightness of its rapid staccato notes will remind you of elves running with such light footfalls that they never even leave footprints. You can easily tell that this is the same composer who wrote that "Elfin Overture" to Shakespeare's *Midsummer Night's Dream*.

The "Dumky" Trio *(Piano Trio in E Minor)* of Dvorak is the second work on our program. "Dumky" is the plural of "Dumka"—a Slavic folk dance that captivated the Czech Dvorak. It will captivate you as well. Each of the six movements in this trio is a different Dumka. It's a wonderful splurge into passionate folk music.

Brahms's exquisite *Piano Trio in B Major* isn't on our program, but you should hear it when you can. Like a magic elixir, its romantic first theme has caused more couples to fall in love than the bachelor Brahms could have ever imagined. Though the work was originally completed in 1854, a mature Brahms thoroughly revised it in 1890.

The piano is strong enough to work with larger groups as well. For quartets, I recommend Mozart's remarkable *Piano Quartet in G Minor*. This lighthearted composer seldom wrote in a minor key, and when he did, his cheerfulness still managed to permeate the music. The dramatic first movement is easily offset by the jubilation of the finale, and the flourish at the end is unforgettable.

## CHAMBER MUSIC PROGRAM #8
## SCHUBERT: PIANO QUINTET IN A MAJOR ("THE TROUT")
## BRAHMS: PIANO QUINTET IN F MINOR

The contest for the most popular piano quintet results in a tie between Schubert's illustrious work "The Trout" *(Piano Quintet in A Major)* and the intense *Piano Quintet in F Minor* of Brahms. The former derives its title from a Schubert song of the same name, using the same fishy theme. Popular with audiences, it's also a special favorite of double-bass players, who are usually left out of chamber music fun.

Brahms's piano quintet surges with enough passion for the entire nineteenth century, but he always keeps our interest with his well-timed changes of mood. This is a piece that will grab and keep your attention.

## CHAMBER MUSIC ADDING WIND INSTRUMENTS

## CHAMBER MUSIC PROGRAM #9
## HAYDN: LONDON FLUTE TRIO NO. 1
## MOZART: CLARINET QUINTET

What about wind players? Aren't they allowed in chamber music parties? Certainly—but their instruments generally developed later than the strings, so they have to wait their turn. The first important non-Baroque works of this kind are by

Haydn and Mozart: the Haydn *Flute Quartets,* his "London" Trios, Mozart's *Oboe Quartet,* as well as his renowned *Clarinet Quintet in A Major.*

Since Haydn wrote music for nearly every instrument he could find, some of his chamber combinations are unique. A popular favorite is his "London" Trios, for two flutes and cello. Forbearing the acrobatics of flute virtuosity, these works are delightful examples of Haydn's clarity of style. When his friend wrote chamber music using woodwinds, Haydn became interested in delving into the new, unexplored aspects of the wind instruments. This is especially noticeable in his use of the extended range of the clarinet.

Considering Mozart's *Clarinet Quintet,* as well as Mozart's promotion of clarinets into the orchestra and his celebrated *Clarinet Concerto,* we might say that this composer did more for that instrument than Benny Goodman.

## CHAMBER MUSIC PROGRAM #10
## BRAHMS: CLARINET TRIO IN A MINOR
## DVORAK: SERENADE IN D MINOR

Another major composer who later discovered and promoted his fascination with the clarinet was Johannes Brahms. In the realm of chamber music, he created two wonderful works employing this instrument, the "Clarinet Trio" *(Piano Trio in A Minor* for clarinet, cello, and piano) and a *Clarinet Quintet,* for clarinet and string quartet. These are wonderful pieces, beloved by clarinetists.

Another great addition to the wind chamber music repertoire (but not on this program) is Brahms's "Horn Trio" *(Piano Trio in E♭ Major)* for violin, horn, and piano.

Winds in greater numbers appear in Haydn's and Mozart's *Divertimenti,* but the best of the larger chamber forms is the so-called "serenade" of the nineteenth century. The most frequently performed are the *Serenade in D Minor* by Dvorak and the two serenades by his friend Brahms. One of the notable aspects of the Dvorak piece is the way he often cleverly uses the instruments to simulate an orchestral sound. For instance, the rapid arpeggios in the clarinets make up for the lack of string accompaniment, and the strong horns substitute for an entire brass choir. You hardly notice that the trumpets are missing, especially in the finale.

These works stretch the term *chamber music* a bit, since their larger ensembles would not fit in most living rooms. But when you don't have a full orchestra handy, these works can give you the same thrill with fewer personnel.

# BAROQUE CHAMBER MUSIC

## CHAMBER MUSIC PROGRAM #11
BACH: TRIO SONATA IN G MAJOR
BACH: THE MUSICAL OFFERING

You Bach fans have been patient with me so far. It's true that when we think of chamber music, our thoughts go to the string quartet—Haydn's time and the years since then. But there's also a wealth of Baroque works to experience in this genre that employ nearly every instrument of their day. Instead of a piano, Baroque composers usually used a harpsichord, often with a cello or gamba (ancestor of the cello) as well. Of the many combinations we can find, the most significant smaller Baroque works are the "trio sonatas."

Bach and his sons wrote plenty of these; so did Corelli, Handel, Vivaldi, Telemann and others. None could be called a sublime masterpiece like Bach's *St. Matthew Passion*. But just as you don't always want to eat steak dinners, sometimes you want a light musical "snack," and Baroque trio sonatas are the perfect choice. On the whole, they're interesting enough to hear in a recital but gentle enough for background music—sort of the original elevator music, and far better than the modern version.

To represent the many Baroque trio sonatas, let's take a brief look at Bach's well-known *Trio Sonata in G Major*. Its four movements alternate in tempos: slow, fast, slow, fast. To some degree, the slower movements seem a kind of introduction to the subsequent quicker ones. That's especially the case with the third, which doesn't quite end, but leaves you waiting for the finale.

The tone of every movement is elegance rather than virtuosity. This music can be delightful either in the concert hall or in the background as you pursue some other activity.

Since we're on Bach, the "culmination of the Baroque," let's end with his *Musical Offering*, the "culmination" of Baroque chamber music. Although Bach lived most of his life in relative obscurity, toward the end of his career he performed for Frederick the Great, king of Prussia. The king—himself a trained musician—presented Bach with a difficult, chromatic theme with which to improvise on the clavier. The results astonished His Majesty. Bach immediately played a complex fugue on the king's theme. Later, he composed a larger work around this theme and presented his "musical offering" to Frederick. In the accompanying letter, the overly modest Bach recalled his ingenius performance this way: "For lack of necessary preparation, the execution of the task did not fare as well as such an excellent theme demanded." I doubt that Frederick was convinced.

# SONATA FORM

For decades, the sonata (sometimes called "sonata form" or "sonata-allegro form") formed the backbone of every symphony, string quartet, solo sonata and countless other works. This was the practice of Haydn, Mozart, Beethoven, most of the nineteenth-century composers and many of those in the twentieth.

Before we go any further, though, we should mention that not all sonatas are sonatas. That is, the earlier Baroque works of this name by composers such as Bach and Scarlatti are not the same as the fully developed "sonata form." Furthermore, the expression "sonata form" can actually refer to either 1) the specific blueprint of the first movement of a classical sonata, or 2) the title and format of the entire four-movement work.

In this second meaning, the four movements of a sonata usually incorporate a standard pattern: 1) a fast movement in sonata form (see below); 2) a slow movement; 3) a minuet and trio, later replaced by a scherzo and trio (often, however, the position of this movement and the slow movement are reversed); and 4) a fast movement, usually in rondo form. All movements may contain great genius and creativity, but the form of the first movement has exalted the art of composition to its highest pinnacle.

The first movement of a sonata is an interesting ABA form. It may have an introduction, and there are many variations to its basic design. But it always contains three principal sections, called the "exposition," "development" and "recapitulation" ("recap" for short)— the last section being a varied restatement of the first. There are always at least two themes given in the exposition, often called the principle theme and the secondary theme. The exposition is often repeated and the recap is usually followed by an extensive amount of extra material called a "coda."

The design looks like this:

| | A | B | A | |
|---|---|---|---|---|
| INTRODUCTION | EXPOSITION | DEVELOPMENT | RECAP | CODA |
| (free | Theme one | Expansion of | Theme one | (free) |
| material) | ("Home" key) | themes one | ("Home" key) | |
| | Theme two | and two | Theme two | |
| | ("related" key) | (many keys) | ("Home" key) | |

Thousands of musical compositions are based on the above blueprint. Like its literary cousin the sonnet, the form of the sonata has captivated hundreds of geniuses. In fact, the sonata has often enabled composers to bring forth their best inspirations.

Why has the sonata form been so popular? Perhaps it finds the perfect balance between the rigidity of too many formal restrictions and the ambiguity of having no guidelines at all.

Composers don't want to invent a new form for every new piece. With the pre-determined sections of a sonata to serve as the blueprint for their composition, musical ideas have a built-in structure. It's as if some of the compositional work is already done for them. And believe me, if you had to produce a sonata by tomorrow for the local prince, you'd accept all the help you could get.

The final product is a collection of interesting fugues, canons and a wonderful trio sonata, all based on the king's theme. No doubt the sovereign's melody was nice, but it is in Bach's hands that the masterpiece was created. I hope you like it—you'll hear it over and over again in the different movements of the *Musical Offering*.

Baroque chamber music on public radio is marvelous to wake up to and provides a pleasant atmosphere for an elegant dinner. For a really nice touch at your next dinner party, turn off your stereo and shell out a few dollars to hire a group of chamber musicians. Now that's *class*—and this is my plug for starving musicians.

## MISCELLANEOUS CHAMBER FORMS

We mentioned earlier the woodwind quintet and the brass quintet as other possibilities in chamber music. These are fashionable ensembles that create fantastic sounds, but before you hear one perform you must know about the magic of "transcriptions" and "arrangements." You see, Handel and Beethoven never actually wrote music for these ensembles, yet wonderful concerts have programmed everything from Handel's "Hallelujah Chorus" for brass quintet to Beethoven's string quartets played by a woodwind quintet.

What happened? Did the performers find some long-lost manuscript? No in each case some enterprising and talented musician transcribed the original music to accommodate the new instruments. Now trombone players can play the Bach *Cello Suites,* saxophone quartets can play Schubert's "Death and the Maiden" string quartet, and electronic synthesizers can play Tchaikovsky symphonies.

If this seems scandalous to you, consider that the best composers throughout history continually have made arrangements and transcriptions, using their own music as well as that of others. Bach, Handel, Mozart, Beethoven—all of them would nonchalantly rework the same material to suit the need of their current situation. So we should have the same liberty, whether at a chamber music party with too few violinists or on the concert stage.

Remember that music is for our enjoyment; it's to serve us, not the other way around. If we ever feel that music—even the most cherished music—is somehow too "sacred" simply to enjoy, then it's time to lighten up. Maybe a tuba ensemble concert would be good for all of us once in a while.

# CHAMBER MUSIC REPERTOIRE

## THE TOP 15

Bartok
  String Quartet No. 5
Beethoven
  Piano Trio in B♭ ("Archduke")
  String Quartet No. 14 in C# Minor
Brahms
  Trio for Violin, Horn and Piano
Debussy
  String Quartet in G Minor
Dvorak
  String Quartet in F ("American")
Haydn
  String Quartet in C Major ("Emperor")
Mendelssohn
  String Octet in E♭ (4 violins, 2 violas, 2 cellos)
Mozart
  Clarinet Quintet in A
  Piano Quartet in G Minor
Schubert
  String Quartet No. 14 in D Minor
    ("Death and the Maiden")
  Piano Quintet in A ("The Trout")
  String Quintet in C
Schumann
  Piano Quintet in E♭
Stravinsky
  L'Histoire du Soldat

## THE TOP 50

Bach, J.S.
  Musical Offering
Bartok
  String Quartet No. 4
  String Quartet No. 5
Beethoven
  String Quartet No. 10 in E♭ ("Harp")
  String Quartet No. 11 in F Minor
  String Quartet No. 13 in B♭
  String Quartet No. 14 in C# Minor
  String Quartet No. 15 in A Minor
  Piano Trio in B♭ ("Archduke")
  Piano Trio in D Minor ("Ghost")
Brahms
  Piano Trio in B Major
  String Quartet in C Minor
  Trio for Violin, Horn and Piano
  Serenade No. 2 in A (2 flutes, 2 oboes, 2
    clarinets, 2 bassoons, 2 horns, viola,
    cello, bass)
  Piano Quintet in F Minor

Debussy
  String Quartet in G Minor
  Sonata for Flute, Viola and Harp
Dvorak
  String Quartet in F ("American")
  Serenade in D Minor (2 oboes, 2 clarinets,
    2 bassoons, 3 horns, cello)
  Piano Trio in E Minor ("Dumky Trio")
  Piano Quintet in A
Haydn
  String Quartet in D Major ("The Lark")
  String Quartet in G Minor ("Quintet")
  String Quartet in C Major ("The Emperor")
  String Quartet in B♭ ("Sunrise")
Mendelssohn
  String Octet in E♭ (4 violins, 2 violas, 2 cellos)
  Piano Trio in D Minor
Mozart
  Flute Quartet
  Oboe Quartet in F
  String Quartet No. 17 in B♭ ("The Hunt")
  String Quartet No. 19 in C ("The Dissonant")
  Clarinet Quintet in A
  String Quintet in C
  Piano Quartet in G Minor
Ravel
  String Quartet in F
  Introduction and Allegro
Schoenberg
  Transfigured Night
Schubert
  Piano Trio No. 2 in E♭
  String Quartet No. 12 in C Minor
    ("Quartett-Satz")
  String Quartet No. 13 in A Minor
  String Quartet No. 14 in D Minor
    ("Death and the Maiden")
  String Quintet in C
  Piano Quintet in A ("The Trout")
Schumann
  Piano Quintet in E♭
  Piano Quartet in E♭
Smetana
  String Quartet No. 1 in E Minor
    ("From My Life")
Stravinsky
  Octet for Winds
  L'Histoire du Soldat
Tchaikovsky
  Souvenir de Florence
  Piano Trio in A Minor

*Haydn, "the father of the string quartet," leading a rehearsal.*

*The opening to Mendelssohn's famous Octet for Strings, written when the composer was 16. Does this look like the work of a teenaged musician?*

# 7

# SONG

*When I compose a song, my concern is not to make music but, first and foremost, to do justice to the poem's intentions. I have tried to let the poem reveal itself, and indeed to raise it to a higher power.*

—Edvard Grieg

The poet Tennyson once wrote, "I do but sing because I must," and he spoke for all of us. We have evidence of people singing songs from the beginning of recorded history. In fact, we've all heard songs ever since our mothers murmured our first lullabies, and sooner than we may remember we joined in with them.

With the advent of recorded music in the twentieth century, a deluge of popular songs began to fill everyone's ears. If you think about it, almost all of what we might categorize as "non-classical" music—that is, typical popular music of today—is in the song category. No doubt we have a few rock operas, and within the jazz world instrumental forms exist. But the overwhelming bulk of pop music consists of songs.

In fact, you may even assume that the song genre belongs to folks like Elvis or the Beatles, while classical composers spend all their time on opera and symphonies. Yet long before the invention of the stereo or even the old-time gramophone, the world's greatest composers were busy writing songs. In the classical world, the form is loosely referred to as lied (LEED, German for "song") or lieder (LEE-der, "songs").

What were these classical songs about? You name it, they wrote about it. As with opera, songs frequently focus on romantic love, but they can also tell of heaven and hell, historical events, death, life, liberty and the pursuit of happiness. We have spiritual songs from biblical texts and dramatic songs from Shakespearean texts. Great poetry from Goethe to Dickinson has been set to music. The sky's the limit on subject matter for lieder.

Unlike our modern Lennon-and-McCartney-type songwriters, classical composers seldom wrote their own lyrics. Usually, they would take a pre-existing poem and set it to their original music. That's why you sometimes find the same song (same title, same text) written by several different composers. A good example is Goethe's lovely poem *Kennst du das Land?* ("Do You Know the Country?"), which was set to music by Beethoven, Schubert, Schumann, Liszt, Spohr, Rubinstein, Spontini, Wolf and Tchaikovsky, among others.

Don't worry that the foreign language texts will be a barrier, even though most of the greatest classical songs are in German, Italian and French. You can enjoy these pieces the same way you enjoy foreign language opera—with a little preparation. In most cases, you'll need to do far less homework than is necessary for opera.

To begin with, songs are conspicuously shorter than operas. Sometimes the entire text is but a few lines.

Furthermore, songs are by necessity beautiful to hear, because they exist for their own sake. Like the arias of opera, they're not written for the sake of something else, such as propelling a plot. When they're sung by a skillful singer, they can provoke in you the same ecstasy as a brilliant instrument, even if you *don't* recognize the words.

I've heard recordings of lieder singers Ely Ameling, Janet Baker or Dietrich Fischer-Dieskau that are so beautiful, I didn't even care about the text. I simply lay back, closed my eyes and let the gorgeous sound wash over me. They could have been singing about Joe's Bar and Grill and I wouldn't have minded, as long as they sound *that* good.

Nevertheless, the world of song can be deep and therefore somewhat bewildering at first. There's much more here than initially meets the ear. The distinguished singer Janet Baker once observed, "Singing lieder is like putting a piece of music under a microscope." But you can find an abundance of beauty under that microscope if you approach it in the right manner.

Before you race off to your first song recital or buy your first CD, you need to know about the "song cycle." Composers sometimes write individual songs as independent works, but often they create a group of related songs called a "cycle." These song cycles are much like mini-operas, and they first came to prominence in the early nineteenth century. Beethoven's *An du ferne Geliebte* ("To the Distant Beloved") was the first, but Schubert, Schumann and others perfected this form. They're still popular both in concerts and on recordings.

We'll move slowly into the song world, moving from the familiar to the uncommon. As with opera, certain composers seem to have majored in writing lieder, and we'll spend most of our time with them. By the time we finish, you may be well on your way to writing your *own* version of *Kennst du das Land.*

## GERMAN SONGS

Although almost every composer has written at least one song, some wrote more than others. Let's begin in Germany, the greatest land of song. The major song composers from this country you need to know are the two "Schu's"—Schubert and Schumann—our old friend Brahms, and a strange new fellow named Hugo Wolf.

This selection might surprise you, especially if you were looking for such "vocal" composers as Mozart or Wagner. These two each wrote songs, but their genius found its best expression in the vastness of opera. It takes a different kind of genius to reveal itself in the beautiful miniatures of song.

## SONG PROGRAM #1
### SCHUBERT: DER ERLKONIG ("THE ERL-KING")
### SCHUBERT: AVE MARIA ("HAIL, MARY")
### SCHUBERT: GRETCHEN AM SPINNRADE
### ("GRETCHEN AT THE SPINNING WHEEL")
### SCHUBERT: DIE SCHOENE MULLERIN
### ("THE BEAUTIFUL MAID OF THE MILL")

## FRANZ SCHUBERT (1797-1828)

Today, when we hear the word *songwriter* most people think of the Bob Dylan variety. In the classical world, thoughts about songwriting turn first to Franz Schubert, the greatest songwriter in all history. He once said, "I am in the world only for the purpose of composing. What I feel in my heart, I give to the world."

In his short life, Schubert wrote over six hundred songs. You'd think that out of so many compositions I might find one or two not to my taste. But to paraphrase Will Rogers, I never met a Schubert song I didn't like.

Three of his most popular lieder have been chosen for our program: *Der Erlkonig* ("The Erl-King"), *Ave Maria* ("Hail, Mary"), and *Gretchen am Spinnrade* ("Gretchen at the Spinning Wheel"). I also want us to examine one of his song cycles, so we'll look at the poignant *Die schoene Mullerin* ("The Beautiful Maid of the Mill").

One day, two of Schubert's friends came visiting and found him reading aloud Goethe's poem "Der Erlkonig." "He paced up and down several times with the book," they reported. "Suddenly he sat down and in no time at all (as quickly as one can write) there was the glorious ballad finished on the paper."

The drama of "Erl-King" is unforgettable. The melodious tones of the father comforting his son contrast starkly with the impassioned cries of the little boy as the mysterious "Erl-King" draws near. Even the piano accompaniment is theatrical, with the repeated octaves depicting the horse's speed as they gallop along. You don't need a full orchestra and opera props to produce excitement—this classic keeps you fully involved.

The text for Schubert's *Ave Maria* is taken neither from the biblical account of Mary and the angel Gabriel (see Luke 1:28) nor from the Roman Catholic prayer, but instead is found in Sir Walter Scott's "The Lady of the Lake." The piece has become a favorite at Christian weddings. Its chordal accompaniment is straightforward, almost plain, but Schubert knew how to write a gorgeous melody. From the first long note we're captivated—especially when performed by a skillful singer (and not just the bride's cousin).

"Meine Ruh ist hin, Mein Herz ist schwer" ("My peace is gone, my heart is heavy") could have been the theme song for all Europe in 1814 when Schubert composed music to accompany that text in *Gretchen am Spinnrade.* Exhausted from the years of suffering that Napoleon's military ambitions had inflicted all across the continent, the nations sent their representatives to a congress in Schubert's hometown, Vienna, to forge what they hoped would be a lasting peace.

Nearby, Schubert busily created this musical context for Goethe's *Faust*, in which the lovesick Gretchen pours out her heart as she sits at her spinning wheel. As you listen, you'll find the tune always fits the words impeccably, and the piano conjures up the image of the treadle of her wheel. This was Schubert's first vocal masterpiece, written at the tender age of seventeen; it gave promise of the many beauties to come from him.

Beethoven may have officially invented the first song cycle with his *An du ferne Geliebte,* but in Schubert's entrancing *Die schoene Mullerin* we could say that the song cycle comes of age. The composer sets twenty poems of a mini-drama (with the subtitle, "Im Winter zu lesen," "To be read in Winter") to tell a moving story of unrequited country love. The cycle revolves around the story of a young apprentice who falls for the miller's daughter. He's convinced the feelings are mutual until a hunter appears, captures the girl's affections and leaves the apprentice to—alas—drown his grief and his person in a convenient brook.

This is perhaps the most perfect archetype of the song cycle. One continual storyline connects all the songs, every one a classic. Many are sung separately at recitals, such as "Wanderschaft" ("Roving") and "Der Mueller und der Bach" ("The Miller and the Brook").

The cycle becomes somewhat of a cross between opera and individual song. There may only be a singer and a pianist on stage, but when *Die schoene Muellerin* reaches its climatic end, you feel as stirred as if you'd attended an entire opera—without the high-priced opera tickets.

With so many beautiful songs flowing from his pen, we shouldn't be surprised to learn that Schubert sometimes lost track of them. One day he gave a new song to a singer friend, who was busy at the time but looked at it later. The singer greatly enjoyed it, transposed it for his voice and had a new copy of it written.

A week or so later, both friends were at a music gathering when the singer nonchalantly brought out his copy of the unheard song. After Schubert listened to the performance, he burst out—with complete sincerity—"Hey! That's a pretty good song. Whose is it, then?"

SONG PROGRAM #2
SCHUMANN: FRAUENLIEBE UND-LEBEN
("WOMAN'S LOVE AND LIFE")
SCHUMANN: DIE LOTOSBLUME ("THE LOTUS FLOWER")
SCHUMANN: DU BIST WIE EINE BLUME
("YOU ARE LIKE A FLOWER")
SCHUMANN: WIDMUNG ("DEDICATION")

## ROBERT SCHUMANN (1810-1856)

Remember the pianist who injured his finger and therefore his concert career? You may also remember that Robert Schumann married a brilliant pianist, Clara Wieck Schumann. After having a difficult time convincing Mr. Wieck that he was good enough to wed his daughter, Schumann found that his inherent romanticism exploded with song compositions. The year of their marriage, 1840, he not only wrote some of his greatest lieder, but also created his three sublime song cycles, *Liederkreis* ("Song Cycle"), *Frauenliebe und-Leben* ("Woman's Love and Life") and *Dichterliebe* ("Poet's Love").

All of these cycles are masterpieces, but my favorite is *Frauenliebe und-Leben.* Perhaps its interest is magnified by the fact that two men—poet Adalbert Von Chasmisso and composer Robert Schumann—tell a convincing story altogether from a woman's point of view. Of course, they had considerable inspiration since both men were blissfully married to remarkable women. In any case, the thousands of women who have sung these songs testify to their heartfelt sincerity.

The text follows a young girl as she falls in love, finds to her elation that the feeling is mutual, delights in cataloging her lover's fine virtues, prepares herself for the wedding, soon afterward happily announces her pregnancy and finds her joy complete in her baby. Then—you guessed it; after all, this is the Romantic period— her husband tragically dies. After the jubilation of the earlier movements, the passion is overwhelming when the young widow sings, "Nun hast du mir den ersten Schmerz getan, Der aber traf" ("Now you have hurt me for the first time, really hurt me").

As with so much Romantic art, talking about the story line makes it sound as silly as a soap opera. But I guarantee that when you hear this cycle sung by a true artist, you'll have goosebumps.

Like other Romantics, when Schumann wrote about love he often used nature's beauties as material for his metaphor. Two typical favorites are *Die Lotosblume* ("The Lotus Flower") and *Du Bist Wie Eine Blume* ("You Are Like a Flower"). Others, like

*Die Grenadiere* ("The Grenadiers"), embrace a patriotic spirit, but this composer could never stay away long from his leading theme of romance. Such love songs as his *Widmung* ("Dedication") have long established his preeminence in the field of Romantic lied.

### SONG PROGRAM #3
### BRAHMS: WIE BIST DU, MEINE KONIGIN
### ("HOW DELIGHTFUL YOU ARE, O MY QUEEN")
### BRAHMS: FOUR SONGS

## JOHANNES BRAHMS (1833-1897)

Thousands of sleepy mothers and fathers will sing a Brahms lied tonight, not in a concert hall, but in their own homes, in their pajamas. When baby wakes up and must be soothed back to sleep, what parent hasn't tried singing the famous words and sweet melody: "Lullaby, and good night..."? Neither the sleepy performer nor the sleepless audience may know that this is properly titled "Wiegenlied," No. 4 from *Funf Lieder*, Opus 49, for voice and piano—but at three in the morning, who cares?

Incidently, this famous melody practically made Brahms rich. It went through so many different arrangements and editions that at one point the composer recommended in jest to his publisher that another version be made: one in a minor key for naughty youngsters.

Though Brahms's "Lullaby" gets more play in the nurseries and music boxes of the world than on concert stages, others of his songs are undeniable classics. Being a bachelor and a loner didn't keep him from composing beautiful love songs; his images of nature are also extraordinary. Don't let his titles deceive you; he typically gave his greatest works dull names like "Four Songs." The titles won't always thrill you, but his music always will.

For example, take Brahms's famous love song, *Wie Bist Du, Meine Konigin* ("How Delightful You Are, O My Queen"), chosen for our program. The lovely melody has a tender climax at the words "Lass mich vergeh'n in deinem Arm!" ("Let me die in your arms!"). This is sung as a separate selection on many recitals, but it's actually part of his longer set, *Nine Songs*. Unless you hear the other eight, you'll miss out on some marvelous beauty.

Also on our program are Brahms's previously mentioned *Four Songs* (another exciting title). Two of them are extremely popular and heard in thousands of recitals; in particular, note the strong devotion of *Von ewige Liebe* ("Of Eternal Love") and the melancholy beauty of *Die Mainacht* ("May Night"). Yet the other two songs of this group are equally attractive and shouldn't be overlooked.

Brahms knew what he was doing when he grouped his songs into sets. So rather than simply hearing a smattering of favorites, you might try to find a CD or a recital that offers an entire set to enjoy. The intense charm of the Brahms lieder is usually an acquired taste, best cultivated by experiencing the works in their original settings.

SONG PROGRAM #4
WOLF: KENNST DU DAS LAND?
("DO YOU KNOW THE COUNTRY?")
WOLF: SPANISH SONG BOOK
WOLF: ITALIAN SONG BOOK

## HUGO WOLF (1860-1903)

Hugo Wolf is surely one of the strangest composers in history. The stereotypical "madman genius," he makes even Wagner look normal. In fact, he became Wagner's biggest fan, and Brahms's biggest critic. Wolf was thrown out of the Vienna Conservatory, made enemies daily, finally went insane, was thrown into an asylum, was released temporarily only to attempt suicide and again be put in the asylum— and finally died there. He wasn't exactly your "most likely to succeed" type.

Yet what a songwriter he was. Hugo Wolf's songs represent the epitome of skill in blending words and music. Perhaps no other composer has ever had such a natural gift for writing melody and harmony that perfectly express a written text. Many modern songwriters, whose words are often awkwardly placed onto unrelated melodies, would do well to study Wolf's compositions. Indeed, songs were almost all he composed—over two hundred and fifty of them. He wrote no symphonies, concerti or sonatas; like Chopin on the piano, Wolf was a "one-genre master."

Since his claim to fame was his ability to set poetry impeccably to music, an understanding of the text is crucial to appreciating the work. One of the easiest ways to keep all his songs straight is by the authors of his texts. For instance, he set to music fifty-one of Goethe's poems, as well as fifty-three of the poet Eduard Friedrich Morike and twenty by Joseph Freiherr von Eichendorff. Add to these his famous "Liederbuchs"—the *Spanish Song Book* (with texts by various Spanish poets) and the *Italian Song Book* (texts by Italian poets)—and you have many of the world's greatest songs.

Let's listen to a few of the must-hear Wolf lieder. Of the many Goethe songs, surely the greatest is *Kennst du das Land?* ("Do you know the country?"), which Wolf also titled *Mignon* (the name of the character who is speaking the text). This exquisite poem is one of the finest in the German language, and Wolf's elaborate setting wins out over all the other renowned composers who gave it a try.

"Do you know the country where the lemon trees bloom?" we are asked dreamily.

When the responses come—"Do you really know it? There! There I would go with you, my beloved"—the effect of Wolf's music is magnificent. What a song!

If anyone you know thinks classical songs are all worldly and secular, play them a few pieces from Wolf's *Spanish Song Book*. (Actually, the words are in German; the poems were translated from the original Spanish before Wolf set them to music; so also with the *Italian Song Book*.) The ten songs taken from sacred Spanish texts are intense with devotion.

My favorite is *Herr, was tragt der Boden hier* ("Lord, what will the earth bring forth"). Set as a dialogue between a sinner and the Lord, the composer flawlessly brings out the contrasts between their words. When Christ closes with the lyrics, "Those made of thorns are for me; those of flowers I give to you," the audience feels less like applauding than kneeling to pray.

How about some humor? Go to the *Italian Song Book*. It's full of comic songs, usually of a light, romantic character. One of the best known is *Nein, junger Herr* ("No, young man!"), in which the young girl reprimands her boyfriend for his "looking around" on holidays. The light-hearted rhythms make you smile and long for your days of youth—that is, if they've already passed you by.

It's a shame Hugo Wolf led such a tragic and unhappy life. But it would also be a shame to neglect his expressive and remarkable music. He offers tightly fused song and poetry that can leave you in high spirits, deeply affected or in profound contemplation.

## OTHER GREAT GERMAN LIEDER COMPOSERS

### SONG PROGRAM #5
### BEETHOVEN: SIX SONGS TO POEMS BY CHRISTIAN GELLERT
### STRAUSS: TRAUM DURCH DIE DAMMERUNG

The German language has been used to produce a great number of songs, by every composer from Bach to Berg. Aside from the "big four" we've already covered, other heavyweights are Richard Strauss and Gustaf Mahler, both of whom liked to write for a vocal soloist and orchestra. You should also hear sometime the songs of Wagner, Mendelssohn, Liszt, Mozart and even Beethoven. I know Beethoven spent most of his time with instruments, but the old guy wrote some lovely songs.

My favorite vocal pieces by Beethoven, chosen for our program, are his *Six Songs to Poems by Christian Gellert*. Composed in 1803, they're the first to show this composer's spiritual side. All have religious texts, and the greatest is surely *Die Ehre Gottes aus der Natur* ("Nature's Praise to God"). Beethoven was a lifelong nature lover; this song reflects both a pastoral and a religious spirit.

Since I want you to discover how the nineteenth century earned its title as the

# TEMPO INDICATIONS

These are the primary tempo indications used in classical music:

| | |
|---|---|
| Largo | Very slow |
| Larghetto | Not quite as slow |
| Adagio | Slow |
| Moderato | Moderately |
| Andante | Moderately (derived from the Italian word for "walking") |
| Andantino | A bit faster than andante |
| Allegretto | Somewhat lively |
| Allegro | Lively, fast (this word is derived from the Italian word for "cheerful") |
| Vivace | Very fast |
| Presto | Very, very fast |
| Prestissimo | As fast as possible; move it! |

These words are all from Italian and have been universally used by composers from different countries. Nevertheless, some composers insist on using their own language, so you'll occasionally see such tempo indications as "tres vite" (French for "very quickly") or "langsam" (German for "slow") or even "fast" (English for "fast").

In printed programs you'll often see these words listed as "titles" of the separate movements to be performed, since composers don't usually give programmatic titles for every piece they write. So you'll hear musicians stating they will play "the Adagio from Beethoven's such-and-such Sonata." Often the tempo will change within a certain movement, and this becomes a marker for the musicians that says: "Let's begin at the Andante."

In 1813, a friend (on some days) of Beethoven, Johann Nepomuk Malzel, invented an adjustable ticking device called the metronome. Since then composers often have given a precise "metronome marking" to indicate their tempo. Every young music student who's ever raced against these machines can attest to their relentless regularity. They're useful tools, but they don't solve all tempo questions. Johannes Brahms once wrote, "The metronome has no value...for I myself have never believed that my blood and a mechanical instrument go well together."

Composers always have been rather irascible on the subject of tempo, at least the tempo in which their music was performed. French composer Camille Saint-Saens once complained that "there are two kinds" of conductors: "One takes the music too fast, and the other too slow. There is no third!"

"German Lied Century," let's jump from its beginning to its end and note the differences. Richard Strauss, when he wasn't composing wild orchestra tone poems, wrote beautiful songs. Interesting examples, written in 1893, are his *Three Songs, op. 29*, containing the famous *Traum Durch die Dammerung* ("Dreaming Through the Twilight"). This is the love song of love songs, the capstone of a Romantic century.

## SONGS IN OTHER LANGUAGES

Weren't any great songs written in something besides German? Of course. There are beautiful songs in every language from Russian to Arabic. But the other principle languages that Western composers have used for this genre are French, Italian and—especially in our century—English.

## FRENCH

France and Germany have seemed to be at odds for centuries. History records numerous wars between these two neighbors, and both their language and their music are poles apart. Nevertheless, well-rounded music lovers learn to appreciate the traditions of both. Their repertoires are different, but both French and German styles have their own particular magnificence. Sometimes you'll be in the mood for Beethoven, but sometimes you'll want Debussy.

As you know, in France the relation between music and the other arts is pronounced. This is especially clear in the French Impressionists, who find their inspiration in the same nature-oriented subjects so loved by the French painters. When you listen to French song, you'll notice this close connection with nature, both in the texts and in the mood of the music.

In the song genre, the five greatest French composers are Berlioz, Gounod, Faure, Debussy and Ravel.

### SONG PROGRAM #6
BERLIOZ: NUITS D'ETE ("Summer Nights")
BACH/GOUNOD: AVE MARIA ("Hail, Mary")
FAURE: APRES UN REVE ("After a Dream")
FAURE: LA BONNE CHANSON ("The Good Song")

## HECTOR BERLIOZ (1803-1869)

Berlioz wrote *songs*? The wild orchestrator who composed pieces that require just under six hundred performers to play them? Yes, Berlioz actually composed a number of lovely French songs.

By far the most popular is the collection of six songs entitled *Nuits d'ete* ("Summer Nights"). Every song here is a gem, but the first is Berlioz's crown jewel, entitled *L'Absence* ("Absence"). Its amorous text could have been subtitled, "Absence makes the heart grow fonder." When the singer beautifully laments, *"Entre nos coeurs tant de distance!"* ("Between our hearts how great the distance!"), our commiseration grows overpowering. A heartbreaker, but a glorious one.

## CHARLES GOUNOD (1818-1893)

The next work isn't exactly a French song—in fact, the words are Latin. But it was shaped by a Frenchman, and it's so famous we can't overlook it.

Charles Gounod is known principally for his opera *Faust,* but he also lays claim to half of an all-time favorite: the "Bach-Gounod Ave Maria." He wrote a lovely melody to the accompaniment of an equally lovely Bach prelude (from the latter's *Well-Tempered Clavier).* Later, the words of the well-known Catholic prayer were added. It all fits together well—and you get two composers for the price of one.

## GABRIEL FAURE (1845-1924)

From Faure my favorites are the sumptuous *Apres un reve* ("After a Dream") and the lovely song cycle *La Bonne Chanson* ("The Good Song"). The texts for this cycle are supplied by Paul Verlaine, who became every French composer's favorite poet. From the first piece, *Une sainte en son aureole* ("A saint with her halo"), to the last, *L'hiver a cesse* ("Winter has passed"), Faure's nine songs give a portrait of a man in joyful love. When at the end of *J'ai presque peur* ("I am almost afraid") the lover finally cries, "*Je t'amie!"* ("I love you!"), every heart in the audience is pounding. Ah, *l'amour!*

### SONG PROGRAM #7
DEBUSSY: BEAU SOIR ("BEAUTIFUL EVENING")
RAVEL: VOCALISE EN FORME DE HABANERA

## CLAUDE DEBUSSY (1862-1918)

In this genre Debussy is again the pinnacle of the French masters. Although such masterpieces as *Beau Soir* ("Beautiful Evening") and *Mandoline* ("Mandolin Serenade") are performed constantly, many of his foremost works are in collections: *Proses Lyriques* ("Lyrical Prose," with texts by the composer); *Fetes Galantes,* sets 1 and 2; and *Chansons de Bilitis* ("Songs of Bilitis," a fictitious Greek name invented by the poet Pierre Louys, a friend of Debussy's). All are ravishing—French at its best.

One reason I want you to hear *Beau Soir* is to illustrate that the day of the young geniuses didn't end with Mozart and Mendelssohn. Debussy wrote this lovely song at the age of fifteen. The text itself is quite mature—reflections, as the evening fades, on enjoying youth while it lasts, "for we are moving on, even as that wave moves; it to the sea, we to the tomb." I'm glad that despite such somber thoughts this prodigy nevertheless lived and composed for many more years.

## MAURICE RAVEL (1875-1937)

As we saw in other genres, when it comes to songs, you seldom hear Debussy's name without soon hearing Ravel's. One of his most interesting works is the

# KEYS AND TONALITY

Non-musicians sometimes are confused by titles such as *Symphony in D Minor* or *Sonata in E♭ Major*. A well-meaning friend may tell them, "Oh, that is what key the piece is in." You politely answer, "Oh, I see." But you may not see, and no wonder. What is all this "key" business, anyway?

You already know that music is composed of pitches, or, as we usually call them, notes. These notes all have letter names from A to G. What you may not know is that in every piece, one note in particular is chosen as the main pitch (what musicians call the "tonal center" or "tonic"), and the other notes are subservient to this main pitch.

Often this main pitch is the first note of a composition and it's almost always the last note. For example, the old children's song "Twinkle, Twinkle, Little Star" begins on the "tonic" ("*Twinkle*") and ends there as well: "How I wonder what you *are*." The pitch you sang on the word *are* is the same pitch as the opening syllable "Twink," and it's obviously the main note of the piece. If you don't think so, try ending the last line early on the word *what* or *you*.

Different singers may begin this little classic on different starting pitches, some lower, some higher. If you begin on the note C, we say that you're singing "Twinkle, Twinkle" in the key of C. If you begin on the note F, you create "Twinkle, Twinkle" in the key of F. In the same way, when you hear Beethoven's *Violin Concerto in D,* the main pitch is D, the opening note is D, the last note you hear is D—and there are lots of D's in between.

Sometimes composers will write a composition in the key of A, sometimes in the key of G, and so forth. It usually depends on the mood they're in. Later, the entire work can be moved up or down to a different degree of the scale. We call this process "transposing" the piece to a different key.

What about terms such as "D *Major*" and "F# *Minor*"? There are "major" keys and "minor" keys for every note. The difference between the two has to do with the make-up of the scales and chords with which the composer chooses to work in that particular composition. What's important to the average listener is that major keys tend to sound bright and cheerful, while minor keys are sad and serious. We need them both.

*Tonality* is what we call the system of writing music in keys that musicians have been working with for hundreds of years. In the twentieth century, many composers have abandoned this system for an unconstrained practice usually called "atonality." To the uninitiated, the first sounds of an atonal composition sound much like babies crying, silverware spilling or tomcats howling.

But don't pass judgment too quickly. Throughout history, composers have always been ahead of their time. The forefathers of today's critics were the same who thought Beethoven's music too weird and modern. Doubtless, much of contemporary classical music is rubbish—that's been the case in *every* era—but there are still musical geniuses at work. If we give some of them a chance, we may find in what they create that there's more than meets the eye, or rather, the ear.

In the meantime, enjoy the charm of C major and the pathos of C minor. And feel free to sing "Twinkle, Twinkle, Little Star," in whichever key you like best.

wordless *Vocalise en Forme de Habanera.* Since an "habanera" is a Spanish dance (you'll remember one in the opera *Carmen*), we have another example of the French composer's fascination with Spain.

Since no text is employed here, all of the interest is on the music itself. The singer has to vocalize without words, performing acrobatic feats that tax the technique of even the greatest virtuosi. Even with this display of vocal skill, the work is musically charming, though the effect is almost instrumental. Perhaps this song belongs in the chapter on concerti.

As with Debussy, some of Ravel's finest works are his song collections, especially the *Histoires Naturelles, Don Quichotte a Dulcinee,* and the ever-popular *Scheherazade.*

Other French composers of song include Henri Duparc, Francis Poulenc and Ernest Chausson. Although their works as a whole are not quite of the same caliber as the other French masters, each have a few exquisite songs that are unforgettable. That's one of the beauties of this genre: Opera and symphonies take months, even years, of work to complete. But sometimes all it takes is one good afternoon and a great song can allow a composer to go down in history.

## ITALIAN

In the chapter on opera you learned that Italians love to sing. Yet they mostly love to sing opera; even the greatest of opera composers wrote few independent songs. Even many of the "Italian art songs" that are on recitals today are actually arias taken from operas. Not surprisingly, the songwriters from Italy are basically the same as those we found in the opera: Rossini, Bellini, Donizetti. (In the interest of space, none of these are on our program.)

The Italians have a great deal of business sense. Composers such as Verdi or Puccini rarely wrote a note of music unless a contract already was signed. For that reason, the lucrative possibilities for opera revenues habitually squeezed out any time that might have been used writing songs. Oh well. A composer has to eat too.

## ENGLISH

### SONG PROGRAM #8
### DOWLAND: COME AGAIN
### VAUGHAN WILLIAMS: FIVE MYSTICAL SONGS
### COPLAND: TWELVE POEMS OF EMILY DICKINSON

## JOHN DOWLAND (1562-1626)

Classical songs in English? You bet. Centuries before the Beatles, a lutenist (lute-player) named John Dowland composed some of the loveliest songs the British Isles would ever produce. I've selected for this program his lively *Come Again.*

Dowland has a gift for simple, clear melody. Being an instrumentalist himself, he made sure that his accompaniments were as interesting as his vocal lines. Notice in

*Come Again* how he alternates the last two lines between voice and instrument to build to a climax. Fun to sing, fun to play, fun to hear.

Another of my Dowland favorites (not on our program) is the tender *Flow, My Tears*. But his songs are like Schubert's lieder—you love them all.

After Dowland, Handel and many of his contemporaries wrote well in the British language. But it wasn't until the twentieth century that English songwriting came into its own.

Our program includes selections from two composers to remember, one from each side of the Atlantic: Ralph Vaughan Williams and Aaron Copland. We'll sample their best: first, Vaughan Williams's deeply moving *Five Mystical Songs,* set to texts of the spiritual poet George Herbert. Actually these were composed for baritone, chorus and orchestra, but now they're usually performed by piano and voice. They're British to the core.

Herbert's seventeenth-century poems fit perfectly into the stately style of Vaughn Williams. This composer is subtle, never bombastic. He has a talent for bringing out the inner meaning of the texts.

Copland's *Twelve Poems of Emily Dickinson* is perhaps the best example of great American poetry set superbly to great American music. They work equally well when accompanied by piano or orchestra. The music is perhaps more unorthodox than some of Copland's most popular works, but his gift for melody is always evident. Although there are some energetic moments, the overall effect is peaceful—beautiful music for the twilight hours.

Also, don't miss a chance to hear Benjamin Britten's sensitive *Holy Sonnets of John Donne,* written in 1945 after a sorrowful journey to visit German concentration camps; and Samuel Barber's interesting *Hermit Songs,* based on medieval texts of Irish monks.

We end the chapter with a question to ponder: What makes all these classical songs different from the millions of contemporary songs played by the Muzak® consumers of the world? Rather than get into an argument over which songs are better than others, consider this: Hundreds of the classical songs are being sung decades and even centuries after they were composed. This doesn't often happen with even the greatest of pop songs; how many Bing Crosby records do you have?

So perhaps there's something intrinsically enduring about these songs that have moved listeners for so long. The more you get into them, the more they will move *you* too. To paraphrase Tennyson, these composers wrote songs because they felt they must; and when we learn to appreciate them, we may find as did millions before us that we *listen* to them because we must—their beauty compels us.

# SONG REPERTOIRE
## (song cycles and collections are in italics)

### THE TOP 15
Brahms
  *Four Songs*
Debussy
  Beau Soir
  *Chansons de Bilitis*
Faure
  Apres un Reve
Schubert
  Ave Maria
  Gretchen am Spinnrade
  *Die schoene Muellerin*
  Der Erlkoenig
Schumann
  *Liederkreis*
  *Frauenliebe und-Leben*
  *Dichterliebe*
Strauss, R.
  *Four Last Songs*
Wolf
  Kennst du das Land?
  *Spanish Song Book*
  *Italian Song Book*

### THE TOP 50
Bach, J.S.
  Bist du bei mir
Barber
  *Hermit Songs*
Beethoven
  *An du ferne Geliebte*
  Adelaide
Berlioz
  *Les Nuits d'ete*
Brahms
  *Four Songs*
  Wiegenlied
  Sapphische Ode
Britten
  *A Charm of Lullabies*
Chausson
  Les temps des lilas
Copland
  *Old American Songs*
Debussy
  Beau Soir
  *Chansons de Bilitis*
Duparc
  Chanson triste
Dvorak
  *Gypsy Songs*

Faure
  Apres un reve
Gounod
  Ave Maria
Haydn
  She Never Told Her Love
Liszt
  O lieb, so lang du lieben kannst
Mahler
  Liebst du um Schonheit
Mendelssohn
  On Wings of Song
Mozart
  Abendempfindung
  Das Veilchen
Purcell
  Music for a While
Rachmaninov
  Vocalise
Rossini
  *Soirees Musicales*
Scarlatti, A.
  Gia il sole dal Gange
Schubert
  An den Mond
  Ave Maria
  Die Allmacht
  *Die schoene Muellerin*
  *Die Winterreise*
  Nacht und Traume
  Der Erlkoenig
  Gretchen am Spinnrade
  Heidenroslein
  An die Musik
  Gesang an Sylvia
Schumann
  *Liederkreis*
  *Frauenliebe und-Leben*
  *Dichterliebe*
Strauss, R.
  Zueignung
  *Four Last Songs*
Tchaikovsky
  None But the Lonely Heart
Wagner
  *Wesendonklieder*
Wolf
  Kennst du das Land?
  *Spanish Song Book*
  *Italian Song Book*
  *Morike Songs*

*Schubert was painfully under-appreciated in his day;*
*he had to take any audience he could get.*

*Schubert's spidery handwriting shows the speed at which he composed his many songs, such as this lovely "Gretchen am Spinnrade."*

# 8

# SOLO LITERATURE

---

*I am not handsome, but when*
*women hear me play, they come crawling to my feet.*

—Niccolo Paganini, the nineteenth century's most renowned violinist

Many of us have memories—fond or horrid—of piano lessons, usually given by the little old lady down the street. Some may have had trumpet lessons in school band, maybe even violin in the school youth orchestra. If you have fond memories of music lessons, that's great—our exploration of solo literature may create some nostalgia for you. But if you had a bad experience as a child with a music teacher who rubbed you the wrong way, please try to put it behind you. It's time to hear solo music—perhaps some of the same pieces you agonized through—with a new set of ears.

Instead of the drudgery of practicing scales, we'll get a taste of some fantastic musical literature. Some of the greatest compositions ever written were designed for one instrument, or one instrument plus accompaniment. It is one of life's wonders that one person can walk onto a huge stage in a concert hall packed with thousands, and by simply playing a single instrument keep the audience absolutely enthralled. Yet it's done every night in halls all over the world.

In every other genre of music, an individual performer is only one element of the production. Those who play are dependent on all the other performers to make the whole complete, and if any of them tried to perform alone, the part would sound rather limited.

Not so with soloists. They walk out, take a bow and do the entire show by themselves. They can even be alone at home and still perform the entire piece. For them, all the fascination of a full orchestra is contained in a much smaller space.

Thousands of compositions have been written for precisely that purpose. Beethoven's piano pieces reflect as much genius and spur as much interest as his symphonies. Sometimes I'm in the mood for Bach's *Brandenburg Concerti,* but sometimes I'd rather hear his solo organ preludes. That's the marvel of it: Great music is great music, whether it's played by one performer or one hundred.

So let's look at the solo literature—or "almost solo," in some cases. You see, a pianist, organist or guitarist might take the stage alone. But a violinist, clarinetist or trumpeter usually brings a friend, a piano accompanist, as solo singers do.

Why the difference? Keyboard instrumentalists and guitarists can play more than one melody at the same time; they can accompany themselves. But "single line" instruments, such as an oboe or trombone, usually depend on another instrument for accompaniment.

For that reason, the solo literature discussed here will be either for one instrument or two. It will include, for example, both a Chopin piano piece and a Brahms sonata for violin and piano. In fact, Baroque music "solo" recitals often use *three* players. The two who accompany the soloist are usually a harpsichord and a cello, playing the music we call the "continuo" part.

We'll divide our material according to the instruments employed. Of course, there's music for *every* instrument, so we'll have to be selective. If I omit your favorite, please forgive me.

One of my goals is to prepare you to enjoy the concerts that are available, and let's face it—many more violin recitals are performed than bassoon recitals. Some orchestral instruments lend themselves to solo work more than others, whether we like it or not. So on behalf of the composers of the world, I apologize to those who play viola, trombone or another instrument that has fewer solo pieces to play.

Not surprisingly, we'll begin with the keyboard instruments, the piano, the organ and the harpsichord. Keyboard literature is roughly eighty-five percent piano, ten percent organ and five percent harpsichord. But it's one hundred percent wonderful. Since you've all heard pianos in homes and organs in churches, perhaps we'll break some new ground by starting with one of my favorite instruments, the harpsichord.

## THE HARPSICHORD AND THE ORGAN

The evolution of keyboard instruments that culminated in the piano goes back five hundred years or so. The first practical instrument of this type was the clavichord, later the harpsichord and finally the piano. On the outside, each is similar in concept: The musician presses a key down to make music, and the keys are placed in a long row called the keyboard.

But what happens on the inside of each instrument is quite different. In the clavichord, pressing a key causes a metal hammer to strike a string, but the resulting sound is thin and inadequate. The inventors had to tinker a bit to come up with a new idea.

By the Baroque era they were making a keyboard mechanism that, instead of striking the strings with a metal hammer, "plucked" the string with a small plectrum—the same concept that brought us the guitar pick. The newfangled instrument was called a harpsichord, and it sounded far more promising than its predecessor. Composers took to it like a duck to water, and thousands of harpsichord pieces are still played today.

In fact, if you check your local newspaper, you'll probably find occasional harpsichord recitals; and if you check your local phonebook, you may even find full-time harpsichordists. I hope you'll soon have the privilege to hear a harpsichord live. But in the meantime, I'll recommend some pieces to enjoy on recordings at home.

## SOLO PROGRAM #1
### SCARLATTI: HARPSICHORD SONATA IN G MINOR
### BACH: ITALIAN CONCERTO
### BACH: GOLDBERG VARIATIONS

History has given us many major (and minor) composers of harpsichord music: Jean-Philippe Rameau, Francois Couperin, Jean Baptiste Lully, Henry Purcell, even G. F. Handel. But the two greatest exponents of the instument to remember are Domenico Scarlatti and our old friend J. S. Bach.

### DOMENICO SCARLATTI (1685-1787)

Scarlatti's father also wrote music, so we'd better be clear about which one we mean. The dad (Alessandro Scarlatti) wrote Italian opera, song and church music, but his son (Domenico) composed over five hundred sonatas for harpsichord. Today you often hear them played on piano, guitar or harp. These one-movement pieces aren't of the same four-movement form that later emerged in the classical period, but they're just as entertaining.

My favorite is the famous *Sonata in G Minor,* better known as the "Cat Fugue." As you listen, notice the wide leaps in the melody; apparently they reminded some listener of the sounds resulting when a cat walks across a keyboard. That sounds odd, but you're sure to love it; Scarlatti sonatas are like Schubert songs: You seldom find one you don't like.

### JOHANN SEBASTIAN BACH (1685-1750)

This guy Bach shows up everywhere, and for good reason. In every regard, he's the master. Legends and anecdotes, even jokes, revolve around his obscure life. A classic:

Did you know that Bach gave us a new addition to concert hall architecture? He was climbing a ladder one day while a friend was at the organ and noticed how much better the music sounded up there. So he suggested building a new row of seats above the floor, which are now named after him and always cost more than all the other seats in the hall. Haven't you ever heard of *Bach's* seats?" (Now you make up your own dumb jokes about a *"Bach's* lunch.")

Anyway, some of his best efforts were played by his own hands on the clavier. (Bach wrote many works for the "clavier"; it simply means "keyboard" in a non-specific sense, whatever you happen to have available.) Depending upon how far you went with your piano lessons, you probably remember his *Two-Part* and *Three-Part Inventions.*

If you went a little further you may have played one of his *French Suites* or *English Suites.* Maybe you even went so far as to play one of his all-time best—the *Italian Concerto,* which I've selected for our program. This solo piece is not a concerto in the typical sense of a soloist with an orchestra, but its three movements have such wonderful contrasts that it gives you the same effect.

Two other Bach keyboard works merit attention. The first, chosen for our program, is the *Aria with Thirty Variations,* usually known as the "Goldberg Variations." This beautiful composition owes its existence to the insomnia of a count in Leipzig, Germany.

The count asked Bach to write a special piece for his musician, named Goldberg, to play on harpsichord to help him go to sleep. The result was a hit. Bach received a golden goblet filled with a hundred gold coins, and you and I gained one of the greatest "theme and variations" works in the world of music.

The *Well-Tempered Clavier* (not on our program) never rewarded its composer with a golden goblet or coins, but it's nevertheless a landmark in musical history. "Well-Tempered" refers not to laid-back keyboard players, but has to do with the type of tuning system used to tune an instrument. In Bach's time, several possibilities were in vogue; the one Bach advocated, called "equal temperament," is the one we still use today.

To demonstrate its benefits, Bach wrote a prelude and fugue in each key. They not only sound in tune; they sound fabulous. From the beautiful broken chords of the first *Prelude* to the virtuosity of the *Fugue in C# Minor,* you'll hear in the "WTC" the soul of J. S. Bach.

# SOLO PROGRAM #2
## BACH: TOCCATA AND FUGUE IN D MINOR
## BACH: "LITTLE" FUGUE IN G MINOR
## BACH: PASSACAGLIA IN C MINOR

Of course, if you want to know Bach's soul, you can also listen to a good organist play his works. The great pipe organ was Johann's ultimate instrument, and his organ compositions form the core of nearly every organ recital.

Schubert once commented, "Johann Sebastian Bach has done everything completely; he was a man through and through." That thoroughness can be heard especially in his organ works. Bach wanted so much from an organ, it was said that sometimes when he played he not only employed both hands on the keyboards and both feet on the pedals, but he even pushed down other keys with a stick held in his mouth.

You've probably already heard the famous *Toccata and Fugue in D Minor,* which I've chosen for our program. It's been used in everything from Disney's *Fantasia* to horror movies. The enigmatic opening is compelling and the perfect introduction to the improvisational nature of a toccata. The fugue that follows is also quite dramatic. Since so many of the masters like Bach wrote innumerable fugues, perhaps we should talk a little more about that particular music form.

As our example, let's listen to Bach's famous *"Little" Fugue in G Minor.* In it you'll hear an unaccompanied melody (called the "fugue subject"), followed by another part playing that same fugue subject in a lower register with a new accompaniment in the first part. Later, the fugue subject appears in other parts, and finally you'll hear a climactic section (called the "stretto") in which the fugue subject is superimposed upon itself in several parts simultaneously—what an ending!

Many of Bach's organ works start quietly and build to an overwhelming finish. The best example of this pattern is his *Passacaglia in C Minor.* The organ pedal mysteriously presents the celebrated theme then simply repeats it again and again while the organist's hands begin to add more, and more, and more until the effect is spectacular. You'll think the organist is growing new fingers.

As you listen to this one, you'll understand the comment about Bach's organ music made by the German poet Goethe: "It is as though eternal harmony were conversing with itself, as it may have happened in God's bosom shortly before creating the world."

Of course, there's much more to organ music than just Bach. Handel, Mozart, Mendelssohn, Franck and a host of lesser composers have given us great organ repertoire. With the advent of electricity and modern electronic organs, the instrument is attracting more and more composers in our century. But it all goes back to Bach, the master organist.

You really must attend an organ recital sometime. Being a rather non-portable instrument, it doesn't travel to concert halls, so you must do the traveling, usually to a large church. Furthermore, you often see neither the performer nor the instrument, since the organ is usually in the choir loft and you're in the pew. No matter. Simply close your eyes and be surrounded by music. Being massaged by the mammoth sound and infinite variety of a cathedral organ is an unforgettable experience.

## PIANO LITERATURE

Now I'm really in trouble. There's *so* much great piano music that this book could go on for years. Just about every composer wrote for this instrument, and most wrote extensively for it.

What to do? I'll simply whet your appetite, push you into the recital hall (or CD store), and let you go for it. We'll hear only from the top piano composers of the ages, and let you sample a few of their greatest hits. Let's look at piano music by Mozart, Beethoven, Chopin, Brahms and Debussy—all great composers and great pianists as well.

SOLO PROGRAM #3
MOZART: PIANO SONATA IN C MAJOR, K. 545
MOZART: PIANO SONATA IN A MAJOR, K. 331
MOZART: "AH, VOUS DIRAI-JE MAMAN" VARIATIONS

## WOLFGANG AMADEUS MOZART (1756-1791)

Our beloved child prodigy wrote seventeen piano sonatas as well as a number of other important solos for piano. His sonatas range from the incredibly difficult *Sonata in D Major,* K. 311, to the ever-popular *Sonata in C Major,* K. 545 (chosen for our program), which he called "a little sonata for beginners."

The beauty of this latter piece lies in its simplicity. Since it's not technically difficult, many piano students often perform it. Yet no virtuoso performer is ever bored by this work, which is so full of charm and elegance.

When you listen to the most frequently performed of Mozart's piano sonatas—*Sonata in A Major*—note that it has only three movements instead of the classical four. This piece opens with an elaborate theme and variations, one of Mozart's favorite techniques. But wait until you hear the popular last movement—a band-like march marked "alla turca" ("in the Turkish style"). You'll know why the great pianist Vladimir Horowitz considered this work "the apotheosis of gallantry and grace."

Perhaps the most famous example is his twelve charming variations on the French nursery rhyme, "Ah, vous dirai-je maman" (K. 265). Don't let the French fool you; you'll recognize this tune as "Twinkle, Twinkle, Little Star." Classic Wolfgang at the keyboard.

# SOLO PROGRAM #4
## BEETHOVEN: PIANO SONATA NO. 8 IN C MINOR ("PATHETIQUE")
## BEETHOVEN: PIANO SONATA NO. 14 IN C# MINOR ("MOONLIGHT")
## BEETHOVEN: PIANO SONATA NO. 23 IN F MINOR ("APPASSIONATA")

### LUDWIG VAN BEETHOVEN (1770-1827)

With Beethoven the piano composition turns the corner from the Classic era to the Romantic. He composed a great deal for this instrument, including thirty-two masterpiece sonatas. As with Haydn's symphonies, the easiest way to keep them straight is by titles; each of his most celebrated sonatas has one: "Pathetique" *(Sonata No. 8 in C Minor),* "Funeral March" *(Sonata No. 12 in A♭ Major),* "Moonlight" *(Sonata No. 14 in C# Minor),* "Pastoral" *(Sonata No. 15 in D Major),* "Tempest" *(Sonata No. 17 in D Major),* "Waldstein" *(Sonata No. 21 in C Major),* "Appassionata" *(Sonata No. 23 in F Minor),* "Les Adieux" *(Sonata No. 26 in E♭ Major),* and "Hammerklavier" *(Sonata No. 29 in A Major).*

Sometimes Beethoven himself gave a title, such as when he dedicated his *Sonata No. 21 in C Major* to his patron, Count Waldstein. Other titles were added later, notably the enigmatic Moonlight Sonata. Years after the composer's death, a music critic said this piece reminded him of "a boat passing the scenery of Lake Lucerne in the moonlight," and from that time on the work was named.

Most of the titles have a somewhat loose reference to the music. For example, when asked what his *Sonata No. 17 in D Major* was about, the composer answered brusquely, "Read Shakespeare's *Tempest.*" Now we call it the "Tempest" sonata.

A fascinating representation of Beethoven as a stormy young man is found in his "Pathetique" Sonata *(Sonata No. 8 in C Minor).* Composed while in his late twenties, its three movements give brazen indication of the conflicts his life will provoke. You'll hear the work open with a slow, dramatic introduction, repeatedly referred to throughout the tempestuous first movement. In contrast, the following movement is the zenith of lyrical beauty. Finally, the third movement is almost Mozartian in its cheerful vitality. Ah, the many-sided Beethoven.

Beethoven actually entitled the "Moonlight" piece "Sonata quasi una Fantasia" ("Sonata like a Fantasia")—and for good reason. The famous opening movement is slow, meditative, even improvisational in its effect. Many people can play this movement, but it takes a true master to perform the last movement, presto agitato— a frenzy of notes that run well into the thousands. My favorite movement is the peaceful second, which Liszt aptly dubbed "a flower between two abysses." As you listen to the rest of the work, you'll discover what he meant.

The next composition on our program is called the "Appassionata" ("impassioned"), a word that actually describes both this sonata as a whole and its composer. It opens in the low register, with ominous portents of the fury to come. As if to add to the drama, we soon hear the "fate knocking at the door" rhythm from the composer's *Fifth Symphony.* This massive movement ends with an equally massive coda—almost as if the piece doesn't want to stop.

The andante movement that follows is much simpler in character, constructed of a theme and four variations. Two connecting chords plunge us into the energetic finale, which gives us the feeling of perpetual motion. Again, look for the huge, Beethovenesque coda—once more at high speed.

## SOLO PROGRAM #5
### CHOPIN: WALTZ, OP. 64, NO. 1 ("MINUTE WALTZ")
### CHOPIN: PRELUDE IN D♭ MAJOR, OP. 28, NO. 15 ("RAINDROP")
### CHOPIN: POLONAISE IN A MAJOR, OP. 40, NO. 1
### ("MILITARY POLONAISE")
### CHOPIN: ETUDE IN E MAJOR, OP. 10, NO. 3

### FREDERIC CHOPIN (1810-1849)

One of my favorite composers is Chopin, the poet of the piano. Born in Poland of a French father and a Polish mother, he has become Poland's leading musical son. Chopin composed almost exclusively for this instrument, and his piano works are among the finest ever written. In many musical forms, he holds an indisputable first place: nocturnes, etudes, preludes, impromptus, scherzos, ballades (see the glossary for definitions of these), polonaises and mazurkas (these last two are Polish dances). His sonatas are equally original, and the Chopin waltzes are popular around the world.

You *must* own at least one all-Chopin CD, containing either a smattering of "greatest hits" or a collection of one musical form (such as an "all-preludes" CD or an "all-nocturnes" CD). As with Beethoven, many of his best-known pieces have programmatic titles. The "Minute Waltz" (Waltz, op. 64, no. 1) is a favorite display for the show-off pianist trying to beat the clock. Chopin's *Prelude in D♭ Major,* op. 28, no. 15, is called "Raindrop," supposedly because he was inspired by the sound of raindrops falling on his window—listen for yourself. The martial spirit of his "Military Polonaise" *(Polonaise in A Major,* op. 40, no. 1) is wonderfully self-evident.

Yet don't simply look for titles, or you'll miss some of Chopin's finest efforts. Many beauties are found in works with such unassuming names as *Nocturne in D♭*

## MUSICAL TITLES, OR "WHAT'S AN OPUS?"

Throughout this book, and throughout the world of classical music, you'll encounter such titles as Brahms's *Four Songs,* op. 43, or Bach's *Sonata for Clavier and Violin No. 3 in E,* BWV 1016, or Mozart's *Clarinet Quintet in A,* K. 581. We've talked about the meaning of keys and we've described forms such as sonata and quintet; but what do those other abbreviations and numbers mean—things like "op." and "K." and "BWV"?

These and similar terms are for cataloging a composer's work chronologically. That way, just by looking at a title, we can see if the piece is a work written when the composer was quite young (such as an op. 1) or a mature composer (maybe op. 500).

The principle abbreviation used is "op.," which stands for "opus," the Latin word for "work." Many composers kept an ongoing chronological list of their pieces, naming them consecutively opus 1, opus 2, opus 3, and beyond. Often, an opus can be an entire set of pieces, such as the first six string quartets of Beethoven, titled "Opus 18, No. 1," "Opus 18, No. 2," and so on.

Unfortunately, some composers never kept such good records. Thus editors have had to collect and then painstakingly arrange in chronological order their complete works. For instance, the man who first did this for Mozart's music was Ludwig Kochel, so Mozart's works are usually followed by a "K." number. Schubert's works were similarly arranged by Otto Erich Deutsch, and therefore are followed by a "D." number. Wolfgang Schmieder's thematic catalogue of Bach's music is called the *Bach Werke Verzeichnis,* with a "BWV" number.

There are a number of peculiar exceptions to this orderly concept. One of my favorites concerns those nine wonderful Dvorak symphonies. For years, only the last five were published, and the publisher called them Nos. 1–5. The famous *New World Symphony*—Dvorak's last—was therefore called *Symphony No. 5.* Now that all nine are performed, they've been renumbered. For instance, the old No. 1 became the new No. 6, No. 2 became No. 7, yet No. 5 became No. 4.

Wouldn't it have been simpler if all these works had nice, easy-to-remember programmatic names? Alas for composers' inconsistencies. Now you see why music lovers are always assigning nicknames to regular titles. It's a lot harder to remember the title Haydn's *String Quartet in D Major,* op. 64, no. 5, than it is to recall "The Lark."

Major, op. 27, no. 2; *Mazurka in F# Minor,* op. 6, no. 1; or *Sonata in B Minor,* op. 58. All of these pieces are classics in the art of keyboard music.

Sometimes you can make up your own titles when so inspired. The exquisite melody of Chopin's *Etude in E Major,* op. 10, no. 3 (chosen for our program) might be called an "Etude for the Soul." It's simple, yet profound. After the peace of its opening, the wild cadenza later in the work is like a sudden storm. Fortunately, the skies soon clear, and when the original theme reappears, we welcome it back like an old friend.

As with Schubert songs or Scarlotti harpsichord sonatas, you'll seldom find a Chopin piano work that you don't love.

## SOLO PROGRAM #6
## LISZT: ANNEES DE PELERINAGE
## LISZT: LIEBESTRAUM
## LISZT: HUNGARIAN RHAPSODY NO. 2

### FRANZ LISZT (1811-1886)

Chopin's friend, admirer and biographer Franz Liszt is cut from a different cloth. Defying convention in both his personal life and his music, he divided his time into writing such virtuosic showpieces as his *Transcendental Etudes* and quasi-religious works like the *Harmonies Poetiques et Religieuses*. His music revels in pure Romanticism; Liszt loved to break out of a lovely section into an unrestrained cadenza. He once commented, "You cannot imagine how it spoils one to have been a child prodigy."

Although much has been written about Liszt's massive *Sonata in B Minor*, for our program I've selected my favorite of his larger works, the *Annees de Pelerinage* ("Years of Pilgrimage"), published in three volumes. If you must settle for just one set, go for the second, which includes such beauties as *Il Penseroso* ("The Thoughtful One") and the lovely *Canzonetta del Salvator Rosa*.

These two works show different sides of their multifaceted composer. The former is so chromatic you may think it's from the twentieth century, while the latter's beauty is manifest in its simplicity.

Liszt also wrote many smaller pieces and piano arrangements. I've chosen for our program the most famous, the romantic *Liebestraum*. Even if you don't recognize this title, you'll recognize the music. Hollywood borrowed its melody for many a love scene.

You won't want to miss a single one of Liszt's illustrious *Hungarian Rhapsodies*. These pieces have overwhelmed audiences for years with color and vitality. The well-known number two is on our program. Again, you'll find that you know this music. Its famous themes have been arranged for every conceivable ensemble, from guitar quartet to marching band. And no wonder—this is fun music, and we can't let only pianists have all the fun.

# SOLO PROGRAM #7
## BRAHMS: VARIATIONS ON A THEME BY PAGANINI
## BRAHMS: WALTZ, OP. 39, NO. 1
## BRAHMS: HUNGARIAN DANCE NO. 5

## JOHANNES BRAHMS (1833-1897)

No piano recital is complete without a piece by Johannes Brahms. Like the works of Liszt and Chopin, his piano music is difficult to play, but not because of virtuoso showmanship, which he loathed. Instead, its musical complexity is the challenge.

Brahms's piano works are luxuriant, crammed with an almost orchestral array of ideas. He could also be touchy about *how* his music was played. For instance, he scorned the use of placing metronome markings for his tempos. "Idiot!" he once shouted. "Do you think I want to hear my music always played at the same speed?!"

After three youthful sonatas, Brahms turned away from this archetype and embraced the theme-and-variations form. Some of his best works are of this type: *Variations on a Theme of Robert Schumann; Variations and Fugue on a Theme of Handel; Variations on an Original Theme; Variations on a Hungarian Song;* the huge *Variations on a Theme by Paganini* (chosen for our program); and the celebrated *Variations on a Theme of Haydn.* This last work was written for two pianos and later beautifully orchestrated by the composer.

The two volumes of Paganini variations are built on a simple melody by the violin virtuoso, Niccolo Paganini (1782-1840), whose notorious quote introduced this chapter. Paganini employed this theme to perform technical acrobatics; Brahms used it to create profound music.

Surely Brahms's most popular piano works are his sixteen *Waltzes.* As you listen to these, you'll hear the composer in his lighter moments. The now-familiar melodies have kept piano students and music-box makers busy for years.

Brahms's *Hungarian Dances* are also quite fashionable. I've chosen the especially popular number five for our program. Originally these dances were written for two pianos, but the composer later adapted many for piano solo—some even for orchestra. The themes are genuine Hungarian tunes, which Brahms didn't compose himself, but rather arranged with ingenius creativity. All are exciting, but the fire of number five makes it one of this composer's most popular works.

Brahms's solo literature for piano includes even more. Like Chopin before him, he personalized a number of musical forms and became their master. These include his *Ballades,* the *Rhapsodies,* the three books of *Klavierstucke* ("keyboard pieces"), the *Phantasien,* and my favorite, the three enchanting *Intermezzi.* Listen to them all when you can. You may have to learn a few new terms when you go to a Brahms piano recital, but it's worth it.

# DANCE MOVEMENTS FOUND IN CLASSICAL MUSIC

Throughout music history, composers have used dance forms to express their instrumental ideas, even though they realized there was no chance of anyone actually dancing to the music.

Yet these dance forms enable composers to create masterpieces. All have a distinctive rhythm and tempo, and most have a peculiar style that's recognizable to the listener.

Here are the principal dance forms:

*Allemande.* A German dance in a moderate to slow 4/4 meter. Very popular in the Baroque era, especially with Bach.

*Bolero.* If it weren't for Maurice Ravel's famous version of this dance, you may never have heard of it. It's of Spanish origin, in a slow 3/4 meter.

*Bourree.* A Baroque dance from France, in a lively 4/4 meter, and always preceded by an upbeat.

*Chaconne.* An unhurried and serious dance in 3/4 meter, usually in "theme and variation" form. Bach and Handel were its supreme exponents.

*Courante.* Literally, "running." A brisk Baroque dance in 3/4 meter.

*Gavotte.* Like its cousin the Bourree, this lively dance in 2/2 time is also from France. It usually begins on the second beat of the opening measure.

*Gigue.* Although popular throughout Europe in the Baroque era, this lively 6/8 dance actually began in the British Isles. It's the classical version of a "jig."

*Hornpipe.* Another import from England (Handel's are the best), this cheerful 4/4 dance has its origin in sailors' ditties.

*Landler.* A stately 3/4 dance from Austria, similar to the waltz. Schubert, as a faithful Viennese composer, wrote the most genuine and beautiful works of this form.

*Mazurka.* A Polish dance that Chopin used with great effect. It's always in 3/4 time, but with accents often on the second or third beat.

*Minuet.* The most celebrated of all dances in the Classical Era, it became the third movement of the standard symphony in a dignified 3/4 meter, until replaced by Beethoven with the faster "scherzo."

*Passacaglia.* A slow and weighty movement in 3/4, used in variation form like the Chaconne. Its classic use was by Bach, in his *Passacaglia in C Minor* for organ.

*Passepied.* A delicate French dance, usually in 6/8 meter.

*Polka.* A popular dance in 2/2 used by composers across Europe, though it originated as a Bohemian dance.

*Polonaise.* A favorite of the Polish composer Chopin, its roots are found in his country more than a century before his birth.

*Rigaudon:* From France, this vigorous dance in 4/4 meter also was popular with Baroque composers of other countries.

*Saraband.* In a stately 3/4 meter, this Spanish dance became the standard slow movement of the Baroque suite.

*Waltz.* Only the minuet has been able to compete with the waltz as the world's most popular dance. Especially in the nineteenth century, this 3/4 dance became the perfect vehicle for such

# SOLO PROGRAM #8
## DEBUSSY: SUITE BERGAMASQUE
## DEBUSSY: CHILDREN'S CORNER
## DEBUSSY: PRELUDES

### CLAUDE DEBUSSY (1862-1918)

As always, to represent France and the great Impressionists, we have Debussy. An excellent pianist, he never quite came to grips with the fact that the piano had hammers that had to strike strings. Debussy wanted a more fluid sound, and when he gave concerts he was hardly heard in the back of the hall. But his compositions for the piano are among the most colorful and exquisite in the repertoire, and they set the stage for the thousands of French works to follow from such illustrious composers as Maurice Ravel.

Debussy's youthful piano solos have become very popular, including the beautiful *Reverie*, the jazzy *Danse* and the lovely *Clair de Lune*—this last piece from his *Suite Bergamasque*. Whether *Clair de Lune* conjures up more visions of lunar luminescence than Beethoven's "Moonlight Sonata" has been debated. But what a beauty this is in any case. Unlike Debussy's later complexities, *Claire de Lune* is charmingly straightforward. The altered harmonies add just enough color to the simple melody—perfectly balanced, delicate, beautiful.

Another favorite of all ages is the set entitled the *Children's Corner*, playfully dedicated to the composer's daughter: "To my dear Chou-Chou, with tender apologies from her father for what is to follow." The movements are each wonderful pictures from a child's life, with such titles as *Serenade for the Doll, Snow Is Dancing* and *The Little Shepherd*. The dancing rhythms of the finale, *Golliwog's Cake-Walk,* will bring you out of your seat.

The true essence of Debussy's genius lies in his serious works, *Pour le Piano, Images* and the two volumes of *Preludes*. Each of the twenty-four preludes has its own character and shows a different side of Debussy's art. One of my favorites among them is the entrancing *La Cathedral engloutie* ("The Engulfed Cathedral"), which seems to engulf the listener with oceans of sound.

A true impressionist, Debussy had a passion for landscapes, as seen in his other preludes *Les Collines d'Anacapri* ("The Hills of Anacapri") and *Le Vent dans la Plaine* ("The Wind in the Plain"). This is music to create an atmosphere, to invoke the imagination. At a concert it might be well to close your eyes and ignore the work of the soloist, lest what you see should distract you from the mesmerizing music.

### VIOLIN LITERATURE

Many years ago at Carnegie Hall in New York City, the great violinist Fritz Kreisler was accompanied by Sergei Rachmaninov at the piano. In the middle of a piece, Kreisler had a sudden memory loss. He frantically whispered to Rachmaninov, "Where are we?"

Without missing a beat, the pianist replied, "In Carnegie Hall."

You may not be able to find nearby a concert by masters of that caliber, but you should be able to find a good violin recital; they're quite common. Violinists have it made; they play the best melodies in the orchestra and the string quartet, they have many concerti to choose from and their solo literature is equally excellent. It's as if composers haven't been satisfied with themselves until they've written at least one violin sonata.

Again, as with the piano literature, the great number of excellent choices forces us to be selective with our composers. And as with so many other genre, the best begins with Bach.

## SOLO PROGRAM #9
## BACH: SONATA FOR CLAVIER AND VIOLIN NO. 3 IN E
## BACH: PARTITA IN D MINOR
## MOZART: VIOLIN SONATA IN A MAJOR

### JOHANN SEBASTIAN BACH (1685-1750)

Bach wrote six sonatas for violin and clavier, and for the unaccompanied violin three sonatas and three partitas. The difference between his sonatas and partitas is simply that the latter are collections of specific dance movements, while the former contain abstract movements with names like "allegro," "adagio" or "presto." When the harpsichord is used with the violin, the effect is that of the trio-sonata we examined as a form of chamber music.

Of the six sonatas Bach composed, my favorite is the *Sonata for Clavier and Violin No. 3 in E,* which I've chosen for our program. You'll enjoy its jazzy fast movements and the delicate charm of its adagio movement.

Playing unaccompanied violin was very different in Bach's day, since the violin's bridge was flatter and the hair of the bow was looser. Thus it was somewhat easier to sustain two, three or even four strings simultaneously. On modern instruments this is nearly impossible. But the music is worth the struggle of accomplishing the impossible, and violinists continue to perform these amazing works.

The most celebrated unaccompanied work of all time is certainly Bach's *Partita in D Minor,* which has been transcribed for every instrument from guitar to harp. Each movement is a gem, but the famous "Chaconne" movement is such a tour de force that it's often heard as a separate solo in virtuoso concerts.

Speaking of older instruments, we should note the recent "original instruments" revival. Until the last decade or so, most people assumed that the most modern instruments and methods of playing were the best. No longer. "Early music" societies have now popularized the practice of performing and recording Baroque and even Classical music on the instruments of those periods.

Whether or not the result is actually closer to the composers' desire is debatable. But the sound is certainly interesting. You may like it, you may not; find a sample recording and decide for yourself.

## WOLFGANG AMADEUS MOZART (1756-1791)

Moving into the Classic Era, our next great violinist is Mozart, who was as much a prodigy on the violin as on the piano. In fact, of his thirty-one violin sonatas, the first four were written when he was only eight years old. (He waited until he was nine to compose the next six.)

Youthful genius shows through all his early works, and his speed of composition is startling. From a letter to his father we know that his *Sonata for Piano and Violin in G Major* was composed one night "between eleven and twelve."

Mozart's last three violin sonatas are his greatest, and his very last, the *Violin Sonata in A Major,* is a true masterpiece. Considering that similar compositions of his day were usually grand piano works with a negligible violin part added, Mozart's use of the two instruments as equals is quite innovative. The movements are well balanced between elegance and vivacity, and the exhilaration of the final movement demonstrates the joy of Mozart at its highest.

## SOLO PROGRAM #10
### BEETHOVEN: SONATA FOR PIANO AND VIOLIN NO. 5 IN F ("SPRING")
### BEETHOVEN: SONATA FOR PIANO AND VIOLIN NO. 9 IN A ("KREUTZER")
### BRAHMS: SONATA FOR PIANO AND VIOLIN NO. 3 IN D MINOR
### FRANCK: VIOLIN SONATA IN A MAJOR

## LUDWIG VAN BEETHOVEN (1770-1827)

The ten violin sonatas of Beethoven are a mix of early works written for money and sublime works written for all time. As you might guess, we're more interested in the latter. Two of this group are easy to remember since they, too, have nicknames.

The first is the popular "Spring Sonata" *(Sonata for Piano and Violin* No. 5 in F), which we've chosen for this program. In this work, you'll find that the ever-stormy Beethoven gives us a fresh and spontaneous gaiety, especially in the first and last movements. Even in this restrained side of his temperament, we can hear Ludwig's humor; the Scherzo contains such rhythmic oddities that you often can't tell whether the violin and piano are playing together or not.

One of Beethoven's most famous compositions is the "Kreutzer Sonata" *(Sonata for Piano and Violin* No. 9 in A). The composer dedicated it to the violinist Rodolphe Kreutzer, who ironically never even performed it. Its literary fame came when Leo Tolstoy wrote his renowned short story "The Kreutzer Sonata," in which Beethoven's dramatic music brings about the murder of a woman by her jealous husband.

Don't let Tolstoy scare you off; this is a grand piece. Even as you experience the frenzy of the last movement—a "tarantella," imitating the furious whirling Italian dance—you probably won't want to murder anyone; you'll want to grab someone's hand and dance.

## JOHANNES BRAHMS (1833-1897)

"You must not complain about the rain," wrote Brahms to a conductor. "It can be set very well to music, something I have tried to do along with spring in a violin sonata." He was referring to the first of his three great violin sonatas, often nicknamed *Regenlied* or "Rain Song."

Whether or not it reminds you of rain, it's a captivating sonata. The last movement uses a rhythmic theme from a Brahms song, also called Regenlied. The composer jokingly asked his publisher whether he could be sued for borrowing from his own music.

I've selected for our program Brahms's last work of this genre, the *Sonata for Piano and Violin* No. 3 in D Minor. This work is the zenith of Romanticism. The composer's friend Clara Schumann said the third movement is "like a beautiful girl frolicking with her lover. Then suddenly, in the midst of it all, a flash of deep passion, only to make way for sweet dalliance once more." What romantic imagination.

This piece is a must-hear. The adagio is Brahms at his impassioned best, and the grand finale makes this work the "Beethoven's Ninth" of violin sonatas.

## CESAR FRANCK (1822-1890)

And now for something completely different. After this spread of heavy monumental German music, we need a little French selection for a light dessert. The perfect finish: Franck's *Violin Sonata in A Major.* Composed when he was sixty-three, this is Franck's *only* sonata, and he put everything he had into it. Many consider it his finest work.

This violin piece has been transcribed for a number of other instruments, notably the flute. Listen for the cyclical themes—that is, related melodies that freely flow in and out of the different movements. Using them, Franck creates moods ranging from the lyrical delicacy of the opening to a later height of intense passion. Pure french, *mais oui.*

# CONCERT ETIQUETTE

*"What do I wear?"* Every town is different and every concert occasion is different, but until you learn the customs of your concert hall's audiences, dress conservatively and take note of the crowd around you. Today, concerts are more and more informal, and men's suits and women's best dresses are usually not necessary. Even ties are optional these days. Chamber music is equally informal, and outdoor concerts encourage jeans.

Nevertheless, at opening nights and gala events, evening gowns and tuxedos come out of the mothballs.

*"Can I bring children?"* Maybe, maybe not. It depends on the child's temperament and maturity. I've always believed that classical music is fun, but not the Saturday morning kind of fun. If your children can silently sit still through two hours of serious music, great! (Please introduce them to *my* kids.) Otherwise, do everyone a favor by getting a baby-sitter.

*"Where do I sit?"* Most concerts have assigned seating, so you need to decide where to sit when you buy your ticket. You want to be able to *see* and *hear* well, but each concert hall is designed differently. A simple rule of thumb: Go for the center. The center of the orchestra seats (those seats on the floor, not the balconies) are best, and so are the center seats of the lower balconies. But always ask advice from the box office; they know their particular hall and are usually happy to help.

*"What if I'm late?"* Never enter when live music is being played. Wait until that movement is over, then find your seats as quickly and inobtrusively as possible.

*"What if I have to leave early?"* Certainly, do *not* get up while music is being played. Wait until the movement or act is over and discretely slip out without disturbing others.

*"Can I talk during the performance?"* Not while music is being performed. Resist the urge; if you have to, write a note. In the superb acoustics of a modern concert hall, whispers can often be heard on the other side of the room. Be considerate of others, and save the conversation for the intermission.

*"When do I applaud?"* When in doubt, don't clap until everyone else does. More specifically: In multi-movement works, whether instrument or vocal...*don't* clap between the movements. Wait until the end of the composition; follow the program in front of you.

In opera you'll find exceptions. Although most applause comes at the end of each scene or act, if at any time a great singer sings a great aria, you're permitted to go wild. They love it!

Before the performance: Whenever an orchestra is present, you applaud separately for the entrance of the concertmaster (first violinist), then the conductor's entrance, and also the entrance of any soloists.

After the performance: Applaud when the final work is over, and keep applauding through the various exits and re-entrances and bows of conductor and soloists. Applaud after each encore, which will not be in your program. *Resist* the urge to sneak away and beat the crowd out of the parking lot.

## CELLO LITERATURE

Remember our discussion of the concerto? Once again we can't escape the emphasis on piano, violin and cello. You can find fabulous music for oboe, trumpet and even percussion recitals, mostly transcriptions of music originally for other instruments. But the masters chose their media judiciously. Not surprisingly, then, it's a lot easier to make a living today as a solo cellist than as a solo bassoonist.

## SOLO PROGRAM #11
### BACH: SONATA FOR VIOLA DA GAMBA NO. 1 IN G MAJOR
### BACH: SUITE FOR UNACCOMPANIED CELLO NO. 1 IN G MAJOR
### BEETHOVEN: SONATA FOR PIANO AND CELLO NO. 3 IN A MAJOR

### JOHANN SEBASTIAN BACH (1685-1750)

The cello repertoire is heavy on "the three B's." (Maybe someday that will be the "four B's," with Bach, Beethoven and Brahms being joined by the Beatles.) Once again we begin with J. S. Bach. He wrote three charming sonatas for an instrument that isn't played much anymore, the viola da gamba (*gamba* is the Italian word for "legs"). This was a sort of six-string fretted cello held up by your knees (try *that* sometime), and its music is usually now performed on the modern cello or viola. Bach's *Sonata for Viola da Gamba No. 1 in G Major* displays such resplendence and contrapuntal interest (that is, employing counterpoint) that you'll be glad it didn't suffer the same fate as its original instrument.

Next are the Bach *Unaccompanied Cello Suites.* Lofty, enigmatic, exalted—for the right feel, just picture the great cellist Pablo Casals late in his long life, quietly playing one of these. Like Bach's *Violin Partitas,* the *Cello Suites* are hard to play and sometimes difficult for the listener to get into. But once you relax and accustom yourself to the austere ambience of this genre, you'll find yourself mesmerized.

Our program starts with the first, *Suite for Unaccompanied Cello No. 1 in G Major.* This one is the most accessible, allowing you to enter into the mammoth caverns of Bach's never-ending creativity.

### LUDWIG VAN BEETHOVEN (1770-1827)

Every cellist bemoans the fact that neither Haydn nor Mozart wrote for cello and piano, but Beethoven makes up for this with his five outstanding sonatas. They're played in cello recitals everywhere, but the most acclaimed is surely the "Beethoven A" (that is, the *Sonata for Piano and Cello No. 3 in A Major),* selected for our program.

Strangely enough, Beethoven wrote on the manuscript of this joyful composition: "Amid tears and sorrow." Those words might describe the "Pathetique Piano Sonata" or the "Kreutzer Violin Sonata," but this cello work is full of animation. Perhaps he'd been recently rejected in love and wrote this to cheer himself up—who knows? In any case, from the nobility of the opening theme to its brilliant conclusion, this work sounds like Beethoven at his happiest.

SOLO PROGRAM #12
SCHUBERT: "ARPEGGIONE" SONATA IN A MAJOR
MENDELSSOHN: SONATA FOR PIANO AND CELLO NO. 2
IN D MAJOR
BRAHMS: SONATA FOR PIANO AND CELLO # 2 IN F MAJOR

## FRANZ SCHUBERT (1797-1828)

Ever heard of the "arpeggione"? The arpeggione (ar-pe-gee-OH-nee) was an instrument that went the way of the dinosaurs. Since it resembled a cello, the beautiful sonata that Schubert composed for the instrument is now firmly in the cello repertoire.

Although it doesn't seem virtuosic—showmanship was remote from Schubert's thinking—the work requires great skill since the cello lacks the extra strings of the arpeggione and finds itself here playing very high in intricate passages. But the work is profound in its Romanticism, beginning in a minor key and later breaking into the sunshine of A Major.

## FELIX MENDELSSOHN (1809-1847)

Liszt once called Felix Mendelssohn "Bach reborn." His friend Robert Schumann called Mendelssohn's first cello sonata "a sonata as beautiful and lucid as anything that has ever emerged from the hands of a great artist." High praise indeed, and for good reason.

Mendelssohn's second effort, the *Sonata for Piano and Cello No. 2 in D Major,* is even better; you'll find it in the repertoire of every concert cellist. As you listen, you'll discover that the composer's joyous energy is immediately established, and even the spooky pizzicatos of the second movement are calculated to bring a smile. Following the chorale-like slow movement, the finale explodes with alacrity that is sustained to the last note.

## JOHANNES BRAHMS (1833-1897)

Once again we must go to Brahms; if you don't like Brahms, you probably don't like music. But every music lover is fond of this old man, especially cellists. His sonatas are on almost every cello recital. The *Sonata for Piano and Cello No. 1 in E Minor* is rather temperamental: one moment stately, the next moment so thickly complex that the cellist has to fight even to be heard.

Brahms's *Sonata for Piano and Cello No. 2 in F Major*, chosen for our program, is pure beauty. The second movement proves that with Brahms, even a pizzicato melody can be dramatic. Following a classic "Allegro Passionato" movement, the finale charms us with its folk-like flavor.

## WORKS FOR TWO OTHER SOLO INSTRUMENTS YOU NEED TO KNOW

### SOLO PROGRAM #13
### BACH: SONATA FOR CEMBALO AND FLUTE IN B MINOR
### BRAHMS: SONATA FOR CLARINET AND PIANO IN E♭ MAJOR

*The Bach Flute Sonatas*

We can't leave solo literature without listening to two of the greatest solo wind compositions ever written. The first is a group of wonderful *Flute Sonatas* from J.S. Bach. The *Sonata for Cembalo and Flute in B Minor* (*cembalo* is an Italian word for *harpsichord*) ranks as the most famous, but you should get a CD set with all of them; each one is excellent.

The first movement of the B minor sonata is one of Bach's most expansive. Notice the ingenius use of mutual imitation between the melodies of the flutes and those of the keyboard. Sometimes the flute goes first and the keyboard echoes the theme; sometimes that process is reversed. Always the effect is amazing—a perfect blend of the emotionally beautiful and the intellectually interesting.

Bach also wrote an enchanting *Sonata for Unaccompanied Flute in A Minor*. We almost lost this work, thanks to Bach's excessive thriftiness. He scribbled all the little notes for it on a blank page of a violin sonata, and it was many years before musicologists discovered this work of profound genius.

*The Brahms Clarinet Works*

Late in life, Brahms met the great clarinetist Richard Muhlfeld. Within a few years he wrote for him two clarinet sonatas, as well as a clarinet trio and a clarinet quintet. Brahms called Muhlfeld the greatest wind player of his day, and he must have been outstanding to have inspired such interesting works.

As Bach is to flutists, Brahms is to clarinetists; they love him and love these late works. Both sonatas are often played in recital. My favorite, chosen for our program, is the *Sonata for Clarinet and Piano in E♭ Major*.

Remember how we said earlier that Brahms likes the "theme and variation" concept? Wait until you hear the last movement of this piece; the theme and six variations constitute one of his most beautiful efforts.

## OTHER SOLO INSTRUMENTS

Toward the end of our discussion of chamber music we mentioned performing transcriptions. That is, some ensembles arrange music from other ensembles to make it fit their own. The same is true for solo recitals. An oboist will play the Bach flute sonatas and a trombonist will play the Bach cello suites. Sometimes the composer even does the work for you; the Brahms clarinet sonatas we just discussed were transcribed for the viola by the composer—to the delight of every violist.

Indeed, two of the most popular recital instruments are the harp and the classical guitar. These folks love to play Bach, too, along with Beethoven, Schubert and the rest of the masters who, sadly enough, seldom or never composed for these instruments. Although some original music exists for every instrument, many recitals are almost entirely made up of transcriptions.

After all, no composer had the time to write for everything. Why should Mozart be unknown to guitarists, or Chopin to harpists?

Besides, transcriptions sometimes sound better than the original. Anyone who's ever heard the great guitarist Andreas Segovia play the famous Bach "Chaconne" knows that it sounds more suitable to a guitar than to the original violin. In fact, Brahms even arranged this work for the piano.

So the sky's the limit. Find a good solo recital this month to attend and note the program carefully. Whether using transcriptions or originals, a gifted performer will leave you spellbound.

## SOLO REPERTOIRE

*All works listed here, unless otherwise stated, are for solo keyboard, usually piano.*

### THE TOP 15
Bach
The Well-Tempered Clavier
Beethoven
Piano Sonata op. 13 in C Minor ("Pathetique")
Piano Sonata, op. 27, No.2 in C# Minor ("Sonata quasi una Fantasia," also called "Moonlight Sonata")
Sonata for Piano and Violin No. 9 in A "Kreutzer"
Brahms
Waltzes, op. 39P
Sonata for Piano and Violin No. 3 in D Minor
Chopin
Twenty-four Preludes
Polonaise, op. 53 in A-flat Major
Waltz, op. 64, No. 1, "Minute Waltz"

Debussy
Suite Bergamasque
Liszt
Sonata in B Minor
Mozart
Piano Sonata in C Major, K. 545
Ravel
Tombeau de Couperin
Schubert
Moments Musicale
Schumann
Carnaval

## The Top 50

Bach
 The Well-Tempered Clavier
 The Goldberg Variations
 Italian Concerto
 Sonata for Cembalo and Flute in B Minor
 Partita for Unaccompanied Violin in D Minor
 Suite for Unaccompanied Cello No. 1 in G Major
Bartok
 Mikrokosmos
Beethoven
 Piano Sonata, op. 13 in C Minor
  ("Pathetique")
 Piano Sonata, op. 27, No. 2 in C# Minor
  ("Sonata quasi una Fantasia," also called
  "Moonlight Sonata")
 Piano Sonata, op. 28 in D Major ("Pastoral
  Sonata")
 Piano Sonata, op. 53 in C Major ("Waldstein")
 Piano Sonata, op. 57 in F Minor ("Appassionata")
 "Fuer Elise" ("Piece in A Minor")
 Sonata for Piano and Violin No. 5 in F "Spring"
 Sonata for Piano and Violin No. 9 in A "Kreutzer"
Brahms
 Variations on a Theme by Paganini, Waltzes,
  op. 39
 Sonata for Piano and Violin No. 3 in D Minor
Chopin
 Twenty-four Preludes
 Etudes, op. 25
 Nocturne, op. 48, No. 1
 Fantasy Impromptu, op. 66
 Polonaise in A♭ Major, op. 53
 Mazurka, op. 24, No. 1
 Waltz, op. 64, No. 1, ("Minute Waltz")
 Piano Sonata in B Minor, op. 58

Debussy
 Suite Bergamasque
 Pour le Piano
 Children's Corner
 Preludes, vol. 1 and 2
Franck
 Violin Sonata in A Major
Ives
 Concord Sonata
Liszt
 Transcendental Etudes
 Annees de Pelerinage
 Sonata in B Minor
Mendelssohn
 Songs without Words
 Sonata for Piano and Cello No. 2 in D Major
Mozart
 Piano Sonata in C Major, K. 545
 Violin Sonata in A Major, K. 526
Mussorgsky
 Pictures at an Exhibition
Rachmaninov
 Prelude in C# Minor, op. 3, No. 2
Ravel
 Miroirs
 Tombeau de Couperin
 Pavane pour une Infante defunte
Satie
 Gymnopedies
Schubert
 Moments Musicals
 Piano Sonata in A Major, op. 120
Schumann
 Album for the Young
 Carnaval
 Papillons

*(Above) A caricature of the "piano-smashing" Liszt.*

*(Left) The Baroque period was a smorgasbord of ornamentation, as this grand Baroque organ illustrates.*

# 9

# EPILOGUE:
# WHERE DO WE GO FROM HERE?

---

*Music exists to elevate us as far as possible above everyday existence.*

—Gabriel Faure

I know what you're thinking. By now you're saying, "Okay, you've sold me. I recognize that there's a whole world of great classical music out there waiting for me. But what can I do to go beyond the good start I've made and get further into that world? Or better yet, how I can reshape *my* world to bring this wonderful music into it?"

There's a good strategy for doing just that, and it won't even cost you an arm and a leg. Nor will you have to give up your career and enroll in a music conservatory. In fact, these ideas can easily fit into your present lifestyle, and they'll more than pay for themselves with the happiness they add to your life.

Actually, I suggest three ways you can enjoy more fine music than you've ever thought possible: listening to radio; developing a personal library of recordings; and attending live concerts. Let's look more closely at each of these.

## 1. THE MIRACLE OF RADIO

You can't live at a concert hall, nor can you always have your stereo nearby. And even if you could, you wouldn't have time to make all the necessary selections to enjoy the best of classical music.

That's what the radio's for. Every major city has at least one classical radio station. (I live near Washington, D.C., and my radio can pick up four.) You need to find their frequencies on the radio dial (usually FM) and start listening right away. Simply check the arts and entertainment section of your local newspaper for listings. Or call someone you know who likes classical music, or even a music store or school.

Try the local yellow pages as well. Someone knows about your nearby classical radio stations. If nothing else works, get an FM radio, and slowly turn the dial until you hear something that sounds like Beethoven.

The classical radio station or stations you find will become important in your cultivation of musical enjoyment. Try keeping the radio on, in the background, all the time, or as often as is practically possible—during your meals, all day at the office, while exercising, in the car, even in the shower.

People sometimes ask me how I know so many hundreds of classical pieces. They think it must be from all those years in music school. But it's not. I've become familiar with much of that music from years of having the radio on throughout the day, day after day. Though it's usually in the background, when I want to pay attention, I can.

Think of the advantages. This way, I'm constantly learning. Since I have no control over what music the station will play, they often play a work with which I'm not familiar.

When I do hear something unfamiliar, I listen more carefully, and I always pay special attention when the piece is over. Then the announcer says something like, "We've been listening to Mahler's *Seventh Symphony,* played by the New York Philharmonic, and..." I've learned something new. Next time I hear this piece, it's a bit more familiar.

It's like a perpetual free education. Radio stations have an extensive CD library, so all day long they play thousands of works by hundreds of performers—all free to us. So easy, too. Simply have your radio pre-tuned to your station, and the greatest music in the world will be just a button-push away.

In fact, there are two times each day when classical music is especially beneficial. The first is when you wake up in the morning. So you need a clock-radio that lets you wake up to classical music. Then, instead of being startled each morning by a loud ring or buzzer, you can start the day with Haydn and Schubert. Your whole morning will be more relaxed.

Studies have shown the influence of what we listen to while we fall asleep as well, so I always set my clock-radio timer to play quietly thirty or forty minutes at bedtime. It soothes me and takes my mind off any worries. I know that people's sleep habits vary, but I think some needless tossing and turning could be avoided by a little restful Mendelssohn or Debussy.

I should also make a plug for the many wonderful concerts that are now offered on television, especially since the proliferation of cable channels. Like radio, it's free and effortless—plus you get the visual viewpoint as well. Check your local listings; I can usually find a symphony or an opera every week. TV doesn't work as well at the office (a good way to get fired) or in the car (a good way to get killed). So music lovers will always have a need for the radio.

With that in mind, get a radio and find your classical music station. They may even publish a programming guide available for a modest subscription price. With a guide you can know in advance what great pieces are in store for you each day. The easiest, cheapest and most educational method of learning classical music is at your fingertips.

## 2. YOUR VERY OWN RECORDED MUSIC

For hundreds of years before our own century, if you wanted to hear music you had to hear it live. With the advent of recorded music, audiences have multiplied from those sitting in a concert hall to the millions listening to music at this moment. Claude Debussy was one of the first to realize the magnitude of this newfangled invention: "The gramophone seems to me a marvelous instrument. Moreover, it assures music of a complete and meticulous immortality."

For those of you who want a bit of this immortality, you need a gramophone, or rather one of our more modern versions, the stereo. Since you'll want to plan some of the music you'll listen to in your home or office, rather than listening only to what the radio offers, you'll want to start a compact disc collection. Why CDs rather than audiocassettes or even those LP albums we've collected for so many years? I know how you must feel; I spent decades creating an outstanding LP collection, and now no one even sells classical LPs anymore. I've also had to start over, building a CD collection from scratch. But I know that it will be worth it for two reasons: sound quality and ease.

For great sound quality, nothing can compete with the CD. No needle scratching over a phonograph record or tape turning slowly in a cassette gives you the ultra-clarity of a laser beam silently gliding over a CD. And what ease. These little disks can contain over an hour's worth of music; they don't scratch, they don't get broken, they don't even melt when you leave them in the car on a hot summer day.

To be sure, cassette tapes are also easy to play, and I also recommend them. They don't have the perfect sound of a CD, but they're still convenient at times and less expensive too. They also have the advantage that you can use them to record something. Until they come out with an affordable CD that you can record yourself, cassette tapes will still be in use.

How do you get started collecting? To begin with, find out what *you* like. Do you want orchestral music, opera, chamber music, a little of everything?

If you're still unsure, buy collections. These can be either a composer's "greatest hits" or one of the many "everyone's favorites" classical music collections. I still remember my first such set, given to me in high school. If I live to be a hundred, whenever I hear Beethoven's *Fifth Symphony* or Schubert's "Death and the Maiden" String Quartet, I'll still remember being fascinated by my first big collection of scratchy albums.

Another approach to starting your CD stash is to combine your purchases with your concert attendance (more on this subject in a moment). Suppose, for example, that you're planning to attend a concert of the Beethoven "Emperor" Piano Concerto. First, run down to the local music store and pick up a recording of the work. This way, you'll prepare yourself to enjoy the concert more and you'll build your CD collection at the same time.

You might also want to join one of the many CD clubs advertised in newspapers and through direct mail. You know the kind: You buy several CDs for a penny at first, then agree to buy a new one each month at the full price. This way you're building up your collection on a regular basis, and they usually give you a good variety of CDs from which to choose.

There are several excellent companies in business. If you can't find an ad for one, call your local music store and ask them for recommendations.

What music should you buy? That's a good question, and everyone should have different answers. But to get started, consider the lists of the "top fifteen" compositions I've provided at the end of each chapter. You certainly don't have to purchase each of them, but any of these are unquestionably superb choices to add to your library. Of course, feel free at any time to acquire something on one of my larger lists as well, or any other great works you can find.

Which recording should you choose? That is, what do you do if you want the Bach *Brandenburg Concerti* and you find that your CD store has *eight* different recordings of this work by eight different orchestras? Not to worry. At this point, any will do. Later on, you may decide you prefer European orchestras to American, or recordings with the original instruments instead of modern ones, or even specific conductors, singers or instrumentalists.

But for now, getting into the music itself is the object. I suppose I could mention some of my favorite orchestras or artists, but such a list would immediately be dated. New artists are constantly appearing, and besides, you should soon develop your *own* preferences. Don't worry about getting a "bad" recording. For building a basic collection of CDs, *all* of the professional musicians who are on recordings will be more than adequate to fill your life with wonderful music.

Once you own a few of your own CDs, you can be much more particular about the music you want in your life. Here are a few examples to help you begin, and then your own imagination can take over:

1. A little earlier, I recommended a clock-radio to start and end the day with music. An even better choice is a clock-radio with a built-in cassette tape player. Then you can choose exactly which works to soothe you to sleep and which to wake you up. For instance, I love to fall asleep with the relaxing tones of Gregorian chant or medieval choruses. For waking up, there's nothing quite like the cheerfulness of Haydn and Mozart. Give it a try.

2. Another wonderful invention...the "walkman" style CD or cassette player. Small is beautiful. These light little gizmos allow you to listen to your favorite concerto or opera while you're working, exercising or jogging down the street. There are even classical exercise tapes available. Warning: While wearing tiny headphones you might not realize that you're singing loudly along with your favorite aria!

3. Employers: If you want happier, more productive workers, get rid of the junk background music you presently have piped in and replace it with Bach, Chopin and Brahms. You'll soon notice the difference; scores of studies confirm that classical music increases productivity. And please, if you have music played over your phone system while your customers are on hold, give them some great classical music. Some music lovers (like me) hang up (and cancel our orders) when we're attacked by the obnoxious "music" that blares on many phone systems.

4. Shop owners: Give your store a little class. Everyone who walks in your establishment will immediately sense a touch of elegance when Mozart plays in the background.

My wife and I have walked out of restaurants because of the nauseating sounds coming from their loudspeakers. Yet when we find an establishment playing Bach and Beethoven, we consciously give them our business and become regular customers. No doubt thousands of other music lovers have similar habits.

Classical music has power to cleanse, calm and stimulate the mind. Don't take my word for it, ask the Edmonton, Alberta police department. I recently read in the newspaper about a rough section in that Canadian town where the local police had for years been unsuccessful in eliminating drug pushers, prostitutes and other malefactors.

When nothing else worked, they set up huge outdoor loudspeakers and played classical music to the gangs. Within a month, the criminal elements completely disappeared.

Don't be discouraged if your music collection still looks rather small after several trips to the CD store. It takes time. Remember, find your favorites first, then start to expand. Soon each member of your private collection will be loved as an intimate friend. In the meantime, there's always the radio—plus the pleasure of live performances.

## 3. THE JOY OF LIVE PERFORMANCES

Whether you live in the eighteenth century or the twenty-first, the pinnacle of musical delight will always be the live concert. I don't care how perfect your speakers sound, there's simply no substitute for the experience of live sound created before your eyes. You can't attend every night, so there's certainly a place for recorded music. But if you want more happiness, exhilaration and sheer ecstasy in your life, attend more concerts.

How do you find out about these concerts? Here's how to get started:

Obviously, your options depend to a great extent on where you live. New York City has thousands more concerts than Frog Jump, Tennessee (well, more *classical* concerts, anyway). But I've found brass quintets in the mountains of New Hampshire and string quartets in the hills of North Carolina. A friend in a touring orchestra recently performed for the Eskimo population of Barrow, Alaska—the northernmost point of the United States. And they loved the music.

Wherever you live, great music is being performed on either a professional or an amateur level. But you need to know what's out there and where to find it.

*What's Out There?*

Here's a list of the most common types of performances and their settings:

### ORCHESTRA

*Professional symphony orchestras*—found in major concert halls; every major city has at least one.

*Chamber orchestras*—in concert halls or churches.

*Outdoor concerts*—becoming more and more popular, enjoyed with picnic suppers; often free.

*College orchestras*—wherever there's a college music department; performances are free and usually on campus.

*Community orchestras*—often sound quite good, usually free and performing in community centers or schools.

*Youth orchestras*—fun to support and fun to hear, usually free and performing in schools.

*Bands*—some excellent band performances also can be found at the college, community and school levels, usually free.

### CHORAL

*Professional chorus and orchestra performances*—in either concert halls or large churches.

*Community choruses with keyboard accompaniment*—usually free and performing in churches.

*College and high school choruses*—these can be fabulous; usually free and performing in schools.

*Madrigal groups and chamber choirs*—usually free and performing in schools or churches.

*Church choir performances*—usually free and performing in churches.

## CONCERTO

These appear in the same settings as orchestra music. An outstanding instrumental soloist will sometimes tour doing solo recitals and also concerti with the local orchestra. Having a world-class soloist in town for a concerto can be the climax of the orchestra's season.

## OPERA

*Professional opera companies*—either your local company if your city is large enough, or one of the larger companies that tour.

*College opera productions*—performances on campus; that's where all those professional opera stars came from.

*Community opera productions*—often "light opera" and can be marvelous; performances usually found in community theaters or schools, sometimes free.

## CHAMBER

*Professional chamber ensembles*—usually touring string quartets or piano trios; performances in concert halls or recital halls.

*Local chamber ensembles*—performances in recital halls, schools or churches, often free.

*College chamber ensembles*—performances usually free and on campus.

## SONG

*Professional song recitalists*—usually touring with an accompanist, sometimes appearing with the local orchestra; performances in concert halls or recital halls.

*Local or college faculty recitalists*—free performances in recital halls, schools or churches.

*Student recitalists*—free performances in recital halls, schools, churches or teachers' homes.

## SOLO

*Professional soloists*—usually touring with an accompanist, sometimes appearing in a concerto with the local orchestra; performances in concert halls or recital halls.

*Local or college faculty soloists*—free performances in recital halls, schools or churches.

*Student recitals*—performances in recital halls, schools, churches or teachers' homes, usually free.

## BALLET

In this book we've chosen not to treat the music written for ballet as a separate unit, since the music itself is usually performed (without dance) on the concert stage. Nevertheless, dance and music are obviously related and I encourage you to enjoy the beauty of ballet performances. You'll not only appreciate the music; you'll enter into the magnificent world of dance.

*How to Locate Performances*

1. Look in the local newspaper for information. Most papers have an arts and entertainment section, especially on the weekends, where you'll find:
   - *advertisements*—Most major concerts will place ads in your newspaper, some well in advance.
   - *calendars*—At least once each week, most newspapers list all upcoming concerts, including free ones.
   - *feature articles*—A great way to see behind the scenes, such as when a touring soloist is interviewed.
2. Listen to the radio and watch TV for information.
   - *advertisements*—Again, be alert for the ads; be ready to jot down a phone number for more information.
   - *public service announcements (PSAs)*—Radio stations often read lists of upcoming concerts, including many free ones.
   - *interviews*—Even better than a newspaper article because you get to hear the performer speak.
3. Get on mailing lists. The best way to get early notification of performances in your area is to get on the mailing lists of performing organizations. Simply call your local concert hall, orchestra, chamber ensemble(s), music school, and so on, asking to be placed on their mailing lists. They'll be glad to oblige; selling tickets is how they exist.
4. Buy a subscription. To get the best seats, you may want to buy a subscription—that is, season tickets for a series of concerts. This is advantageous once you determine which type of music you want to explore.

Suppose you are after orchestra music this year. Call the local symphony orchestra and order some season tickets. Now your seats are reserved all year, and you have a method to your concert-going. You'll get first notice of future events and you'll even make new friends; other subscribers will consistently sit near you.

5. Check with music schools and the music departments of universities. If you live anywhere near a college with a music department, there are hidden treasures on campus you should know about. Every music major—both instrumentalists and singers—has to give recitals.

Since the students work months on these concerts, many of them are outstanding, yet few are well advertised. Even the college orchestra and chamber ensemble concerts are often unannounced to the general public. Call the main office of your local music department and ask about upcoming concerts. You'll find wonderful variety—everything from percussion ensembles to innovative works by student composers. And most are free.

6. Seek out music teachers and amateur music groups. Suppose you live in a rural setting where none of these organizations are nearby. I guarantee that there's at least one music teacher in the vicinity. Thousands of teachers require their millions of students to perform recitals, and they'd be delighted for you to attend.

Sometimes you may also come across amateur chamber groups, such as the four computer hackers who meet every week to play string quartets. They'd love to have an audience. All you have to do is ask.

For that matter, one of the most interesting ways to experience live music is not at the performance itself, but in rehearsals. Many of the concert situations we've described occasionally have open rehearsals that are not only entertaining but educational. Perhaps the conductor will behave and not scream too loudly at the performers. And if he or she does, that will only make it more entertaining for you.

## OTHER WAYS TO CULTIVATE YOUR LOVE OF MUSIC

In addition to radio, recordings and live concerts, you can dig deeper into classical music in other ways, especially once you determine which type of music you want to highlight.

For instance, you can fill your bookcases with a host of new titles on the subject. Thousands of wonderful books are in print that deal with every aspect of musical life.

A good start is to collect biographies of your favorite composers. (See the bibliography in the back of this book for suggestions.) Then, branch out to music histories, books on your favorite genre (opera, chamber music, or whatever), even books of musical anecdotes. They all make for great reading, and your appreciation of the music will skyrocket.

There are even music-lovers' magazines to which you can subscribe. Begin with a general periodical such as *Ovation,* then move to a magazine that covers your specific preferences. Opera buffs love *Opera News,* while my cellist wife enjoys *Strings.* It's fun to read about the latest developments in music, and the interviews with your favorite performers are fascinating.

The sky's the limit. The important thing is to be individual in your tastes and your musical habits. Just because your family all enjoys singing in choirs doesn't mean that you can't become a chamber music fan. Try it all, find your focus and go for it.

Music is here to love. I hope your musical odyssey fills your world with a new and extraordinary joy. Spend your life learning to love it.

# 10

# A LIFETIME OF LISTENING: YOUR FIRST THOUSAND PIECES

*Music is enough for a lifetime, but a lifetime is not enough for music.*

—Sergei Rachmaninov

Since there's so much great music waiting for you, I want to give you a master list of masterpieces—a thousand works or so—to keep you joyfully listening for years to come. This list may also help you build your CD collection and plan your concert schedule.

This master list brings together the lists that have appeared at the end of previous chapters—what I would consider the top one hundred and fifty works for each of the seven genres of music we've discussed. To make it an even thousand, I've also added fifty "extras" that didn't quite fit into the other categories. Like all musical lists, these selections are sometimes a bit arbitrary, and my personal tastes are obviously revealed. In any case, I depended on two basic criteria in selection: the composition's popularity (frequency of performance) and its importance in music history.

Consult these lists occasionally to keep you well-rounded. For instance, maybe you've been hearing a lot of opera lately and it's been a long time since you heard a good concerto. Find one that's new to you. Or maybe you've been indulging in Baroque music almost exclusively and you need to check out the twentieth century for a while. Scan the lists and find yourself a new musical adventure.

Whatever you do, find the music you *love*. Education is wonderful, but ultimately, music isn't here to make us smarter. It's here to give us more pleasure, to encourage our souls, to cultivate our love of the beautiful, to help us experience deeper feelings and the sensitivities of the composer and the performer.

For that reason, if you're not enjoying a certain work, and you've given it a fair chance to captivate you, forget it and move on to some music you can embrace. Happily, the world of classical music is *vast*. There's plenty for all of us. Explore, discover, cherish, savor and explore again.

# THE TOP 150 ORCHESTRAL WORKS

## ALBENIZ

Suite Espanola

## BACH

Orchestra Suite No. 1
Orchestra Suite No. 2
Orchestra Suite No. 3
Orchestra Suite No. 4

## BARTOK

Concerto for Orchestra

## BEETHOVEN

Symphony No. 1
Symphony No. 2
Symphony No. 3 ("Eroica")
Symphony No. 4
Symphony No. 5
Symphony No. 6 ("Pastoral")
Symphony No. 7
Symphony No. 8
Symphony No. 9 ("Choral")
Leonore Overture No. 3
Egmont Overture

## BERLIOZ

Symphonie Fantastique
Roman Carnival Overture

## BERNSTEIN

Symphony No. 1 ("Jeremiah")
Symphony No. 2
   ("The Age of Anxiety")
Overture to Candide
Fancy Free

## BIZET

Symphony in C

Borodin
Symphony No. 2

## BRAHMS

Symphony No. 1
Symphony No. 2
Symphony No. 3
Symphony No. 4
Variations on a Theme of Haydn
Academic Festival Overture

## BRITTEN

Young People's Guide to the Orchestra
Sinfonia da Requiem

## BRUCKNER

Symphony No. 4 ("Romantic")
Symphony No. 8
Symphony No. 9

## COPLAND

Appalachian Spring
A Lincoln Portrait

## DE FALLA

The Three-Cornered Hat

## DEBUSSY

Prelude to the Afternoon of the Faun
Nocturnes
La Mer
Images

## DVORAK

Slavonic Dances
Symphony No. 6
Symphony No. 8
Symphony No. 9
   ("From the New World")

## ELGAR

Enigma Variations
Pomp and Circumstance Marches

## FRANCK

Symphony in D Minor

## GERSHWIN

An American in Paris

Rhapsody in Blue

## GRANADOS

Intermezzo

## GRIEG

Peer Gynt Suites

## HANDEL

Water Music

Royal Fireworks Music

## HAYDN

Symphony No. 45 ("Farewell")

Symphony No. 83 ("The Chicken")

Symphony No. 94 ("Surprise")

Symphony No. 100 ("Military")

Symphony No. 101 ("Clock")

Symphony No. 103 ("Drum Roll")

Symphony No. 104 ("London")

## HINDEMITH

Mathis der Maler

## HOLST

The Planets

## IVES

Three Places in New England

The Unanswered Question

Holidays Symphony

## LISZT

Les Preludes

## MAHLER

Symphony No. 1 ("The Titan")

Symphony No. 2 ("Resurrection")

Symphony No. 4

Symphony No. 5

Symphony No. 8
   ("Symphony of a Thousand")

Symphony No. 9

## MENDELSSOHN

Symphony No. 2 ("Hymn of Praise")

Symphony No. 3 ("Scotch")

Symphony No. 4 ("Italian")

Symphony No. 5 ("Reformation")

Midsummer Night's Dream Overture

Fingal's Cave Overture

## MOZART

Symphony No. 31 ("Paris")

Symphony No. 35 ("Haffner")

Symphony No. 36 ("Linz")

Symphony No. 38 ("Prague")

Symphony No. 40

Symphony No. 41 ("Jupiter")

A Little Night Music

## MUSSORGSKY/RAVEL

Pictures at an Exhibition

## NIELSEN

Symphony No. 2
   ("The Four Temperaments")

## PROKOVIEV

Classical Symphony

Symphony No. 5

Peter and the Wolf

## RACHMANINOFF

Symphony No. 2

Symphonic Dances

## RAVEL

Daphnis and Chloe, Suite No.2

Bolero

Mother Goose Suite

Le Tombeau de Couperin

## RESPIGHI

The Pines of Rome
Ancient Airs and Dances
Rimsky-Korsakov
Scheherazade
Russian Easter Overture
Saint-Saens
Symphony No. 3 ("Organ")
Carnival of the Animals

## SCHOENBERG

Transfigured Night
Five Pieces for Orchestra

## SCHUBERT

Symphony No. 4 ("Tragic")
Symphony No. 5
Symphony No. 8 ("Unfinished")
Symphony No. 9 ("The Great")

## SCHUMANN

Symphony No. 1 ("Spring")
Symphony No. 3 ("Rhenish")
Symphony No. 4
Manfred Overture

## SHOSTAKOVICH

Symphony No. 4
Symphony No. 5
Symphony No. 7 ("Leningrad")

## SIBELIUS

Finlandia

## SMETANA

The Moldau

## STRAUSS, J.

Blue Danube Waltz

## STRAUSS, R.

Till Eulenspiegel's Merry Pranks
Also Sprach Zarathustra
Ein Heldenleben
Death and Transfiguration
Don Juan
Don Quixote

## STRAVINSKY

The Firebird
Petrushka
The Rite of Spring
Symphony in C

## TCHAIKOWSKY

Symphony No. 2 ("Little Russian")
Symphony No. 4
Symphony No. 5
Symphony No. 6 ("Pathetique")
Nutcracker Suite
Romeo and Juliet Overture
1812 Overture
Marche Slav
Sleeping Beauty
Swan Lake
Vaughan Williams
Fantasia on a Theme by Thomas Tallis
Symphony No. 1 ("Sea Symphony")
Symphony No. 2 ("A London
    Symphony")

## WAGNER

Tannhauser Overture
The Mastersinger Overture
The Flying Dutchman Overture
Lohengrin Overture
Tristan und Isolde Prelude
Siegfried Idyll

# THE TOP 150
# CHORAL WORKS

## BACH

Magnificat

Mass in B Minor

Jesu meine Freude

Komm, Jesu, komm

Christmas Oratorio

Passion According to St. John

Passion According to St. Matthew

Wir danken dir, Gott, wir danken dir
(Cantata No. 29)

Ein' feste Burg ist unser Gott
(Cantata No. 80)

Jesus schlaft, was soll ich hoffen
(Cantata No. 81)

Gottes Zeit ist die allerbeste Zeit
(Cantata No. 106)

Wachet auf, ruft uns die Stimme
(Cantata No. 140)

Mer hahn en neue Oberkeet
(Cantata No. 212 - "Peasant
Cantata")

Schweigt stille, plaudert nicht
(Cantata No. 211 - "Coffee
Cantata")

## BEETHOVEN

Christ on the Mount of Olives

Mass in C Major

Missa Solemnis

## BERLIOZ

L'Enfance du Christ

Requiem

Te Deum

## BLOCH

Sacred Service

## BRAHMS

Ave Maria

Deutsches Requiem

Motet (Op. 110)

Alto Rhapsody

Lieberslieder Waltzes

Triumphlied

## BRITTEN

A Ceremony of Carols

Hymn to St. Cecilia

Rejoice in the Lamb

St. Nicolas

## BRUCKNER

Mass in E Minor

Mass in F Minor

Te Deum

Psalm 150

## BUXTEHUDE

In Dulci Jubilo

Magnificat in D

## BYRD

Ave verum

Psalmes, Sonets and Songs

## CARISSIMI

Jephtha

## CHERUBINI

Requiem Mass in C Minor

## DELIUS

Requiem

## DUBOIS

Seven Last Words of Christ

## DVORAK

Requiem
Stabat Mater
Te Deum

## ELGAR

King Olaf
The Apostles
The Dream of Gerontius

## FAURE

Messe de Requiem

## FRANCK

Les Beatitudes
Redemption

## GIBBONS

This is the Record of John

## HANDEL

Coronation Anthem
Dixit Dominus
Belshazzar
Esther
Israel in Egypt
Jephtha
Judas Maccabaeus
La resurrezione
Messiah
Samson
Saul
Solomon
Susanna
Theodora
Brockes' Passion
St. John
Te Deum
Christmas Cantata

## HAYDN

Harmoniemesse
Paukenmesse ("Missa in tempore belli")
Schopfungsmesse
Theresienmesse
The Creation
The Seasons
Lord Nelson Mass
Te Deum

## HAYDN, MICHAEL

Missa Brevis

## HOLST

Hymn of Jesus

## HONEGGER

Jeanne d'Arc au Bucher
King David

## JANACEK

Festliche Messe

## KODALY

Psalmus Hungaricus

## LASSUS

Magnificat

## LISZT

Christus
Coronation Mass
The Legend of the Holy Elizabeth

## MENDELSSOHN

Elijah
Loreley
St. Paul

## MILHAUD

Service Sacree
Monteverdi
Laetatus sum

## MADRIGALS

Messa a 4 voci
Vespers

## MOUSSORGSKY

The Destruction of Sennacheraib

## MOZART

Missa Brevis (K.192)
Coronation Mass (K.317)
Mass in C minor (K.427)
"Organ-solo" Mass (K.259)
Ave Verum Corpus
Requiem
Vesperae de Confessore
Davidde penitente

## ORFF

Carmina Burana

## PALESTRINA

Missa L'homme arme'
Missa Papae Marcello
Stabat Mater
Tu es Petrus

## PENDERECKI

Passion According to St. Luke

## PERGOLESI

Stabat Mater

## POULENC

Mass in G

## PURCELL

Blessed is He that Considereth the poor
Hail, Bright Cecelia
Rejoice in the Lord

## REGER

Palm-Sunday morning

## SAINT-SAENS

Messe Solennelle

## SCARLATTI

Christmas Cantata

## SCHOENBERG

Gurre-Lieder
A Survivor from Warsaw

## SCHUBERT

Mass in A♭
Mass in B♭
Mass in C
Mass in E♭
Mass in F
Mass in G
Psalm XCII
Song of Miriam
Stabat Mater

## SCHUTZ

Passion according to St. Luke
Passion according to St. Matthew
Resurrection Oratorio
Seven last words

## SIBELIUS

Songs from Kalevala

## STRAVINSKY

Cantata
Pater Noster
Mass
Symphony of Psalms

## TCHAIKOVSKY

Legend

## VAUGHAN WILLIAMS

Mass in G minor
O vos omnes

## VERDI

Ave Maria
Requiem
Stabat Mater
Te Deum

## VICTORIA

Ave Maria

## VIVALDI

Gloria

## WALTON

Belshazzar's Feast

# THE TOP 150 CONCERTI

## BACH

Brandenburg Concerto No. 1 in
F Major (oboe and violin piccolo)
Brandenburg Concerto No. 2 in
F Major (flute, oboe, trumpet
and violin)
Brandenburg Concerto No. 3 in
G Major (strings - no soloists)
Brandenburg Concerto No. 4 in
G Major (two flutes and violin)
Brandenburg Concerto No. 5 in
D Major (harpsichord)
Brandenburg Concerto No. 6 in
B♭ Major (solo string groups)
Harpsichord Concerto No. 1 in
D Minor
Harpsichord Concerto No. 5 in
F Minor
Concerto for Two Harpsichords in
C Major
Concerto for Four Harpsichords in
A Minor

Violin Concerto No. 1 in A Minor
Violin Concerto No. 2 in E Major
Concerto for Two Violins in D Minor

## BARBER

Piano Concerto, op. 38
Violin Concerto, op. 14
Capricorn Concerto for Flute, Oboe,
Trumpet and Orchestra

## BARTOK

Piano Concerto No. 2
Piano Concerto No. 3
Violin Concerto No. 2
Viola Concerto

## BEETHOVEN

Piano Concerto No. 1 in C Major
Piano Concerto No. 2 in B♭ Major
Piano Concerto No. 3. in C Minor
Piano Concerto No. 4 in G Major
Piano Concerto No. 5 in E♭ Major
Violin Concerto in D Major, op. 61
Concerto for Violin, Cello and Piano
in C Major

## BERG

Violin Concerto

## BERLIOZ

Harold in Italy, for Viola and Orchestra

## BLOCH

Violin Concerto
"Schelomo" for Cello and Orchestra

## BOCCHERINI

Cello Concerto in B♭ Major

## BRAHMS

Piano Concerto No. 1 in D Minor
Piano Concerto No. 2 in B♭ Major
Violin Concerto in D Major

Concerto for Violin and Cello in
A Minor

**BRUCH**

Violin Concerto No. 1 in G Minor
Scottish Fantasy for Violin and
Orchestra
Kol Nidrei, for Cello and Orchestra

**BUSONI**

Piano Concerto
Violin Concerto in D Major

**CHOPIN**

Piano Concerto No. 1 in E Minor
Piano Concerto No. 2 in F Minor

**CRESTON**

Concerto for Trombone

**DEBUSSY**

Dances Sacrees et Profanes, for Harp
and Orchestra

**DELIUS**

Violin Concerto

**DITTERSDORF**

Concerto for Double Bass In E♭ Major

**DVORAK**

Piano Concerto in G Minor
Violin Concerto in A Minor
Cello Concerto in B Minor

**ELGAR**

Violin Concerto in B Minor
Cello Concerto in E Minor

**FAURE**

Elegie, for Cello and Orchestra

**GERSHWIN**

Concerto in F, for Piano and Orchestra

**GLAZUNOV**

Alto Saxophone Concerto
Violin Concerto in A Minor

**GRIEG**

Piano Concerto in A Minor

**HANDEL**

Organ Concerto in B♭ Major,
op. 7, no. 6
Concerto for Harp in B♭ Major

**HAYDN**

Piano Concerto in D Major
Cello Concerto No. 1 in C Major
Cello Concerto No. 2 in D Major
Trumpet Concerto in E♭ Major

**HINDEMITH**

Viola Concerto, op. 36, no. 4

**IBERT**

Concertino da Camera, for Alto
Saxophone and Orchestra

**KHATCHATURYAN**

Piano Concerto
Violin Concerto

**LALO**

Cello Concerto

**LISZT**

Piano Concerto No. 1 in E♭ Major
Piano Concerto No. 2 in A Major

**MARTINU**

Violin Concerto No. 2

**MENDELSSOHN**

Piano Concerto No. 1 in G Minor
Piano Concerto No. 2 in D Minor
Violin Concerto in E Minor

## MOZART

Piano Concerto No. 14 in E♭ Major,
  K. 449

Piano Concerto No. 17 in G Major,
  K. 453

Piano Concerto No. 20 in D Minor,
  K. 466

Piano Concerto No. 21 in C Major,
  "Elvira Madigan," K. 467

Piano Concerto No. 22 in E♭ Major, K.
  482

Piano Concerto No. 23 in A Major,
  K. 488

Piano Concerto No. 24 in C Minor,
  K. 491

Piano Concerto No. 25 in C Major,
  K. 503

Piano Concerto No. 26 in D Major,
  K. 537

Piano Concerto No. 27 in B♭ Major, K.
  595

Concerto for Two Pianos in E♭ Major,
  K. 365

Violin Concerto No. 3 in G Major,
  K. 216

Violin Concerto No. 4 in D Major,
  K. 218

Violin Concerto No. 5 in A Major,
  K. 219

Clarinet Concerto in A Major, K. 622

Bassoon Concerto in B♭ Major, K. 191

Flute Concerto in G Major, K. 313

Oboe Concerto in C Major, K. 314

Horn Concerto No. 1 in D Major,
  K. 412

Horn Concerto No. 2 in E♭ Major,
  K. 417

Horn Concerto No. 3 in E♭ Major,
  K. 447

Horn Concerto No. 4 in E♭ Major,
  K. 495

Concerto for Flute and Harp in
  C Major, K. 299

Sinfonia Concertante for Violin and
  Viola in E♭ Major, K. 364

## NIELSEN

Violin Concerto

Clarinet Concerto

Flute Concerto

## PAGANINI

Violin Concerto No. 1 in D Major, op.
  1, no. 6

Violin Concerto No. 2 in B Minor, op.
  2, no. 7 ("La Chochette")

## PISTON

Viola Concerto

## POULENC

Concert Champetre (Rustic Concerto)
  for Harpsichord and Orchestra

Concerto in G Minor for Organ,
  Strings and Timpani

## PROKOFIEV

Piano Concerto No. 3 in C Major

Piano Concerto No. 5 in G Major

Violin Concerto No. 2 in G Minor

Symphony Concertante, for Cello
  and Orchestra

## RACHMANINOV

Piano Concerto No. 1 in F# Minor

Piano Concerto No. 2 in C Minor

Piano Concerto No. 3 in D Minor

Rhapsody on a Theme of Paganini, for
Piano and Orchestra

## RAVEL

Piano Concerto in G Major

Piano Concerto in D Major for the Left
Hand

## RODRIGO

Concierto de Aranjuez, for Guitar and
Orchestra

## SAINT-SAENS

Piano Concerto No. 2 in G Minor

Cello Concerto No. 1 in A Minor

Violin Concerto No. 3 in B Minor

## SCHOENBERG

Violin Concerto

Piano Concerto

## SCHUMANN

Piano Concerto in A Minor

Cello Concerto in A Minor

Violin Concerto in D Minor

## SCRIABIN

Piano Concerto in F# Minor

## SHOSTAKOVITCH

Concerto No. 1 for Piano in C Minor

Concerto No. 1 for Violin in A Minor

Cello Concerto in E♭ Major

## SIBELIUS

Violin Concerto in D Minor

## STRAUSS

Horn Concerto No. 1 in E♭ Major

Horn Concerto No. 2 in E♭ Major

Oboe Concerto in D Major

## STRAVINSKY

Violin Concerto in D Major

Ebony Concerto

## TCHAIKOVSKY

Piano Concerto No. 1 in B♭ Major

Violin Concerto in D Major

Variations on a Rococo Theme, for
Cello and Orchestra

## VAUGHAN WILLIAMS

The Lark Ascending, for Violin and
Orchestra

Concerto for Tuba

## VILLA-LOBOS

Guitar Concerto

## VIVALDI

The Four Seasons (for violin),
op. 8 (no. 1-4)

Bassoon Concerto in E Minor, op. 137

Flute Concerto in E Minor, op. 10,
no. 3 ("Bullfinch")

Oboe Concerto in F Major, op. 306

Concerto for Two Cellos in G Minor,
op. 411

## WALTON

Viola Concerto

## WEBER

Piano Concerto No. 1 in C Major

Clarinet Concerto No. 1 in F Minor

Bassoon Concerto in F Major

# THE TOP 150 OPERAS

## BARBER
Vanessa

## BARTOK
Bluebeard's Castle

## BEETHOVEN
Fidelio

## BELLINI
I Puritani
La Sonnambula
Norma

## BERLIOZ
Les Troyens
Damnation of Faust

## BERG
Lulu
Wozzeck

## BIZET
Carmen
The Pearl Fishers

## BOITO
Mefistofele

## BORODIN
Prince Igor

## BRITTEN
Midsummer Night's Dream
Billy Budd
The Turn of the Screw
Albert Herring
Peter Grimes

## CATALANI
La Wally

## CHARPENTIER
Louise

## CILEA
Adriana Lecouvreur

## CIMAROSA
The Secret Marriage

## DEBUSSY
Pelleas et Melisande

## DONIZETTI
Don Pasquale
La Fille du Regiment
La Favorita
Lucia di Lammermoor
The Elixir of Love

## DVORAK
Rusalka

## FALLA
La Vida Breve

## FLOTOW
Martha

## GERSHWIN
Porgy and Bess

## GIORDANO
Andrea Chenier
Fedora

## GLINKA
Russlan and Ludmilla
A Life for the Czar

## GLUCK
Armide
Alceste
Orfeo ed Euridice

## GOUNOD

Faust
Romeo and Juliet

## HANDEL

Julius Caesar
Semele
Rinaldo

## HUMPERDINCK

Hansel und Gretel

## JANACEK

The Cunning Little Vixen

## LEONCAVALLO

Pagliacci

## LULLY

Alceste
Acis et Galatee

## MASCAGNI

Cavalleria Rusticana
L'Amico Fritz

## MASSENET

Manon
Le Cid
Thais
Werther

## MENOTTI

The Consul
The Telephone
The Saint of Bleeker Street
Amahl and the Night Visiters

## MEYERBEER

L'Africaine
Le Prophete
Les Huguenots
Dinorah

## MONTEMEZZI

L'Amore dei Tre Re

## MONTEVERDI

Orfeo
Arianne
L'Incoronazione di Poppea

## MOORE

The Ballad of Baby Doe

## MOZART

Cosi Fan Tutte
Don Giovanni
Idomeneo
La Clemenza di Tito
The Impresario
The Abduction from the Seraglio
The Magic Flute
The Marriage of Figaro

## MUSSORGSKY

Boris Godounov

## NICOLAI

The Merry Wives of Windsor

## OFFENBACH

Orpheus in the Underworld
The Tales of Hoffmann

## PERGOLESI

La Serva Padrona

## PONCHIELLI

La Gioconda

## POULENC

The Dialogues of the Carmelites

## PROKOFIEV

The Love of Three Oranges

## PUCCINI

Gianni Schicchi
Il Tabarro
La Boheme
La Fanciulla del West
La Rondine
Madame Butterfly
Manon Lescaut
Suor Angelica
Turandot
Tosca

## PURCELL

Dido and Aeneas

## RAMEAU

Hippolyte

## RAVEL

L'heure Espagnole
L'Enfant et les Sortileges

## RIMSKY-KORSAKOV

Le Coq d'Or
The Czar's Bride
The Snow Maiden

## ROSSINI

L'Italiana in Algeri
La Cenerentola
Semiramide
The Barber of Seville
William Tell

## SAINT-SAENS

Samson et Dalila

## SCHOENBERG

Moses and Aaron

## SMETANA

The Bartered Bride

## STRAUSS, J.

Die Fledermaus
The Gypsy Baron

## STRAUSS, R.

Arabella
Ariadne auf Naxos
Der Rosenkavalier
Elektra
Salomé

## STRAVINSKY

The Rake's Progress
Le Rossignol
Oedipus Rex

## TCHAIKOVSKY

Eugene Onegin
The Queen of Spades

## THOMAS

Mignon

## THOMPSON

The Mother of Us All

## VERDI

Aida
A Masked Ball
Don Carlo
Falstaff
Il Trovatore
I Vespri Siciliani
La Forza del Destino
La Traviata
Luisa Miller
Macbeth
Nabucco
Rigoletto
Otello
Simon Boccanegra

## WAGNER

The Ring of the Nibelungs
  (4 opera series)
    Das Rheingold
    Die Walkure
    Siegfried
    Gotterdammerung
Die Meistersinger
Lohengrin
Parsifal
Rienzi
Tannhauser
The Flying Dutchman
Tristan und Isolde

## WEBER

Der Freischutz
Euryanthe
Oberon

## WOLF-FERRARI

The Jewels of the Madonna

# THE TOP 150 CHAMBER MUSIC WORKS

## BACH, J.S.

Trio Sonata in G
Trio Sonata in C
Musical Offering

## BACH, C.P.E.

Trio Sonata in D Minor

## BARBER

String Quartet, op. 11

## BARTOK

String Quartet No. 4
String Quartet No. 5

String Quartet No. 6

## BEETHOVEN

Trio for flute, violin and viola, op. 25
String Quartet No. 1 in F
String Quartet No. 4 in C Minor
String Quartet No. 7 in F, op. 59
String Quartet No. 9 in C, op. 59
String Quartet No. 10 in E♭
String Quartet No. 11 in F Minor
String Quartet No. 12 in E♭
String Quartet No. 13 in B♭
String Quartet No. 14 in C# Minor
String Quartet No. 15 in A Minor
String Quartet No. 16 in F
String Quintet
Piano Trio in B♭, op. 97 ("Archduke")
Piano Trio in D Minor, op. 70,
  no. 1 ("Ghost")
Quartet for piano and winds,
  op. 16 in E♭
Piano Quintet in E♭, op. 16

## BLOCH

Piano Quintet No. 2

## BOCCHERINI

Guitar Quintet (Guitar and String
  Quartet)
String Quintet in D Minor, op. 62,
  no. 5

## BORODIN

String Quartet No. 2 in D Major
Piano Quintet in C Minor

## BRAHMS

Piano Trio in B Major
String Quartet in C Minor
String Quartet in A Minor

## BRAHMS - *Continued*

String Quartet in B♭
String Quintet in B Minor
Trio for Violin, Horn and Piano
Serenade 2 in A (2 Fl, 2 Ob, 2 Cl, 2
   Bsn, 2 Hn, Vla, Cello, Bass)
Piano Quartet in C Minor
Piano Quintet in F Minor

## DOHNANYI

Serenade in C, op. 10 (String Trio)

## CARTER

String Quartet No. 3

## CASTELNUOVO-TEDESCO

Guitar Quintet, op. 143 (guitar and
   string quartet)

## CHOPIN

Piano Trio in G Minor

## COPLAND

Piano Quartet
Nonet for Strings

## CORELLI

Sonata da Cheisa, op. 3, no. 5

## DEBUSSY

String Quartet in G Minor, op. 10
Sonata for Flute, Viola, and Harp

## DVORAK

String Quartet in C, op. 61
String Quartet in F, op. 96
   ("American")
String Quintet in E♭, op. 97
Serenade in D Minor, op. 44 (2 Ob, 2
   Cl, 2 Bsn, 3 Hn and Cello)
Piano Trio, op. 90 ("Dumky Trio")
Piano Quartet in E♭, op. 87
Piano Quintet in A, op. 81

## FAURE

Piano Trio, op. 120
Piano Quintet No. 2, op. 11

## FRANCK

String Quartet in D
Piano Quintet in F Minor

## GLIERE

String Quartet No. 4, op. 83

## GLINKA

String Quartet No. 2 in F
Piano Trio ("Pathetique")

## GRIEG

String Quartet in G Minor, op. 27

## HANDEL

Trio Sonata in B♭, op. 2, no. 4

## HAYDN

London Trios (2 flutes, cello)
String Trio op. 32, no. 3 in C
String Quartet in C Minor, op. 33,
   no. 3 ("The Bird")
String Quartet in C Minor, op. 55,
   no. 2 ("The Razor")
String Quartet in D Major, op. 64,
   no. 5 ("The Lark")
String Quartet in G Minor, op. 76,
   no. 2 ("Quintet")
String Quartet in C Major, op. 76,
   no. 3 ("The Emperor")
String Quartet in B♭, op. 76,
   no. 4 ("Sunrise")
Piano Trio No. 31 in G

## HONEGGER

String Quartet No. 3

## HOVHANESS

Piano Trio in E Minor, op. 3

## IVES

String Quartet No. 1
String Quartet No. 2

## KODALY

String Quartet No. 2, op. 10

## MENDELSSOHN

String Quartet in E♭, op. 12
String Quartet in E♭, op. 44, no. 1
String Quartet in E Minor, op. 44, no. 2
String Quartet in E♭, op. 44, no. 3
String Octet in E♭, op. 20
  (4 Vn, 2 Vla, 2 Cello)
Piano Trio in D Minor, op. 49
Piano Trio in C Minor, op. 66
Sextet in D Minor, op. 110
  (Vn, 2 Vla, Cello, Bass and Piano)

## MILHAUD

String Quartet No. 18

## MOZART

String Trio in B♭, K. 266
Flute Quartet, K. 285
Oboe Quartet in F, K. 370
String Quartet No. 17 in B♭, K. 458
  ("The Hunt")
String Quartet No. 19 in C, K. 465
  ("The Dissonant")
String Quartet No. 21 in D, K. 575
String Quartet No. 23 in F, K. 590
Clarinet Quintet in A, K. 581
Horn Quintet in E♭, K. 407
String Quintet in C, K. 515
Piano Trio No. 5 in G, K. 564
Piano Trio No. 8 in D Minor, K. 442
Piano Quartet in G Minor, K. 478
Piano Quintet in C, K. 415

## NIELSEN

String Quartet in F Minor, op. 44

## PISTON

String Quartet No. 5

## PROKOFIEV

String Quartet No. 2, op. 92
Overture on Jewish Themes, op. 34
  (Clarinet, String Quartet and Piano)

## RACHMANINOFF

Piano Trio Elegiaque, op. 9

## RAVEL

String Quartet in F
Introduction and Allegro
Piano Trio

## SAINT-SAENS

String Quartet No. 2
Piano Trio in F, op. 18
Piano Quartet, op. 41

## SCHOENBERG

Transfigured Night
String Quartet No. 4, op. 37

## SCHUBERT

String Trio No. 1 in B♭
String Trio No. 2 in B♭
Piano Trio No. 1 in B♭
Piano Trio No. 2 in E♭
String Quartet in E♭
String Quartet in E Minor
String Quartet 12 in C Minor
  ("Quartett-Satz")
String Quartet 13 in A Minor
String Quartet 14 in D Minor
  ("Death and the Maiden")
String Quintet in C
Piano Quintet in A ("The Trout")

## SCHUMANN

String Quartet in A Minor, op. 41, no. 1

String Quartet in F, op. 41, no. 2

String Quartet in A, op. 41, no. 3

Piano Trio, op. 110

Piano Quintet in E♭, op. 44

Piano Quartet in E♭, op. 47

## SHOSTAKOVICH

String Quartet No. 1, op. 49

## SIBELIUS

String Quartet in D Minor, op. 56 ("Voces Intimae")

## SMETANA

String Quartet No. 1 in E Minor ("From My Life")

Piano Trio in G Minor, op. 15

## STRAUSS

Piano Quartet in C Minor, op. 13

## STRAVINSKY

3 Pieces for String Quartet

Octet for Winds

L'Histoire du Soldat

Septet (Cl in A, Hn, Vn, Vla, Cello and Piano)

## TCHAIKOVSKY

String Quartet in B♭, op. posth

Souvenir de Florence

Piano Trio in A Minor

## TELEMANN

Trio Sonata in G

## VERDI

String Quartet in E Minor

## VILLA-LOBOS

String Quartet No. 7

## VIVALDI

Trio Sonata in E Minor, op. 1, no. 2

## WEBER

Piano Quartet, op. 8

## WEBERN

String Quartet, op. 28

## WOLF

Italian Serenade (String Quartet)

# THE TOP 150 SONGS OR SONG CYCLES
**(song cycles and collections are in italics)**

## ARGENTO

Six Elizabethan Songs

## BACH, J.S.

Bist du bei mir

## BARBER

Hermit Songs

Sure on This Shining Night

## BEETHOVEN

Die Ehre Gottes aus der Natur

Adelaide

An die ferne Geliebte

## BELLINI

Sei ariette

## BERLIOZ

Les Nuits d'ete

## BIZET

Chanson d'Avril

Ouvre ton coeur

**BORODIN**

The Sleeping Princess

**BRAHMS**

Wie bist du, meine Konigin?

Fifteen Romances from Magelone,
  op. 33

Four Songs, op. 43

Sapphische Ode

Wiegenlied

Vier ernste Gasange

**BRITTEN**

Seven Sonnets of Michelangelo

A Charm of Lullabies

Tenor Serenade

**CANTALOUBE**

Chants d'Auvergne

**CARPENTER**

Gitanjali

**CASTELNUOVO-TEDESCO**

Three Sonnets from the Portuguese

Ninna-Nanna

**CHABRIER**

Six Melodies

**CHAUSSON**

Le temps des lilas

Le colibri

Chanson perpetuelle

**COPLAND**

Twelve Poems of Emily Dickinson

Old American Songs

**DEBUSSY**

Fetes Galantes, sets 1 and 2

Proses lyriques

Ariettes Oubliees

Chansons de Bilitis

Beau Soir

Mandoline

**DONIZETTI**

La Chanson de L'Abeille

L'Amor mio

**DOWLAND**

Come Again

Flow, My Tears

**DUPARC**

Chanson triste

L'Invitation au Voyage

Phidyle

La vie anterieure

**DVORAK**

Gypsy Songs, op. 55

Biblical Songs, op. 99

**FALLA**

Siete Canciones Populares Espanolas

**FAURE**

Tristesse

Apres un reve

Cinq Melodies, op. 58

Four Songs, op. 39

La Bonne Chanson, op. 61

La chanson d'Eve

**FRANCK**

Nocturne

**GLINKA**

Doubt

**GLUCK**

Die fruhen Graber

**GIORDANI**

Caro mio ben

## GOUNOD

Ave Maria

## GRIEG

Ein Traum

Vaaren

## HAYDN

Das Leben ist ein Traum

She Never Told Her love

## HANDEL

Dank sei Dir, Herr

## IVES

General William Booth Enters into
    Heaven

The Circus Band

## LEONCAVALLO

Mattinata

## LISZT

Three Petrarch Sonnets

Es muss ein Wunderbares sein

O lieb, so lang du lieben kannst

## MACDOWELL

Six Love Songs

## MAHLER

Kindertotenlieder

Lieder eines fahrenden Gesellen

Des Knaben Wunderhorn

Liebst du um Schonheit

## MENDELSSOHN

Neue Liebe

Das erste Veilchen

On Wings of Song

## MONTSALVATGE

Canciones Negras

## MOZART

Abendempfindung

Das Veilchen

Als Luise die Briefe ihres ungetreuen
    Liebhabers verbrannte

## MUSSORGSKY

Songs and Dances of Death

Song of the Flea

## POULENC

Fiancailles pour Rire

Banalites

## PUCCINI

E L'uccellino

## PURCELL

Ah, How Pleasant 'Tis To Love

Music for a while

I'll Sail upon the Dog Star

## RACHMANINOV

Vocalise

Spring Waters

Twelve Songs, op. 21

Lilacs

## RAVEL

Don Quichotte a Dulcinee

Histoires Naturelles

Scheherazade

Sainte

Vocalise en Forme de Habanera

## RESPIGHI

Nebbie

## RIMSKY-KORSAKOV

In Spring

## ROSSINI

Soirees Musicales

La Regata Veneziana

## SCARLATTI, A.

Le violette
Gia il sole dal Gange

## SCHUBERT, FRANZ

Gretchen am Spinnrade
Heidenroslein
Rastlose Liebe
Der Erlkonig
An Den Mond
Die Forelle
Litanei
Der Wanderer
Der Tod und das Madchen
An die Musik
Du bist die Ruh
Standchen
Auf dem Wasser zu Singen
Die schone Mullerin
Die Winterreise
Die junge Nonne
Nacht und Traume
Die Allmacht
Ave Maria
Gesang an Sylvia
Der Doppelganger

## SCHUMANN

Widmung
Die Lotosblume
Du bist wie eine Blume
Liederkreis
Frauenliebe un Leben
Dichterliebe

## STRAUSS

Four Last Songs
Allerseelen
Du meines Herzens Kronelein
Ich trage meine Minne

Zueignung
Four songs, op. 27

## TCHAIKOVSKY

None But the Weary Heart
Six songs, op. 38

## VAUGHAN WILLIAMS

Songs of Travel
Five Mystical Songs

## VERDI

Il poveretto
Lo spazzacamino

## WAGNER

Wesendonklieder

## WOLF

Morike songs
Spanish Song Book
Italian Song Book
Eichendorff Songs
Kennst du das Land?

# THE TOP 150 SOLO WORKS

## ALBENIZ

Iberia

## BACH

The Well-Tempered Clavier
French Suites
English Suites
The Goldberg Variations
Italian Concerto
Sonata for Cembalo and Flute in
    B Minor
Sonata for Unaccompanied Flute in
    A Minor

## BACH - *Continued*

Sonata for Clavier and Violin
No. 3 in E
Sonata for Unaccompanied Violin in
G Minor
Sonata for Viola da Gamba No. 1 in
G Major

## BARBER

Piano Sonata, op. 26

## BARTOK

Allegro barbaro
Mikrokosmo

## BEETHOVEN

Piano Sonata in C Minor
("Pathetique")
Piano Sonata in C# Minor
("Sonata quasi una Fantasia")
(also called "Moonlight Sonata")
Piano Sonata in D Major
("Pastoral Sonata")
Piano Sonata in C Major ("Waldstein")
Piano Sonata in F Minor
("Appassionata")
Piano Sonata in Bb Major
("Hammer-Klavier")
Piano Sonata in E Major
Piano Sonata in Ab Major
Piano Sonata, op. 111 in C Minor
"Fur Elise" ("Piece in A Minor")
"Diabelli" Variations
"Eroica" Variations (Fifteen Variations
in Eb Major, op. 35)
Sonata for Piano and Cello No. 3 in A
Sonata for Piano and Violin No. 5 in F,
"Spring"
Sonata for Piano and Violin No. 9 in
A, "Kreutzer"

## BORODIN

Petite Suite

## BRAHMS

Variations and Fugue on a Theme of
Handel
Variations on a Theme by Paganini
Intermezzi, op. 117
Two Rhapsodies, op. 79
Waltzes, op. 39P
Sonata for Clarinet and Piano in
F Minor
Sonata for Piano and Violin
No. 3 in D Minor
Sonata for Piano and Cello
No. 2 in F Major

## C.P.E. BACH

Sonata in G Minor

## CHABRIER

Pieces pittoresques

## CHOPIN

Twenty-four Preludes
Etudes, op. 10
Etudes, op. 25
Nocturne, op. 27, No. 2, in Db Major
Nocturne, op. 37, No. 2
Nocturne, op. 48, No. 1
Fantasy Impromptu, op. 66
Polonaise, op. 26, No. 2, in Eb Minor
Military Polonaise, op. 40, No. 1, in
A Major
Grandes Polonaise, op. 44 in F# Minor
Polonaise, op. 53 in Ab Major
Polonaise-Fantaisie, op. 61
Mazurka, op. 24, No. 1
Waltz, op. 69, No. 1

Waltz, op. 64, No. 1, ("Minute Waltz")
Piano Sonata, op. 35 in B♭ Minor
Piano Sonata, op. 58 in B Minor
Ballade, op. 23
Scherzo No. 2, in B♭ Minor
Sonata for Cello and Piano in G Minor,
    op. 65

## COPLAND

Piano Variations

## CORELLI

Violin and Harpsichord Sonata op. 5,
    No. 12, "La Folia"

## COUPERIN

Le Rossignol en Amour

## D'INDY

Sonata

## DEBUSSY

Suite Bergamasque
Pour le Piano
Children's Corner
Preludes, vol. 1 and 2
Sonata for Cello and Piano
Sonata for Violin and Piano
Syrinx (for unaccompanied flute)

## DVORAK

Humoresque

## FAURE

Barcarolles
Nocturnes
Sonata for Violin and Piano No. 1 in A

## FRANCK

Prelude, Choral and Fugue
Violin Sonata in A

## GRIEG

Pictures from Folk Life
Lyric Pieces (second set)
Sonata No. 3 for Violin and Piano

## HANDEL

Harmonious Blacksmith

## HAYDN

Piano Sonata No. 20 in C Minor
Piano Sonata No. 37 in D Major
Piano Sonata No. 52 in E♭ Major

## HINDEMITH

Ludus Tonalis

## IVES

Concord Sonata
Violin and Piano Sonata No. 4,
    "Children's Day at the Camp
    Meeting"

## KABALEVSKY

Children's Pieces

## KHACHATURIAN

Toccata

## KODALY

Sonata for Unaccompanied Cello

## LISZT

Transcendental Etudes
Annees de Pelerinage
Sonata in B Minor

## MACDOWELL

Woodland Sketches

## MENDELSSOHN

Songs Without Words
Sonata in B♭ Major
Six Preludes and Fugues

## MENDELSSOHN - *Continued*

Sonata for Piano and Cello No. 2 in D Major

Sonata for Organ No. 1 in F Minor

## MESSIAEN

Vingt regards sur l'Enfant Jesus

## MILHAUD

Le Candelabre a Sept Branche

## MOZART

Piano Sonata in D Major, K. 284

Piano Sonata in C Major, K. 309

Piano Sonata in A Major, K. 331

Piano Sonata in F Major, K. 332

Piano Sonata in C Minor, K. 457

Piano Sonata in C Major, K. 545

Piano Sonata in D Major, K. 576

Violin Sonata in E Minor, K. 304 (300c)

Violin Sonata in B♭ Major, K. 454

Violin Sonata in E♭ Major, K. 481

Violin Sonata in A Major, K. 526

"Ah, vous dirai-je maman," K. 265

Fantasy, K. 475

## MUSSORGSKY

Pictures at an Exhibition

## POULENC

Les Soirees de Nazelles

Sonata for Flute and Piano

Sonata for Clarinet and Piano

Sonata for Oboe and Piano

## PROKOFIEV

Ten Little Piano Pieces, op. 12

Sonata in A Minor, op. 28

Sonata in A Major, op. 82

Sonata for Cello and Piano, op. 119

Sonata for Flute and Piano, op. 94

Sonata for Violin and Piano, No. 1 in F Minor op. 80

Sonata for Unaccompanied Violin in D, op. 11

## PURCELL

Trumpet Tune in D major

## RACHMANINOV

Prelude, op. 23

Prelude, op. 32

Prelude in C# Minor, op. 3, no. 2

Sonata in B♭ Minor op. 36

Sonata for Cello and Piano in G Minor, op. 19

## RAMEAU

Nouvelles Suites de Pieces de Clavecin

## RAVEL

Miroirs

Gaspard de la Nuit

Valses nobles et sentmentales

Tombeau de Couperin

Pavane pour une Infante defunte

Sonata for Violin and Piano

## SAINT-SAENS

Six Etudes, op. 111

## SATIE

Gymnopedies

## SCARLATTI

Sonata in C Major, L. 104

Sonata in G Minor (L. 499) "Cat Fugue"

## SCHONBERG

Five Piano Pieces, op. 23

## SCHOSTAKOVITCH

Twenty-Four Preludes and Fugues, op. 87
Sonata for Viola and Piano, op. 147

## SCHUBERT

Moments Musicals
Impromptu No. 3 in B♭ Major
Piano Sonata in A Minor
Piano Sonata in D Major
Piano Sonata in A Major
Piano Sonata in C Major
Cello Sonata, D. 821 ("Arpeggione")
Violin Sonata in D, D. 381
Violin Sonata in G Minor, D. 408

## SCHUMANN

Albumblatter
Album for the Young
Carnaval
Kinderscenen
Papillons
Sonata in F# Minor
Sonata in G Minor
Etudes Symphoniques, op. 13
Violin Sonata No. 2 in D Minor,
    op. 121

## STRAUSS

Sonata for Cello and Piano in F, op. 6
Sonata for Violin and Piano in E♭,
    op. 18

## STRAVINSKY

Sonata

## VIVALDI

Sonatas for Cello and Harpsichord,

## WEBER

Invitation to the Dance, op. 65

## WEBERN

Piano Variations, op. 27

The last fifty of my recommendations are miscellaneous "extras." Some of them are combinations of genres that don't fall into easy categories, such as Schubert's *Shepherd on the Rock,* for soprano, clarinet and piano. Others are works that didn't quite make the top 150 lists, but are nonetheless wonderful pieces I hope you have the opportunity to hear. Still others are rather peculiar pieces—Mozart's fascinating *Music for Glass Harmonica,* for example—that have become musical curiosities.

All of these and thousands of others are waiting to enthrall you. When you finish your first thousand, give me a call. I'll send you a few thousand more. Enjoy!

## THE "EXTRA" 50

## BACH

Art of the Fugue
    (the instrumentation is unspecified)
Lute Suite in E Minor
Cantata #208 ("Sheep May
    Safely Graze")

## BEACH

Gaelic Symphony

## BEETHOVEN

Duet in E♭ with Two Eyeglass
    Obbligato (viola and cello)
Coriolanus Overture (for orchestra)
Octet for wind instruments, op. 103
Trio for 2 oboes and English horn, op. 87
Equale for four trombones, WoO 30

## BERG

Three Pieces for orchestra

## BIZET

L'Arlesienne Suites (for orchestra)

## BRAHMS

Two Songs for contralto and piano, with viola obbligato, op. 91
Tragic Overture

## DEBUSSY

Rapsodie for saxophone and piano
Petite Piece for clarinet and piano
Jeux (for orchestra)
La Martyre de saint Sebastian (for orchestra)

## DVORAK

Serenade for Strings
Scherzo Capriccioso (for orchestra)

## FRANCK

Redemption (for chorus and orchestra)

## HAYDN

Guitar Quartet in D Major
Nonet (2 oboes, 2 horns, 2 violins, 2 violas, bass)
Six Sonatas for Violin and Viola

## IVES

Central Park in the Dark (for orchestra)

## MAHLER

Lieder eines Fahrenden Gesellen ("Songs of a Wayfarer")
Das Lied von der Erde ("The Song of the Earth")

## MILHAUD

The Creation of the World (for orchestra)

## MOZART

Music for Glass Harmonica
Adagio for 2 Clarinets and 3 Basset Horns, K. 411
Serenade in Bb Major for 13 winds, K. 361
Sonata for Bassoon and Cello, K. 292
Adagio and Allegro for Mechanical Organ in F Minor, K. 594

## PACHELBEL

Canon in D Major

## PROKOFIEV

The Love of Three Oranges Suite (for orchestra)
Lieutenant Kije Suite (for orchestra)
Romeo and Juliet Suite (for orchestra)

## RAVEL

Sonata for Violin and Cello

## RIMSKY-KORSAKOV

Capriccio Espagnol

## RUGGLES

Sun-Treader

## SCHOENBERG

Pierrot Lunaire
Variations for orchestra, op. 31

## SCHUBERT

The Shepherd on the Rock (soprano, clarinet and piano)

## SMETANA

Overture to The Bartered Bride

## STRAVINSKY

Canticum Sacrum
Symphony of Wind Instruments

## TCHAIKOVSKY

Symphony #3 in D Major ("Polish")
Serenade for Strings
Capriccio Italien

## VILLA LOBOS

Bachianas Brasileiras

## WAGNER

The Love Feast of the Twelve Apostles

# APPENDIX:
# THE MAJOR COMPOSERS

**Johann Sebastian Bach**
born: Eisenach, Thuringia, March 21, 1685
died: Leipzig, Germany, July 28, 1750

**Samuel Barber**
born: West Chester, Pennsylvania, March 9, 1910
died: New York, New York, January 23, 1981

**Bela Bartok**
born: Nagyszentmiklos, Hungary, March 25, 1881
died: New York, New York, September 26, 1945

**Ludwig van Beethoven**
born: Bonn, Germany, December 16, 1770
died: Vienna, Austria, March 26, 1827

**Alban Berg**
born: Vienna, Austria, February 9, 1885
died: Vienna, Austria, December 24, 1935

**Hector Berlioz**
born: La Cote-Saint-Andre, France,
    December 11, 1803
died: Paris, France, March 8, 1869

**Georges Bizet**
born: Paris, France, October 25, 1838
died: Bougival, near Paris, France, June 3, 1875

**Ernest Bloch**
born: Geneva, Switzerland, July 24, 1880
died: Portland, Oregon, July 15, 1959

**Alexander Borodin**
born: St. Petersburg, Russia, November 11, 1833
died: St. Petersburg, Russia, February 27, 1887

**Johannes Brahms**
born: Hamburg, Germany, May 7, 1833
died: Vienna, Austria, April 3, 1897

**Benjamin Britten**
born: Lowestoft, Suffolk, England, November 22, 1913
died: Aldeburgh, England, December 4, 1976

**Anton Bruckner**
born: Ansfelden, Austria, September 4, 1824
died: Vienna, Austria, October 11, 1896

**Ernest Chausson**
born: Paris, France, January 21, 1855
died: Limay, Seine-et-Oise, France, June 10, 1899

**Frederic Chopin**
born: Zelazowa Wola, near Warsaw, Poland,
    February 22, 1810
died: Paris, France, October 17, 1849

**Aaron Copland**
born: Brooklyn, New York, November 14, 1900
died: North Tarrytown, New York,
    December 2, 1990

**Claude Debussy**
born: Saint-Germain-en-Laye, near Paris, France,
    August 22, 1862
died: Paris, France, March 25, 1918

**Gaetano Donizetti**
born: Bergamo, Italy, November 29, 1797
died: Bergamo, Italy, April 8, 1848

**Paul Dukas**
born: Paris, France, October 1, 1865
died: Paris, France, May 17, 1935

**Antonin Dvorak**
born: Nelahozeves, Bohemia, September 8, 1841
died: Prague, Czechoslovakia, May 1, 1904

**Sir Edward Elgar**
born: Broadheath, near Worcester, England,
    June 2, 1857
died: Worcester, England, February 23, 1934

**Manuel de Falla**
born: Cadiz, Spain, November 23, 1876
died: Alta Garcia, Argentina, November 14, 1946

**Gabriel Faure**
born: Pamiers, Ariege, France, May 12, 1845
died: Paris, France, November 4, 1924

**Cesar Franck**
born: Liege, Belgium, December 10, 1822
died: Paris, France, November 8, 1890

**George Gershwin**
born: Brooklyn, New York, September 26, 1898
died: Hollywood, California, July 11, 1937

**Christoph Willibald Gluck**
born: Erasbach, Upper Palatinate, July 2, 1714
died: Vienna, Austria, November 15, 1787

**Charles Gounod**
born: Paris, France, June 17, 1818
died: Paris, France, October 18, 1893

**Edvard Grieg**
born: Bergen, Norway, June 15, 1843
died: Bergen, Norway, September 4, 190

**George Friederic Handel**
born: Halle, Saxony, February 23, 1685
died: London, England, April 14, 1759

**Joseph Haydn**
born: Rohrau, Lower Austria, March 31, 17
died: Vienna, Austria, May 31, 1809

**Paul Hindemith**
born: Hanau, Germany, November 16, 1895
died: Frankfurt, Germany, December 28, 196

**Arthur Honegger**
born: Le Havre, France, March 10, 1892
died: Paris, France, November 27, 1955

**Vincent d'Indy**
born: Paris, France, March 27, 1851
died: Paris, France, December 2, 1931

**Zoltan Kodaly**
born: Keczkemer, Hungary, December 16, 1882
died: Budapest, Hungary, March 6, 1967

**Edouard Lalo**
born: Lille, France, January 27, 1823
died: Paris, France, April 22, 1892

**Ruggiero Leoncavallo**
born: Naples, Italy, March 8, 1858
died: Montecatini, Tuscany, August 9, 1919

**Franz Liszt**
born: Raiding, Hungary, October 22, 1811
died: Bayreuth, Bavaria, July 31, 1886

**Gustav Mahler**
born: Kalischt, Bohemia, July 7, 1860
died: Vienna, Austria, May 18, 1911

**Jules Massenet**
born: Montaud, France, May 12, 1842
died: Paris, France, August 13, 1912

**Felix Mendelssohn**
born: Hamburg, Germany, February 3, 1809
died: Leipzig, Germany, November 4, 1847

**Giacomo Meyerbeer**
born: Berlin, Germany, September 5, 1791
died: Paris, France, May 2, 1864

**Darius Milhaud**
born: Aix, Provence, September 4, 1892
died: Geneva, Switzerland, June 22, 1974

**Wolf**

... Ekaterinoslav, Ukraine, April 23, 1891
died: Moscow, Russia, March 4, 1953

**Giacomo Puccini**
born: Lucca, Italy, December 22, 1858
died: Brussels, Belgium, November 29, 1924

**Serge Rachmaninoff**
born: Onega, Novgorod district, Russia, April 1, 1873
died: Beverly Hills, California, March 28, 1943

**Maurice Ravel**
borrn: Ciboure, France, March 7, 1875
died: Paris, France, December 28, 1937

**Ottorino Respighi**
born: Bologna, Italy, July 9, 1879
died: Rome, Italy, April 18, 1936

**Nicholas Rimsky-Korsakov**
born: Tikhvin, Novgorod district, Russia,
    March 18, 1844
died: St. Petersburg, Russia, June 21, 1908

**Gioacchino Rossini**
born: Pesaro, Italy, February 29, 1792
died: Passy, France, November 13, 1868

**Camille Saint-Saens**
born: Paris, France, October 9, 1835
died: Algiers, Algeria, December 16, 1921

**Arnold Schoenberg**
born: Vienna, Austria, September 13, 1874
died: Brentwood, California, July 13, 1951

**Franz Schubert**
born: Vienna, Austria, January 31, 1797
died: Vienna, Austria, November 19, 1828

**Robert Schumann**
born: Zwickau, Germany, June 8, 1810
died: Endenich, near Bonn, Germany, July 29, 1856

**Alexander Scriabin**
born: Moscow, Russia, January 6, 1872
died: Moscow, Russia, April 27, 1915

**Dmitri Shostokovich**
born: Leningrad, Russia, September 25, 1906
died: Moscow, Russia, August 9, 1975

**Jean Sibelius**
born: Tavastehus, Finland, December 8, 1865
died: Jarvenpaa, Finland, September 20, 1957

**Bedrich Smetana**
born: Litomischl, Bohemia, March 2, 1824
died: Prague, Czechoslovakia, May 12, 1884

**Richard Strauss**
born: Munich, Germany, June 11, 1864
died: Garmisch-Partenkirchen, Bavaria,
    September 8, 1949

**Igor Stravinsky**
born: Oranienbaum, Russia, June 17, 1882
died: New York, New York, April 6, 1971

**Peter Ilyich Tchaikovsky**
born: Votinsk, Russia, May 7, 1840
died: St. Petersburg, Russia, November 6, 1893

**Ralph Vaughan Williams**
born: Down Ampney, England, October 12, 1872
died: London, England, August 26, 1958

**Giuseppe Verdi**
born: Le Roncole, Italy, October 10, 1813
died: Milan, Italy, January 27, 1901

**Heitor Villa-Lobos**
born: Rio de Janeiro, Brazil, March 5, 1887
died: Rio de Janeiro, Brazil, November, 17, 1959

**Richard Wagner**
born: Leipzig, Germany, May 22, 1813
died: Venice, Italy, February 13, 1883

**William Walton**
born: Oldham, Lancashire, March 29, 1902
died: Ischia, Italy, March 8, 1983

**Karl Maria von Weber**
born: Eutin, Oldenburg, November 18, 1786
died: London, England, June 5, 1826

**Hugo Wolf**
born: Windischgraz, Austria, March 13, 1860
died: Vienna, Austria, February 22, 1903

# FOR FURTHER READING

Here's a short reading list for more information about the composers whose works we've encountered in this volume, plus a few more.

**J. S. Bach**

Geiringer, Karl, *Johann Sebastian Bach—The Culmination of an Era*. New York: Oxford University Press, 1966.

Grew, E.M., and S. Grew, *Bach*. New York: Collier, 1962.

Schrade, Leo, *The Conflict Between the Sacred and the Secular*. 1955. Reprint. New York: Da Capo, 1973.

Schweitzer, Albert, *J. S. Bach,* trans. Ernest Newman. Boston: Humphries, 1964. 2 vols.

Spitta, Philipp, *Johann Sebastian Bach, His Work and Influence on the Music of Germany,* trans. Clara Bell and J. A. Fuller-Maitland. New York: Dover, 1951.

Terry, Charles Sanford, *Bach: The Historical Approach*. New York: Oxford University Press, 1930.

**Bartok**

Kroo, Gyorgy, *A Guide to Bartok,* trans. Ruth Pataki and Maria Steiner. trans. rev. Elizabeth West. Budapest: Corvina, 1974.

Lesznai, Lajos, *Bartok,* trans. Percy M. Young. New York: Octagon, 1973.

Stevens, Halsey, *The Life and Music of Bela Bartok,* rev. ed. New York: Oxford University Press, l964.

**Beethoven**

Knight, Frida, *Beethoven and the Age of Revolution*. London: Lawrence & Wishart, 1973.

Marek, George, *Beethoven: Biography of a Genius*. New York: Funk & Wagnalls, l969.

Scott, Marion, *Beethoven*. New York: Farrar Straus & Giroux, 1960.

Sullivan, J. W. N., *Beethoven: His Spiritual Development*. New York: New American Library, Mentor Books, 1954.

Thayer, Alexander Wheelock, *The Life of Beethoven,* rev. and ed. Elliott Forbes. Princeton, N.J.: Princeton University Press, 1964. 2 vols.

Tovey, Donald F., *Beethoven,* ed. H. J. Foss. New York: Oxford University Press, 1965.

Turner, William J., *Beethoven*. London: J. M. Dent, 1945.

**Berg**

Redlich, H. F., *Alban Berg, The Man and His Music*. New York: Abelard-Schuman, 1957.

Reich, Willi, *The Life and Work of Alban Berg,* trans. Cornelius Cardew. London: Thames & Hudson, 1965.

**Berlioz**

Barzun, Jacques, *Berlioz and the Romantic Century,* 3rd ed. New York: Columbia University Press, 1969.

Dickenson, A. E. F., *The Music of Berlioz,* rev. ed. New York: Farrar, Straus & Giroux, 1967.

Primmer, Brian, *Berlioz' Style*. New York: Oxford University Press, 1973.

Turner, Walter J., *Berlioz, The Man and His Work*. New York: Vienna House, 1974.

**Bizet**

Curtiss, Mina, *Bizet and His World*. New York: Knopf, 1958.

Dean, Winton, *Bizet*. London: J. M. Dent, 1965.

Parker, Douglas C., *Georges Bizet, His Life and Works*. Freeport, N. Y.: Books for Libraries Press, 1969.

**Brahms**

Evans, Edwin, *Handbook to the Works of Johannes Brahms*. 1912. Reprint. New York: Lenox Hill, 1970. 4 vols.

Geiringer, Karl, *Brahms, His Life and Work,* trans. H. B. Weiner and Bernard Miall, 2nd ed., rev. and enl. London: Allen & Unwin, 1963.

Latham, Peter, *Brahms*. New York: Collier, 1962.

**Britten**

Howard, Patricia, *The Operas of Benjamin Britten—An Introduction*. New York: Praeger, 1969.

Kendall, Alan, *Benjamin Britten*. London: Macmillan, 1973.

Mitchell, Donald, and Hans Keller, eds., *Britten: A Commentary on His Works from a Group of Specialists*. New York: Philosophical Library, 1950.

White, Eric Walter, *Benjamin Britten, A Sketch of His Life and Works,* rev. and enl. ed. London: Boosey & Hawkes, 1954.

White, Eric Walter, *Benjamin Britten, His Life and Operas.* Berkeley, Calif.: University of California Press, 1970.

**Bruckner**

Doernberg, Erwin, *The Life and Symphonies of Anton Bruckner.* New York: Dover, 1960.

Newlin, Dika, *Bruckner, Mahler, Schoenberg.* New York: Columbia University Press, 1947.

Simpson, Robert, *The Essence of Bruckner.* Philadelphia: Chilton, 1968.

**Cage**

Kostalanetz, Richard, *John Cage.* New York: Praeger, 1970.

**Chopin**

Abraham, Gerald, *Chopin's Musical Style.* New York: Oxford University Press, 1960.

Chissell, Joan, *Chopin.* London: Faber & Faber, 1965.

Hedley, Arthur, *Chopin,* ed. and rev. Maurice J. E. Brown. London: J. M. Dent, 1974.

Walker, Alan, ed., *The Chopin Companion, Profiles of the Man and the Musician.* New York: Norton, 1973.

**Copland**

Berger, Arthur, *Aaron Copland.* New York: Oxford University Press, 1953.

**Corelli**

Pincherle, Marc, *Corelli: His Life, His Work,* trans. Hubert Russell. New York: Norton, 1956.

**Debussy**

Lockspeiser, Edward, *Debussy,* 4th ed. New York: Collier, 1962.

Lockspeiser, Edward, *Debussy, His Life and Mind.* London: Cassell, 1962, 1965. 2 vols.

Vallas, Leon, *Claude Debussy, His Life and Works,* trans. Marie O'Brien. 1933. Reprint. New York: Dover, 1973.

**Dvorak**

Clapham, John, *Antonin Dvorak.* London: St. Martin's, 1966.

Hughes, Gervase, *Dvorak: His Life and Music.* New York: Dodd, Mead, 1967.

Robertson, Alec, *Dvorak.* New York: Collier, 1962.

**Elgar**

Kennedy, Michael, *Portrait of Elgar.* New York: Oxford University Press, 1968.

Parrott, Ian, *Elgar.* New York: Octagon, 1971.

Young, Percy M., *Elgar, O. M.; A Study of a Musician,* rev. ed. London: White Lion, 1973.

**Faure**

Suckling, Norman, *Faure.* London: J. M. Dent, 1951.

**Franck**

Demuth, Norman, *Cesar Franck.* London: Dobson, 1964.

Vallas, Leon, *Cesar Franck,* trans. Hubert Foss. 1951. Reprint. Westport, Conn.: Greenwood, 1973.

**Gershwin**

Jablonski, Edward, and Lawrence D. Stewart, *The Gershwin Years.* Garden City, N. Y.: Doubleday, 1973.

Kimball, Robert, and Alfred Simon, *The Gershwins.* New York: Atheneum, 1973.

New York Times Gershwin Years in Song. New York: Quadrangle, 1973.

Schwartz, Charles M., *George Gershwin: His Life and Music.* New York: Bobbs-Merrill, 1973.

**Gluck**

Einstein, Alfred, *Gluck.* New York: Collier, 1962.

Howard, Patricia, *Gluck and the Birth of Modern Opera.* New York: St. Martin's, 1964.

**Gounod**

Harding, James, *Gounod.* New York: Stein & Day, 1973.

**Grieg**

Horton, John, *Grieg.* London: J. M. Dent, 1974.

Johansen, David Monrad, *Edvard Grieg,* trans. Madge Robertson. Princeton, N. J.: Princeton University Press, 1938.

**Handel**

Abraham, Gerald, *Handel: A Symposium.* London: Oxford University Press, 1954.

Dean, Winton, *Handel and the Opera Seria.* Berkeley, Calif.: University of California Press, 1969.

Lang, Paul Henry, *George Frideric Handel.* New York: Norton, 1966.

Young, Percy M., *Handel,* rev. ed. New York: Farrar, Straus & Giroux, 1965.

## Haydn

Geiringer, Karl, in collaboration with Irene Geiringer, *Haydn: A Creative Life in Music,* 2nd ed., rev. and enl. Berkeley, Calif.: University of California Press, 1968.

Hughes, Rosemary, *Haydn.* New York: Collier, 1962.

## Ives

Cowell, Henry, and Sydney Cowell, *Charles Ives and His Music.* New York: Oxford University Press, 1955.

Ives, Charles, *Memos.* ed. John Kirkpatrick. New York: Norton, 1972.

Perry, Rosalie S., *Charles Ives and the American Mind.* Kent, Ohio: Kent State University Press, 1974.

Wooldridge, David, *From the Steeples and Mountains: A Study of Charles Ives.* New York: Knopf, 1974.

## Liszt

Beckett, Walter, *Liszt.* New York: Collier, 1961.

Perenyi, Eleanor, *Liszt: The Artist As Romantic Hero.* Boston: Little, Brown, 1974.

Rostand, Claude, *Liszt,* trans. John Victor. New York: Grossman, 1972.

Searle, Humphrey, *The Music of Liszt,* 2nd ed. Gloucester, Mass.: Peter Smith, 1968.

Sitwell, Sacheverell, *Liszt.* New York: Dover, 1967.

Walker, Alan, ed., *Franz Liszt, The Man and His Music.* New York: Taplinger, 1970.

## Mahler

Blaukopf, Kurt, *Gustav Mahler,* trans. Inge Goodwin. New York: Praeger, 1973.

De La Grange, Henry-Louis, *Mahler.* New York: Doubleday, 1973.

Kennedy, Michael, *Mahler.* London: J. M. Dent, 1974.

Newlin, Dika, *Bruckner, Mahler, Schoenberg.* New York: Columbia University Press, 1947.

## Mendelssohn

Jacob, Heinrich E., *Felix Mendelssohn and His Times,* trans. Richard Weston and Clara Weston. Westport, Conn.: Greenwood Press, 1973.

Radcliffe, Philip, *Mendelssohn,* rev. ed. New York: Collier, 1967.

Werner, Eric, *Mendelssohn: A New Image of the Composer and His Age.* trans. Dika Newlin. New York: Free Press, 1963.

## Monteverdi

Arnold, Denis, *Monteverdi.* New York: Farrar, Straus & Giroux, 1963.

Arnold, Denis, and Nigel Fortune, eds., *The Monteverdi Companion.* London: Faber & Faber, 1968.

Schrade, Leo, *Monteverdi, Creator of Modern Music.* New York: Norton, 1950.

## Mozart

Blom, Eric, *Mozart.* New York: Collier, 1962.

Brophy, Brigid, *Mozart, the Dramatist.* New York: Harcourt, Brace & World, 1964.

Dent, Edward J., *Mozart's Operas,* 2nd ed. London: Oxford University Press, 1960.

Einstein, Alfred, *Mozart: His Character, His Work,* trans. Arthur Mendel and Nathan Broder. New York: Oxford University Press, 1945.

King, A. Hyatt, *Mozart in Retrospect,* 3rd ed. London: Oxford University Press, 1970.

Landon, H. C. Robbins, ed., *The Mozart Companion.* London: Oxford University Press, 1956.

Turner, Walter J., *Mozart: The Man and His Works,* rev. and ed. Christopher Raeburn. New York: Barnes & Noble, 1966.

## Mussorgsky

Calvocoressi, M. D., *Mussorgsky,* completed and rev. G. Abraham. London: J. M. Dent, 1974.

## Palestrina

Coates, Henry, *Palestrina.* London: J. M. Dent, 1948.

Roche, Jerome, *Palestrina.* London: Oxford University Press, 1971.

## Poulenc

Hell, Henri, *Francis Poulenc,* trans. Edward Lockspeiser. New York: Grove Press, 1959.

## Prokofiev

Nestyev, Israel V., *Prokofiev,* trans. Florence Jonas. Stanford, Calif.: Stanford University Press, 1961.

## Puccini

Ashbrook, William, *The Operas of Puccini.* New York: Oxford University Press, 1968.

Carner, Mosco, *Puccini: A Critical Biography.* New York: Knopf, 1959.

## Purcell

Westrup, J. A., *Purcell.* New York: Collier, 1962.

Zimmerman, Franklin B., *Henry Purcell, 1659-1695: His Life and Times.* New York: St. Martin's, 1967.

## Rachmaninoff

Bertensson, Sergei, and Jay Leyda, *Sergei Rachmaninoff: A Lifetime in Music.* New York: New York University Press, 1956.

Threfall, Robert, *Sergei Rachmaninoff: His Life and Music.* London: Boosey & Hawkes, 1973.

## Ravel

Demuth, Norman, *Ravel.* New York: Collier, 1962.

Roland-Manuel, Alexis, *Maurice Ravel,* trans. Cynthia Jolly. London: Dobsdon, 1947.

Stuckenschmidt, H. H., *Maurice Ravel—Variations on His Life and Work,* trans. Samuel R. Rosenbaum. Philadelphia: Chilton, 1968.

## Rossini

Toye, Francis, *Rossini: A Study in Tragi-Comedy.* New York: Norton, 1963.

Weinstock, Herbert, *Rossini.* New York: Knopf, 1968.

## Satie

Mayers, Rollo H., *Erik Satie.* New York: Dover, 1968.

## A. Scarlatti

Dent, Edward J., *Alessandro Scarlatti: His Life and Work.* London: Edward Arnold, 1960.

## D. Scarlatti

Kirkpatrick, Ralph, *Domenico Scarlatti,* rev. ed. Princeton, N. J.: Princeton University Press, 1955.

## Schoenberg

Newlin, Dika, *Bruckner, Mahler, Schoenberg.* New York: Columbia University Press, 1947.

Payne, Anthony, *Schoenberg.* New York: Oxford University Press, 1968.

Reich, Willi, *Schoenberg, A Critical Biography,* trans. Leo Black. New York: Praeger, 1972.

## Schubert

Abraham, Gerald, ed., *The Music of Schubert.* New York: Norton, 1947.

Brown, Maurice J. E., *Schubert: A Critical Biography.* London: Macmillan, 1958.

Capell, Richard, *Schubert's Songs,* 3rd ed. London: Gerald Duckworth, 1973.

Hutchings, Arthur, *Schubert,* rev. ed. New York: Octagon, 1973.

## Schumann

Abraham, Gerald, ed., *Schumann: A Symposium.* New York: Oxford University Press, 1952.

Brion, Marcel, *Schumann and the Romantic Age,* trans. Geoffrey Sainsbury. New York: Macmillan, 1956.

Chissell, Joan, *Schumann,* rev. ed. New York: Collier, 1967.

Plantinga, Leon B., *Schumann as Critic.* New Haven: Yale University Press, 1967.

Walsh, Stephen, *The Lieder of Schumann.* New York: Praeger, 1971.

## Schutz

Moser, Hans Joachim, *Heinrich Schutz: His Life and Work,* trans. Carl F. Pfatteicher. St. Louis: Concordia, 1959.

## Sibelius

Abraham, Gerald, ed., *Sibelius: A Symposium.* London: Drummond, 1948.

Johnson, Harold E., *Jean Sibelius.* New York: Knopf, 1959.

## Smetana

Clapham, John, *Smetana.* New York: Octagon, 1972.

Large, Brian, *Smetana.* New York: Praeger, 1971.

## Stockhausen

Harvey, Jonathan, *The Music of Stockhausen: An Introduction.* Berkeley, Calif.: University of California Press, 1974.

Worner, Karl H., *Stockhausen: Life and Work,* intro., trans., and ed. Bill Hopkins. Berkeley, Calif.: University of California Press, 1973.

## R. Strauss

Del Mar, Norman, *Richard Strauss: A Critical Commentary on His Life and Works.* Philadelphia: Chilton, 1962-72. 3 vols.

Mann, William, *Richard Strauss: A Critical Study of the Operas.* New York: Oxford University Press, 1966.

Marek, George Richard, *Richard Strauss: The Life of a Non-Hero.* New York: Simon & Schuster, 1967.

## Stravinsky

Strobel, Heinrich, *Stravinsky: Classic Humanist,* trans. Hans Rosenwald. 1955. Reprint. New York: Da Capo, 1973.

Vlad, Roman, *Stravinsky,* trans. Frederick Fuller and Ann Fuller, 2nd ed. New York: Oxford University Press, 1967.

White, Eric Walter, *Stravinsky: The Composer and His Works.* Berkeley, Calif.: University of California Press, 1966.

## Tchaikovsky

Abraham, Gerald, ed., *Tchaikovsky: A Symposium.* London: Drummond, 1946.

Abraham, Gerald, ed., *The Music of Tchaikovsky.* 1969. Reprint. New York: Norton, 1974.

Evans, Edwin, *Tchaikovsky,* rev. ed. New York: Farrar, Straus & Giroux, 1966.

Hanson, Laurence, and Elisabeth Hanson, *Tchaikovsky: The Man Behind the Music.* New York: Dodd, Mead, 1966.

Tchaikovsky, Modeste, *The Life and Letters of Peter Ilyich Tchaikovsky,* ed. and trans. Rosa Newmarch. New York: Dodd, Mead, 1924.

Warrack, John, *Tchaikovsky.* London: Hamilton, 1973.

**Varese**

Oullette, Fernand, *Edgard Varese,* trans. Derek Coltman. New York: Orion Press, l966.

Varese, Louise, *Varese, A Looking-Glass Diary,* Vol. 1: 1883-1928. New York: Norton, 1972.

**Vaughan Williams**

Day, James, *Vaughan Williams.* London: J. M. Dent, 1972.

Dickinson, A. E. F., *Vaughan Williams.* London: Faber & Faber, 1963.

Foss, Hubert, *Ralph Vaughan Williams: A Study.* London: Harrap, 1950.

**Verdi**

Budden, Julian, *The Operas of Verdi.* London: Cassell, 1973—. 2 vols. to date.

Gatti, Carlo, *Verdi: The Man and His Music,* trans. Elisabeth Abbott. New York: Putnam's, 1955.

Hughes, Spike, *Famous Verdi Operas.* Philadelphia: Chilton, 1968.

Hussey, Dyneley, *Verdi,* rev. ed. London: J. M. Dent, 1974.

Martin, George, *Verdi: His Music, Life and Times.* New York: Dodd, Mead, 1963.

Osborne, Charles, *The Complete Operas of Verdi.* New York: Knopf, 1970.

Toye, Francis, *Giuseppe Verdi: His Life and Works.* New York: Random House, 1946.

Walker, Frank, *The Man Verdi.* New York: Knopf, 1962.

**Vivaldi**

Kolneder, Walter, *Antonio Vivaldi: His Life and Work,* trans. Bill Hopkins. Berkeley, Calif.: University of California Press, 1970.

Pincherle, Marc, *Vivaldi: Genius of the Baroque,* trans. Christopher Hatch. New York: Norton, 1962.

**Wagner**

Donington, Robert, *Wagner's "Ring" and Its Symbols—The Music and the Myth.* 3rd ed.

London: Faber & Faber, 1974.

Gutman, Robert W., *Richard Wagner: The Man, His Mind and His Music.* New York: Harcourt Brace Jovanovich, 1968.

Jacobs, Robert L., *Wagner,* rev. ed. New York: Collier, 1965.

Newman, Ernest, *The Life of Richard Wagner.* New York: Knopf, 1949. 4 vols.

Newman, Ernest, *Wagner as Man and Artist.* New York: Random House, 1960.

Shaw, George A. Bernard, *The Perfect Wagnerite—A Commentary on the Nibelung's Ring.* 1923. Reprint. New York: Dover, 1967.

Stein, Jack, *Richard Wagner and the Synthesis of the Arts.* Detroit: Wayne State University Press, 1960.

White, Chappell, *An Introduction to the Life and Works of Richard Wagner.* Englewood Cliffs, N.J.: Prentice-Hall, 1967.

Winkler, Franz E., *For Freedom Destined: Mysteries of Man's Evolution in the Mythology of Wagner's Ring Operas and Parsifal.* Garden City, N.Y.: Waldorf, 1974.

**Weber**

Saunders, William, *Weber.* New York: Dutton, 1940.

Stebbins, Lucy Poate, and Richard Poate Stebbins, *Enchanted Wanderer: The Life of Carl Maria von Weber.* New York: Putnam's, 1940.

Warrack, John Hamilton, *Carl Maria von Weber.* New York: Macmillan, 1968.

**Webern**

Kolneder, Walter, *Anton Webern: An Introduction to His Works,* trans. Humphrey Searle. Berkeley, Calif.: University of California Press, 1968.

Moldenhauer, H., comp., M. and D. Irvine, ed., *Anton Webern: Perspectives.* Seattle: University of Washington Press, 1966.

Wildgans, Friedrich, *Anton Webern,* trans. Edith Temple Roberts and Humphrey Searle. New York: October House, 1967.

**Wolf**

Sams, Eric, *The Songs of Hugo Wolf.* London: Methuen, 1961.

Walker, Frank, *Hugo Wolf,* 2nd ed. New York: Knopf, 1968.

# GLOSSARY

*A cappella (lit., "in church style")*. Singing without instrumental accompaniment.

*A tempo*. At the original tempo; used after a change of speed.

*Absolute music*. Music that does not have a programmatic title or depend on literary or other associations.

*Accelerando*. Increase the speed gradually.

*Accent*. A strong beat, normally the first beat of each measure; rhythmic stress at any place in a piece of music.

*Accidental*. A symbol placed before a note to raise or lower the tone, usually by a half step (flats, sharps and naturals).

*Accompaniment*. A part supporting the leading melody.

*Acoustics*. The branch of physics that studies the laws and phenomena of sound; also, the sound-affecting properties of an auditorium, concert hall or other performing space.

*Ad libitum (lit., "at will")*. An indication telling performers that they may employ a tempo or an expression that suits their pleasure.

*Agitato*. Agitated, excited.

*Air*. A song or melody. See Aria.

*Ala breve*. An indication that the music that follows is to be performed twice as fast as its notation would suggest.

*Allargando*. Gradually growing slower and broader.

*Allegro (lit., "cheerful")*. Fast.

*Allegro ma non troppo*. Fast, but not too fast.

*Animato*. With spirit.

*Anthem*. A sacred choral composition.

*Antiphonal*. Two or more choruses or instrumental chords "against" each other, often placed at different parts of the concert hall, stage, or church.

*Aria*. A composition for solo voice and instrumental accompaniment, often taken from an opera or oratorio.

*Arpa*. Harp.

*Arpeggio*. Tones of a chord played one after the other; also called a broken chord.

*Assai*. Very.

*Atonal*. Having no fixed key; not centering on any distinct key.

*Augmented*. 1) Interval—a major or perfect interval enlarged by one half-step. 2) Triad—a chord made up of a major third and an augmented fifth.

*Bagatelle (lit., "a trifle")*. A short piece, usually for the piano, especially peculiar to the nineteenth century.

*Bagpipe*. A wind instrument with a large windbag, reed pipes and drone pipes, and finger holes.

*Balalaika*. Guitar-like instrument with a triangular body.

*Ballerina*. A female ballet dancer.

*Ballet*. A dance composition accompanied by the orchestra, often employing a dramatic thread or story.

*Bar*. A vertical line dividing notes on the staff into measures and indicating that the strong accent falls on the note or notes immediately following.

*Barcarole*. Music written to imitate the song of a Venetian gondolier.

*Baroque*. The music or style of art that prevailed during the seventeenth and the first part of the eighteenth centuries, characterized by the use of grandiose and magnificent forms.

*Bass clef (also called the F clef)*. The sign indicating that F below Middle C is the fourth line of the staff.

*Baton*. A conductor's stick.

*Batterie*. The group of percussion instruments in the orchestra.

*Beat*. The regularly recurring pulse that constitutes a unit of rhythmical measurement in a musical piece.

*Bel canto (lit., "beautiful singing")*. A style of singing made famous by Italian singers in the eighteenth century.

*Berceuse*. A lullaby or music written in the style of a lullaby.

*Binary form.* Music consisting of two distinct sections.

*C clef.* A sign used on the staff to indicate Middle C. It is also called *alto clef* when it is on the third line and *tenor clef* when it is on the fourth line.

*Cadence.* A short series of notes or chords through which a melody or harmony is brought to a temporary or final close.

*Cadenza.* A virtuoso passage for the solo voice or instrument, especially found in a concerto. Originally, cadenzas were improvised by the performer but now are usually written by the composer.

*Cantabile.* In "singing style," an indication usually given to an instrumental line, to be played smoothly in a vocal manner.

*Capriccio.* A lively and sometimes humorous instrumental composition written in free form.

*Carillon.* A set of bells hung in a tower on which melodies are played by striking a keyboard.

*Carol.* A joyous song, originally for dancing, for special seasons of the year.

*Castanets.* A percussion instrument made of a pair of small, hollowed pieces of wood that are clicked together.

*Celesta.* A piano-like instrument whose tones are made by hammers hitting little metal bars.

*Cembalo.* Harpsichord.

*Chant.* A sacred song with many words sung on the same pitch in free rhythm.

*Chimes.* A percussion instrument played by striking a hammer against tuned metal tubes of graduated length suspended from a frame.

*Chord progression.* A succession of distinct chords.

*Chorus.* 1) A large group of singers, usually singing in four parts. 2) The refrain of a song.

*Chromatic.* Melodies or harmonies based on the chromatic scale—that is, based on successive half-steps.

*Church modes.* The scales used in medieval church music.

*Clavecin.* Harpsichord.

*Clavichord.* A stringed keyboard instrument superseded by the piano. The strings were struck by small metal wedges called *tangents.*

*Clavier.* Refers to early keyboard instruments other than the organ, such as clavichords, harpsichords and the early pianos.

*Clef.* A symbol placed at the left of each staff in music to indicate the pitch of the lines and spaces. See *bass clef, treble clef* and *C clef.*

*Coda.* The closing passage of music added to the principal part of the composition.

*Col legno (lit., "with the wood").* An indication directing the string player to strike the string with the wood, not the hair, of the bow.

*Composition.* 1) An original piece of music created by a composer. 2) The study of the principles of composing.

*Con brio.* With fire or passion.

*Con sordino.* Indication that the instrumentalist should play the following passage with a mute.

*Concertmaster.* The leader of the first-violin section of an orchestra.

*Consonance.* A combination of two or more tones that produce an effect pleasing to the ear.

*Counterpoint.* A style of composition with various musical lines being played simultaneously.

*Crescendo.* Play or sing gradually louder.

*Cymbals.* A percussion instrument consisting of a pair of brass or bronze concave plates that are either struck together or suspended on a stand and tapped with drum sticks.

*Dal segno (D.S.).* A sign indicating the performer is to go back to the sign and repeat the subsequent music.

*De capo (D.C.).* A sign indicating the performer is to repeat the composition from the beginning to its end, or to a place marked *fine (da capo al fine).*

*Debut.* The first public appearance of a performing artist.

*Decibel.* A unit for measuring the loudness of sound.

*Decrescendo.* Play or sing gradually softer.

*Development.* A section of a composition that consists of the variation of rhythmic, melodic or harmonic aspects of the theme or themes.

*Diatonic.* A regular major or minor scale of seven tones as distinguished from the chromatic scale of twelve tones.

*Diminished.* 1) Interval—a minor or perfect interval made one half-step smaller. 2) Triad—a chord made up of a minor third and a diminished fifth.

*Diminuendo.* Play or sing gradually softer.

*Divisi ("divided").* A direction to the string section of an orchestra to divide into two or more bodies when playing certain passages.

*Dolce.* Sweetly.

*Dominant.* The fifth degree of the scale. The dominant triad is built on the dominant tone.

*Dominant chord.* A chord built on the fifth degree of the scale.

*Dotted (or dotted-note) rhythm.* A rhythmic pattern in which dotted notes are prominent.

*Double flat.* The sign that lowers the tone following it by one whole-step.

*Double sharp.* The sign that raises the tone following it by one whole-step.

*Double bar.* Two vertical lines placed on the staff to indicate the end of a section, movement or composition.

*Double bass (or "contrabass" or simply "bass").* The largest and lowest-pitched of the bowed stringed instruments.

*Double stops.* In string writing, playing more than one note at the same time. Although *double stops* literally means "two notes," the term is loosely used to mean two, three, or even four notes at the same time.

*Downbeat.* The principal stroke, downward in motion, of the conductor's baton indicating the first beat of a measure.

*Duet.* A composition for two performers, singers or instrumentalists, usually with accompaniment.

*Duple meter.* Rhythmic section of music that is based on two beats per measure.

*Embouchure.* The position and tension of the mouth and lip in playing a wind instrument.

*Encore.* A piece of music repeated or added to the end of a performance in response to the demands of a pleased audience.

*Enharmonic.* A note, chord or interval that sounds the same as another note, chord or interval that is written differently (e.g., C sharp and D flat are enharmonic to each other).

*Ensemble.* 1) A group of musicians who perform together. 2) The general effect of music performed by such a group of musicians.

*Entr'acte.* An interval between acts, or a composition or ballet interpolated between acts of a theatrical performance.

*Ethnomusicology.* The study of comparative culture and the music of various peoples.

*Etude (lit., "study").* An instrumental composition, often involving some technical problem for the instrument concerned.

*Exposition.* The first principal section of the sonata form or fugue that presents the main thematic material.

*Expressionism.* A term borrowed from the art world to refer to early twentieth-century music that aims to present inward feelings in unconventional forms.

*Fanfare.* A short flourish of trumpets or an imitation of their sound to introduce some special event or ceremony.

*Fantasia.* A composition that is free in its form and feeling.

*Fermata.* A sign placed above or below a specific note or rest to indicate that the note is to be held or the pause extended.

*Fife.* A small, high-pitched transverse flute usually played with drums in military groups.

*Finale.* 1) The last movement of an extended work. 2) The concluding portion of an operatic act.

*Fine.* The end.

*Finger board.* A part of the neck of a stringed instrument against which the strings are pressed by the fingers to change the pitch of the various tones.

*Flat.* A sign (♭) placed to the left of a given note that lowers its pitch one half-step.

*Flutter tonguing.* A special type of tonguing employed with woodwind instruments in some twentieth-century music, requiring a rolling movement of the tongue. This tonguing gives a curious "flutter" effect to the tone.

*Form.* The overall structure of a musical composition showing each section as it follows another to make the whole.

*Frets.* Narrow ridges of metal, wood, ivory or other material placed in precise positions across the finger board of such instruments as guitars, banjos and ukeleles. The player presses the strings down upon these frets to change the pitch of the strings.

*Fughetta.* A short fugue.

*Fugue.* An important form of musical composition based on a melody (called the *theme* or *subject)* that is taken up in turn by the different parts (or *voices*). Usually there are three or four voices, and each expresses the theme one after the other while all continue to develop the piece with new material.

*Fuoco.* Forcefully, usually fast.

*Galant.* The light, elegant style of the Rococo Period as distinguished from the heavy, more elaborate style of the Baroque Period.

*Glissando (lit., "sliding").* Very rapid scales executed in such a way to sound as if sliding from one extreme pitch to another, especially on the piano or harp. See also *portamento.*

*Glockenspiel.* A percussion instrument made from a set of tuned metal bars that give a bell-like sound when struck with a small hammer. When mounted on a frame that can be played while carried, it is often called a *bell-lyre.*

*Gong.* A percussion instrument (also called the *Tam-Tam)* consisting of a large circular bronze disk, usually struck with a large, soft mallet.

*Grace note.* A short ornamental note used as an embellishment, often designated in small notation.

*Grave.* Slowly and solemnly.

*Grazioso.* Gracefully.

*Gregorian.* The form of liturgical chanting within the Roman Catholic Church that was codified during the reign of Pope Gregory the Great (A.D. 590-604).

*Half-step.* The smallest interval commonly used in Western music. An example of a half-step can be indicated at the piano by playing any two adjacent keys without skipping any key that might intervene.

*Harmonics.* 1) Harmonic overtones; additional notes produced when a fundamental sound is generated, giving the note its characteristic sound. 2) Flute-like tones produced on a stringed instrument by touching the string lightly with the finger at certain places that divide the length of the string into equal portions.

*Harmonization.* The choosing of chords to accompany a given melody.

*Harmony.* The science of chords and their relationship to one another.

*Harpsichord.* A keyboard stringed instrument in which the strings are plucked by quills to produce tones. The harpsichord, popular as a solo and ensemble instrument from the tenth through the eighteenth centuries, was superseded by the rise of the piano, and began again to be used in the twentieth century.

*Hold.* See *fermata.*

*Homophony.* Music in which one melody stands out and the others accompany in chordal effects.

*Hurdy-gurdy.* An old mechanical folk instrument of melody and drone strings played by a wheel turned by a crank. The notes of the melody are played on a small keyboard that stops the strings.

*Hymn.* A religious song, usually in a slow homophony style, to be sung by a congregation in public worship.

*Imitation.* An important contrapuntal device of employing in one voice a melodic or rhythmic figure that has been stated in another.

*Impressionism.* A term originally referring to a style of painting popular at the end of the nineteenth century, but borrowed to describe a particular style of music as well. Impressionistic music seeks to create descriptive effects or subtle impressions rather than specific concepts. Debussy and Ravel were the two most important composers of Impressionistic music.

*Improvisation.* 1) Music spontaneously created directly from the imagination of the performer. Improvisation was widely used in the Baroque era and is today primarily employed in jazz. 2) The title of an instrumental composition written to give the effect of its having been improvised.

*Incidental music.* Music played during the sections *(incidents)* of a dramatic work.

*Instrumentation.* The choice of instruments for a composition. See also *orchestration.*

*Interlude.* Music written to be played between acts of a play or opera or between other pieces of music.

*Intermezzo.* A short piano piece, common in the nineteenth century, intended or suitable as an interlude.

*Interval.* The distance in pitch between two tones.

*Intonation.* Truth of pitch. Good or bad intonation refers to playing in or out of tune respectively.

*Introduction.* A preliminary section to an extended composition.

*Kapellmeister.* The director of music in eighteenth-century choirs or orchestras. Used in Germany to mean a conductor at the theater or concert hall.

*Kettledrum.* See *tympani.*

*Key.* 1) The system of tones and semitones constituting a scale and built on one selected note (the tonic). This key note or tonic becomes the first note of the scale as well as the name of the key. 2) The black and white digitals of a piano.

*Key signature.* The sharps or flats written at the beginning of each staff, or at any point where the key is changed, to indicate the key of the composition.

*Kithara.* A stringed instrument of the ancient Greeks.

*Koto.* The Japanese stringed zither with thirteen or more silk strings.

*Leading tone.* The name for the seventh tone of the scale, since its tonal quality leads upward to the tonic, a half-step above it.

*Ledger line.* A short line for scoring notes above or below the staff.

*Legato.* An indication that the passage is to be performed in a smooth and connected manner, usually marked by a slur line above or below the notes affected.

*Leitmotiv.* An identifying theme associated with and accompanying a particular character, atmosphere or situation.

*Lento.* Slow, usually between andante and largo.

*Libretto.* The complete text of an opera, cantata or oratorio.

*Lied (plural, "lieder").* Strictly used for the great number of art songs by German composers, but loosely used to refer to the song genre in general.

*Lute.* A plucked stringed instrument that reached its zenith in the sixteenth century. Lutes have a pear-shaped body and from six to thirteen pairs of strings stretched over a fretted finger board.

*Lyre.* An ancient stringed instrument with strings stretched on a frame with a sound box often made from a turtle shell.

*Lyrics.* The words of a song.

*M.M.* Abbreviation for Maelzel's Metronome. Composers often indicate the speed they desire for a composition by writing a note that is to be played at a certain number of beats per minute. See also *metronome.*

*Ma non troppo.* "But not too much." See *Allegro ma non troppo.*

*Madrigal.* An unaccompanied part-song setting of a short lyrical poem written in the language of its composer (especially Italian or English) rather than Latin.

*Maestoso.* Majestic, dignified.

*Mandolin.* A stringed instrument similar to a lute, played with a plectrum on pairs of wire strings over a fretted finger board.

*Marcato.* Marked or accented; that is, each note is to be played with emphasis.

*Marimba.* Percussion instrument similar to but larger than the xylophone and provided with resonators for a more sustained sound.

*Martele.* In bowed stringed instruments, a special type of heavily accented bow stroke.

*Mass.* Musical setting of the Roman Catholic worship service.

*Measure.* A rhythmic group of beats set off by bar-lines.

*Mediant.* The tonal name of the third degree of the scale.

*Meno.* Less.

*Meter.* Any specific pattern of rhythm determined by the number and length of the notes it contains.

*Meter signature.* Two numbers found at the beginning of every composition and also inserted within the composition if and where meter changes. The top number of the meter signature indicates the number of beats in the measure. The lower number of the meter signature indicates the type of note to receive one count.

*Metronome.* A device used to indicate gradations of tempo by sounding regular beats.

*Mezza voce.* With half voice, that is, restrained volume of tone.

*Middle C.* The C note nearest the middle of the piano keyboard and notated on a ledger line lying between the treble and bass clefs.

*Modulation.* The changing from one key to another within a composition.

*Molto.* Very much.

*Mordent.* A musical ornament, usually consisting of a rapid alternation of the written note with the note directly below it.

*Motet.* An unaccompanied vocal composition in contrapuntal style, important from the thirteenth to the seventeenth century, and nearly always using a sacred text in Latin.

*Motive (or motif).* A brief theme or figure that occurs throughout a composition.

*Movement.* A musical division complete in itself, forming part of an extended composition.

*Musette.* 1) A French version of the bagpipe. 2) A short gavotte with a drone bass part imitating the music of the bagpipe.

*Mute.* A device to soften or muffle the tones of a musical instrument.

*Natural.* The sign that cancels either a sharp or flat for the tone before which it appears.

*Neoclassicism.* The anti-Romantic movement in the twentieth century that sought to adapt the objective style of the Classical period to present-day composition.

*Neumes.* Notation signs written in the early Middle Ages above the words of the plainsong. The exact meaning, both rhythmically and melodically, of every neume is still unknown, making them the subject of extensive research and sharp controversies among musicologists.

*Nocturne.* "Night piece." A kind of character piece for piano, popular in the nineteenth century. Typically melancholy, it features an expressive melody over a harmony of broken chords.

*Note.* A sign written on a musical staff to represent a tone.

*Nuance.* A subtle difference in tone color, tempo, intensity or phrasing.

*Obbligato.* Although *obbligato* means obligatory and refers to an indispensable part that cannot be omitted, modern usage has often altered this meaning to denote an accompanying part that may be omitted if necessary.

*Octave.* The interval of eight degrees of a scale. The lower and upper tone of the octave will have the same letter name and, acoustically, the upper tone will have twice the frequency of the lower.

*Opera.* A musical drama sung to the accompaniment of an orchestra.

*Operetta.* A light musical play of popular appeal with vocal and instrumental music, but also including spoken dialogue.

*Opus.* "Work" of a composer. The numbers used with Opus indicate the chronological position of a composition, often with respect to their publication rather than their creation.

*Oratorio.* A composition, usually of religious character, for vocal soloists, chorus and orchestra, sung without costumes, scenery or action.

*Orchestration.* The art of writing or scoring music to be performed by an orchestra.

*Organum.* The earliest attempts at writing for more than one part, beginning in the ninth century. The earlier organum used parts that progressed in parallel fifths and fourths. In the eleventh century, other intervals and parts progressing in contrary motion provided the beginning of modern polyphony.

*Ornaments.* Embellishments of a given melody, usually indicated by specific signs in the score. Examples: trill, modent and turn.

*Ottava (usually abbreviated 8va).* When placed above notes, indicates the notes are to be performed an octave higher than written. When placed below notes, indicates they are to be performed an octave lower.

*Overture.* Instrumental music composed as a musical introduction to an opera, oratorio or suite. The concert overture of the nineteenth century is an independent composition with a programmatic title suggesting a pictorial or literary association.

*Partita.* Used in the seventeenth and eighteenth centuries to mean a suite of non-dance movements.

*Passion.* A musical setting of the story of Christ's death.

*Pedal.* 1) A foot lever on the organ that creates tones. 2) A foot lever on the harp, harpsichord, piano, tympani or other instruments used for tuning, damping, etc. 3) A note sustained below changing harmonies.

*Pentatonic.* A five-tone scale widely used in Oriental music (and in Western music that imitates the Oriental), as well as in American Indian, Negro and Scottish music.

*Percussion instruments.* All instruments with a struck or shaken resonating surface having definite pitch, such as tympani, xylophone, bells and chimes; and instruments producing indefinite pitch, such as drums, triangle, gong, cymbals, castanets and maracas.

*Period.* A complete musical idea, usually 8, 12 or 16 measures, ending with a full cadence.

*Phrase.* A musical thought composed of two or more measures.

*Pianoforte (lit., "loud-soft").* The full Italian name of the piano.

*Piccolo.* A small flute sounding one octave higher than the standard flute.

*Pitch.* The highness or lowness of a tone, determined by the frequency of its vibrating material. For example, if a violinist plays the A string, it vibrates 440 times per second. The first seven letters of the alphabet are used as pitch names, often with the additions of accidentals (sharps, flats and naturals).

*Pizzicato.* In string playing, to pluck the strings with the finger rather than to use the bow on the strings.

*Plainsong.* Another name for Gregorian chant. Derived from cantus planus ("plain song"), unmeasured free chant, as opposed to cantus figuralis ("figured song"), exactly measured music.

*Plectrum.* A pick used to pluck the strings of instruments such as the guitar, mandolin or zither, usually made of thin ivory, plastic or metal.

*Poco.* Little.

*Poco a poco.* Little by little.

*Polyphony.* The combining of two or more melodies.

*Polyrhythm.* The combining of two or more meters with their varying rhythms sounding simultaneously.

*Polytonality.* The combining of two or more keys; that is, the writing of melodies or harmonies that are distinctly in two or more keys.

*Portamento.* A sliding between two pitches without distinguishing any intermediate tones, characteristic of the voice, non-fretted strings and trombone. *Glissando* distinguishes all the intermediate half-steps between two pitches. Thus the piano, harp and guitar can play glissando but not portamento.

*Postlude.* A final number, usually an organ selection, at the close of a church service.

*Prelude.* The first movement of a musical suite, or a musical composition played before another composition, drama or church service.

*Prima donna.* The leading soprano in an opera, or a woman who often sings such leading roles.

*Program music.* Music based on an extramusical theme, such as a literary or associative subject, that is evoked by the music itself and usually given a title referring to its extramusical theme.

*Psaltery.* An ancient stringed instrument, similar to a dulcimer, that is plucked by the fingers or a plectrum.

*Pulse.* The regular beat that underlies music and determines its motion and speed.

*Quarter tone.* One half of a half tone; a microtone used in some twentieth-century music.

*Quartet.* 1) A musical composition for four voices or instruments, especially a string quartet for two violins, viola and cello. 2) An ensemble that performs quartet compositions.

*Rallentando.* Gradually slower.

*Range.* 1) The extreme limits of a voice or instrument with respect to pitch. 2) The extreme pitch limits of the melody in a piece of music.

*Recapitulation.* The third section of a movement in sonata form, which serves to re-present the principal themes as they were originally presented (or in slight variation) in the exposition.

*Recital.* A musical performance by one individual or by a soloist and accompanist.

*Recitative.* A reciting, declamatory style of singing made in imitation of speech. It was popular in seventeenth-century and eighteenth-century opera.

*Recorder.* A straight wooden flute without a reed and made in bass, tenor, treble (alto) and descant (soprano) ranges.

*Reed.* A thin strip of wood, cane or metal placed in an instrument in a position that sets an air current in motion.

*Register.* A specific part of the range of an instrument or a voice. Also, in organ playing, a set of pipes controlled by one stop.

*Repeat.* A section of a composition to be performed again can be indicated by a repeat sign. The performer is to return to the beginning or to the reverse repeat sign.

*Requiem.* The Roman Catholic service for the dead, used by many composers as the form for a large choral work.

*Resolution.* The process of a dissonance progressing to consonance.

*Responsorial.* A style of vocal music in which a soloist (or soloists) is answered by the choir, or vice versa.

*Rest.* A sign in musical notation that represents a pause or cessation of sound. Rests have the same rhythmic value as notes of the same name.

*Rhapsody.* An instrumental composition of free form, often demonstrating national characteristics.

*Rhythm.* 1) organization of time elements in music. 2) The regular recurrence of repeated features in a composition.

*Ripeno.* The full parts played by the entire ensemble (as opposed to a small group or solo) in a Baroque orchestra.

*Ritardando.* Gradually slower.

*Rococo.* The florid, ornamental style that characterized much music of the mid-eighteenth century.

*Romanticism.* A style of composition pervading most of the nineteenth century that places strong emphasis on individual feeling, innovative chromaticism and the personal expression of poetic sentiment.

*Rondeau.* A medieval French song of which portions are repeated as a refrain. Later, this form was imitated instrumentally.

*Rondo.* A form often used as the final movement of a classical sonata or symphony in which the theme of the opening section is repeated alternately with other themes of a different character.

*Root.* The lowest note on which a chord is constructed.

*Round.* A simple kind of vocal canon in which each part enters at different times and sings the entire theme.

*Rubato.* An indication that allows some freedom in performing the music of a special passage to give the musician greater freedom of expression.

*Sacred music.* Music having to do with religion, usually through the meaning of its text.

*Scale.* A succession of tones moving in the same direction, used as the basic material for melodic writing.

*Score.* The complete printed music of an opera, cantata, oratorio, ballet, symphony, concerto or suite.

*Secular music.* Music other than that intended for religious purposes.

*Semitone.* A half-tone.

*Sequence.* The successive repetition of a melodic figure given at different pitch levels.

*Serenade.* A free musical form, originally applied to music suitable for performance in the open air.

*Sforzando.* Sudden force and volume to be applied to a single note or chord.

*Sharp.* The character (#) that raises the pitch of a note by a half-step.

*Skip.* Any two notes in a melody that follow one another by an interval wider than a second.

*Slur.* A curved line grouping two or more notes together and indicating they are to be performed smoothly, with little or no articulation on each note under the slur line.

*Snare drum.* A small drum with two heads, the lower of which has cut strips or wires, called snares, stretched across it to reinforce the tone.

*Solo.* A composition or part of a composition played or sung by a single performer.

*Sonatina.* A "small sonata," usually having fewer or shorter movements, simpler style or less demanding technical requirements than a true sonata.

*Sordino.* An indication for the performers to use mutes.

*Sostenuto.* Sustained.

*Sotto voce.* In an undertone.

*Spiccato.* In string playing, a type of bow stroke in which the bow rebounds lightly off the string.

*Spinet.* 1) A small harpsichord with only one manual. 2) A small upright piano.

*Spiritual.* A religious folk song originating in the southern United States.

*Staccato.* An indication to play notes that are short and detached. The notation is usually a dot over or under each note.

*Staff, stave.* Five horizontal, parallel and equidistant

lines and the included four spaces between them upon which musical symbols are written. Historically, the staff, at one time or another, has had as few as one and as many as eleven lines.

*Stretto.* 1) That part of a composition, especially a fugue, where two or more themes overlap. 2) Also used in compositions other than fugues to indicate a passage of increased speed.

*Subdominant.* The tonal name of the fourth degree of the scale.

*Subito.* Suddenly.

*Submediant.* The tonal name of the sixth degree of the scale.

*Suite.* 1) A set or series of instrumental pieces usually comprised of several dance forms. 2) A set of movements rather loosely connected that may be selected from an opera or ballet.

*Sul ponticello ("on the bridge").* In string playing, a bowing done very close to the bridge, giving a thin, eerie sound.

*Sul G.* In violin playing, an indication to play a passage completely on the G string.

*Supertonic.* Tonal name of the second degree of the scale.

*Symphonic poem.* An extended one-movement orchestral composition in free form, usually based on an extramusical idea, such as a story or a poem.

*Syncopation.* A rhythmic figure in which the musical accent falls on the normally weak beat or portion of a beat.

*Tambourine.* A small, round percussion instrument with metal jingles in a wooden frame.

*Technique.* Mechanical dexterity, training and skill.

*Temperament.* Any system of tuning whose intervals deviate from acoustically pure ones. In equal temperament (the standard used today on the piano), the octave is divided equally into twelve parts, each half-step being equal to every other half step.

*Tempo.* The pace or speed of a composition.

*Tenor.* The highest natural voice part sung by men.

*Tessitura.* The position of a passage or composition within the range of an instrument or voice.

*Theme.* A melody of sufficient length and importance to form a complete musical idea. In compositions such as fugues and sonatas this is called the subject.

*Tie.* A curved line written above or below two adjacent strokes of the same pitch indicating that the sound is to continue unbroken for the total time value of the two notes.

*Timbre.* Tone color.

*Timbrel.* Ancient predecessor of the tambourine.

*Toccata.* A single-movement solo composition written in a brilliant style for a keyboard instrument, usually in free form.

*Tonality.* Music written in a tonic-centered key.

*Tone color.* The blend of overtones that distinguishes a note played on one instrument from the same note played on another instrument.

*Tonic.* The tonal name for the first degree of the scale. The principal tone of the scale and the main tone of any key.

*Tonic chord.* A chord with the tonic note as its root.

*Transcribe.* To arrange or adapt a composition for an instrument other than that for which it was originally written by the composer.

*Transition.* A passage that leads from one principal section to another.

*Transpose.* To put a piece in another key—that is, to change the composition's level of pitch.

*Treble clef.* The sign that fixes the pitch for the highest staff. It is often called the G clef because the treble clef sign centers on the second line of the staff, which represents the G above Middle C.

*Tremolo.* The rapid reiteration of the same pitch on stringed instruments.

*Triad.* A chord of three tones built in successive thirds from the root tone.

*Triangle.* A percussion instrument of extremely high indefinite pitch. It is made from a steel rod bent into a triangular shape and struck with a short metal stick.

*Trill.* An important musical ornament consisting of a rapid alternation of a note with the note that is a half-step or whole-step above.

*Trio.* 1) A group of three performers. 2) The center section of a minuet or scherzo.

*Triplet.* A group of three notes to be performed in place of two of the same value.

*Troppo ("too much").* See Allegro ma non troppo.

*Troubadour.* Poet-minstrels of medieval France, circa 1100-1300.

*Tuning.* The adjustment of strings or tubing to bring an instrument into correct tune with itself and other instruments.

*Turn.* A musical ornament consisting of four or five notes "turning" around the principal (written) note.

*Tympani.* Large hollow, metal, kettle-shaped drums, each with a head that can be stretched and tuned to exact pitches. Two or more are used together by the same player.

*Una corda ("one string").* In piano playing, a direction to depress the soft (left) pedal of the piano in order to shift the striking mechanism so that the hammer hits only one string (una corda) or two instead of all of them.

*Unison.* 1) The simultaneous playing of the same notes or melody by different instruments or voices. 2) A tone of the same pitch as a given tone.

*Upbeat.* 1) Unstressed note or notes beginning a composition before the first bar-line. 2) The raising of the conductor's hand as a preparation for the beginning of a composition or a new section, indicating the last beat of a measure.

*Variations.* Changes given to a theme through melodic, harmonic, rhythmic or orchestrative means.

*Vibraphone.* A musical instrument similar to the marimba but with electrically operated valves in the resonators, producing a controlled vibrato.

*Vibration.* Extremely rapid movements back and forth, such as those of a vibrating string or air column, that produce tones.

*Vibrato.* Slight fluctuation of pitch produced on stringed instruments or in the voice to increase the emotional quality of the tones produced.

*Viol.* A family of ancient bowed stringed instruments popular during the sixteenth and seventeenth centuries.

*Viola da gamba.* One of the larger viol instruments that is held between the knees of the player like a cello.

*Virginal.* A type of early harpsichord encased in an oblong box.

*Virtuoso.* An instrumentalist who excels in the technical mastery of his or her instrument.

*Vivace.* Lively.

*Vocal music.* Music to be performed by singers—even when accompanied by instrumentalists—either as solo, small ensemble or chorus.

*Voice.* 1) The human voice. 2) Separate parts of a chord. 3) Separate parts in a composition.

*Whole step.* The distance in pitch equal to two half-steps.

*Whole-tone scale.* A scale composed only of whole tones.

*Word painting.* The depiction of a text by some appropriate musical means to underline or emphasize the ideas presented in the text.

*Xylophone.* A percussion instrument consisting of a series of wooden bars graduated in length so as to sound the notes of the scale when struck with small wooden sticks.

*Yodel.* A special type of singing characterized by going rapidly from the natural to the falsetto voice.